A
GENEVA
SERIES
COMMENTARY

1 & 2 PETER

AN EXPOSITION OF
1 & 2 PETER

Alexander Nisbet

THE BANNER OF TRUTH TRUST

THE BANNER OF TRUTH TRUST
3 Murrayfield Road, Edinburgh EH12 6EL
P O Box 621, Carlisle, Pennsylvania 17013, U.S.A.

*

First published 1658
First Banner of Truth edition 1982
ISBN 0 85151 338 7

*

Printed and bound in Great Britain at
The Camelot Press Ltd, Southampton

CONTENTS

1 PETER

THE ARGUMENT

Although this Apostle was in a very mean external condition before his calling, Matt. 4:18, and wanted not his manifold failings thereafter, Matt. 16:22 and 26:70, Gal. 2:14, yet by the free grace of God he was honoured to be an eye-witness of Christ's greatest glory on earth, Matt. 17:1, and of His saddest sufferings, Matt. 26:27; to convert many thousand souls, Acts 2:41, to write this excellent Scripture and to die a martyr, 2 Pet. 1:14 compared with John 21:18,19. All which considerations of him may serve to commend to the church the truths delivered by him.

The Epistle is directed to the Christian Jews, of whom he had gotten a special charge, Gal. 2:7, and of whose conversion he had been a prime instrument, Acts 2:9, &c.

The special occasion of his writing to them (as appears by the strain of his doctrine) was the rage of persecution, the prevailing of error, and some decay of grace and holiness among them, together with the present opportunity of a fit messenger to carry the Epistle, 1 Pet. 5:12, who had a calling to interpret and publicly to explain the same to them, 2 Cor. 1:19.

His principal scope is to confirm believers in the truth, to stir them up to constancy and cheerfulness under their sufferings for it, to grow in grace and to adorn their profession by a holy walking in their several relations, as appears by comparing 1 Pet. 5:12 where he resumes his scope in this Epistle with 2 Pet. 3:1 where he expresses his scope in both.

The principal parts of this Epistle are three. In the first (after the Preface, Chap. 1, vv 1,2) the Apostle gives such a description of the excellent spiritual condition of believers, as might provoke them to joy under their saddest sufferings, and engage them to these duties of holiness which he presses in the rest of the Epistle; and this is to the thirteenth verse of the first chapter. The second part contains several exhortations with motives pressing the same, to such duties of holiness as that most excellent state does oblige all Christians unto, whatever their relations or condition be in the world: and this is to the thirteenth verse of the second chapter. In the third part, the

Apostle presses such duties of holiness as are suitable for Christians, considered under their civil, domestic or church relations, and especially such as belong to those who are in a condition of suffering for Christ and His truth; and this is to the tenth verse of the fifth chapter. After which is the close of the whole Epistle.

CHAPTER ONE

The parts of this chapter are two. In the first (after the Preface of the whole Epistle containing a description of the penman of it and of the parties to whom it is directed, (vv. 1,2), the Apostle incites suffering Christians to praise God by raising the song before them: wherein he makes clear how excellent their spiritual estate was; and holds forth what reasons they had from it of cheerfulness and constancy under all their sufferings, to wit [1.] Their regeneration (v 3). [2.] Their matchless inheritance (v 4). [3.] The certainty of their perseverance (v 5) [4.] The shortness and [5.] the necessity of all their sufferings (v 6). [6.] Their spiritual advantage by them, to wit, the trial of their graces, especially of their faith (v 7). [7.] The happy effects of that faith, which by trials is discovered to be sound (vv 8,9). [8.] The excellency of the doctrine of salvation for which they did suffer, which is proved by the great pains and delight of the prophets, apostles and angels in the study thereof (vv 10,11,12).

In the second part are contained several exhortations to the study of holiness with motives pressing the same. As, [1.] seeing they had those excellent privileges formerly mentioned, they should therefore study perseverance, and growth in grace (v 13). [2.] Considering that they were now made children they should therefore study their Father's obedience and not live as they had done formerly (v 14). [3.] Seeing their calling was to be holy and [4.] the holiness of God did oblige them to that study (vv 15,16). [5.] Since their Father was to be their Judge, and [6.] themselves were but strangers in the world, therefore they should live in fear of offending him (v 17). [7.] Considering that they were bought from their former sinful courses with a most excellent price (vv 18,19). [8.] That their Redeemer was from eternity designed for them and more clearly manifested in their time than formerly (v 20). [9.] Seeing the Father has exalted Christ after His sufferings that believers may be the more confident that justice is fully satisfied for them (v 21). And [10.] seeing they had already made some good progress in mortification, therefore they should study to grow, especially in love to the saints (v 22). [11.] Considering that their spiritual original

5

was so excellent (v 23). And lastly, that their spiritual estate was not fading, as the best things in nature are (v 24), but behoved to endure for ever, as the Word, which is the principle of it, does (v 25). Therefore they ought to live to their Father's honour in the study of holiness.

1. **Peter, an apostle of Jesus Christ, to the strangers scattered throughout Pontus, Galatia, Cappadocia, Asia and Bithynia.**

In this part of the inscription, the penman of the Epistle first makes himself known by that new name which Christ gave him, John 1:42, and by his office, common to him with other apostles who had immediate commission, and extraordinary assistance from the Son of God to preach the gospel and to work miracles for confirmation of the same, and were not fixed, as ordinary ministers are, to any particular charge, Matt. 10:1 and 28:19. Next he describes the persons to whom this Epistle was first directed, from their afflicted external condition, to wit, that they were banished from their own country and wonted privileges and scattered in many places of the world, whereof some are here mentioned. From the Apostle's description of himself we may learn [1.] When the ministers of Jesus Christ are entering upon any part of their public employment it is then especially necessary for them to have in their hearts the sensible consideration of what honour Christ has put upon them, what engagements to be faithful to Him, what warrant they have from Him to go about their employment, and what an one He is from whom they have their calling that so they may carry along in their hearts some holy fear of slighting the work of such a one as the Son of God, to whom they must give an account, Heb. 13:17, and may have much encouragement, considering that their commission is from Him, who has all fulness, Col. 1:19, to furnish them and supply the people's necessities: for, the Apostle, entering upon this part of his employment, to wit, the writing of this Epistle, has had in heart the consideration of that new name wherewith Christ honoured him, and whereby He would have him constantly mindful of his duty, that he should be according to the signification of his name, interpreted by Christ, John 1:42, steadfast as a rock or stone in his Master's service; and likewise of his commission from so honourable and glorious a Master, as the anointed Saviour of sinners, while he writes, *Peter an Apostle of Jesus Christ*. [2.] When the message of

Christ's ministers is much slighted and opposed, and their calling much questioned, it is necessary for them openly to avow and assert their authority from Him; that people, perceiving ministers not afraid to avow themselves, and their calling from Christ, upon all hazards, may be encouraged to embrace and adhere to the truths they deliver; and having their minds raised above instruments, the truths delivered may have the greater weight with them: for, upon these grounds we may safely conceive the Apostle to prefix his name to this Epistle, and to avow his office, even in a time of persecution; *Peter an Apostle of Jesus Christ.* [3.] There has never been any supremacy over the rest of the apostles conferred upon Peter, neither did he ever assume any such thing to himself; and consequently did never cast a copy to any minister to usurp, or affect any such thing over their fellow-labourers: for, if there had been any such thing of so great concern as the church of Rome makes it, it cannot be thought, but this Apostle would have found himself bound to assert it: which if he had done any where, it could not be expected in a fitter place than in the entry of his writings, where the prophets and apostles usually assert to themselves as much dignity as the Lord allows them. And yet neither here, nor in the following epistle, is there any such thing, but at the most, *Peter an Apostle* (or messenger) *of Jesus Christ.*

From the first branch of the description of those to whom the Epistle is directed, we may learn, [1.] That exile and separation from outward comforts and privileges may be the lot of the people who are dearest to the Lord of any on earth besides; even those may be corrected and humbled for the abuse of their mercies, Psa. 89:30, and by their means, in their exile and scattering, the Lord minds to spread the seeds of saving knowledge among strangers to Him, Micah 5:7, Zech. 10:9 for which, and the like causes, the Christian Hebrews to whom the Apostle writes were called here *strangers scattered,* &c. [2.] Although the Lord's afflicted people, by reason of their ignorance and unbelief, are very prone to conclude themselves forgotten and forsaken of him, Isa. 49:14, yet those who under their affliction are humbling themselves for sin and cleaving to the truth and way of God may be confident that the Lord not only takes notice of their sad condition and of all the places of their suffering; but that He will provide some subsistence for them there, while He has service for them; and will also, as is needful, follow them through all those places, and all their mis-

7

eries, with real testimonies of His love and respect; whereof He gives here a proof while by the hand of this apostle He sends to those Christian Jews (who, though they were justly for their sins shut out of their own land, yet wanted not means of subsistence in all the places of their exile) so sweet and seasonable a message as this Epistle, directed to the *strangers scattered throughout Pontus, Galatia, Cappadocia, Asia and Bithynia.*

2. **Elect according to the foreknowledge of God the Father, through sanctification of the Spirit, unto obedience and sprinkling of the blood of Jesus Christ: Grace unto you, and peace be multiplied.**

This last part of the inscription contains the second branch of the description of those to whom the Epistle is directed, together with the Apostle's salutation of them. They are here described from their most excellent spiritual condition, to comfort them against their forementioned and outward condition, to wit, that they were wailed out[1] from among others as the word *elect* signifies, which may be safely understood both of the Lord's eternal purpose of love toward them, in which sense the word *elect* is taken, Matt. 20:16, as also of his actual separating of them from the rest of the world in their effectual calling as the word is taken, John 15:16. And that not for any foreseen good that they were to do, but according as the Lord, in his eternal foreknowledge having all *Adam's* posterity in his eye, had freely condescended upon them and appointed them to come by the way of faith and holiness (which his own Spirit was to work in them) to the full enjoyment of all that Christ had purchased for them, by His fulfilling of the law and satisfying for the breach thereof. To these in the salutation the Apostle wishes the proofs of God's favour in a continual increase of all saving graces, and true peace with God, with others and with their own consciences. From this second branch of the description of those to whom the Epistle is directed, we may learn [1.] Although none, in an ordinary way, can infallibly know the election or effectual calling of another, Rev. 2:17, yet it is not impossible for the elect and called themselves to attain to some comfortable measure of the knowledge thereof, the Lord having taken so much pains to

---

[1] 'wailed out' (usually written 'waled'): a word used in Scotland in the 17th century, meaning 'to pick out', 'to choose'.

give the marks of such in His Word and to describe a saving work by the effects thereof, which are proper to the elect and effectually called ones, John 6:37, 2 Pet. 2:7,9; and having promised His Spirit to make His own know their privileges, 1 Cor. 2:12; for it is asserted here, as Christians' chief consolation against their sad outward condition spoken of before, that they are *elect*. Now this could be no more consolation to them that were eternally elected, and effectually called, than to any other members of the church, except they might know themselves to be such as are here described: and there can be no question but their consolation is mainly intended, while they are thus spoken to, *Elect, according to the foreknowledge of God*.

[2.] Where there may be discerned in Christians a serious and constant profession of the truth of Christ, and endeavours to walk suitably thereunto, there is sufficient ground for others to esteem and deal with them as with those that are the elect of God, and in time effectually called: for, though there be no ground to think that all to whom the Apostle writes were such, yet because he intended to edify the elect and regenerate and in charity esteemed them to be serious and constant professors of the truth, even in and to be aiming at an answerable walking thereunto, he calls them here, *Elect, according to the foreknowledge of God*. [3.] Those who are powerfully drawn to believe in Jesus Christ and are changed by His Spirit and have His Spirit present, manifesting their change to be such as the Word approves for saving, have a well-grounded confidence of their election or effectual calling: for, those whom the Apostle here calls *Elect, according to the foreknowledge of God* are afterward at large described to be such as had a saving work of grace in them, to wit, saving faith in Christ (v 6), some good degree of mortification (v 22) and were daily employers of Christ for growth in grace and holiness (2:4), and had the Spirit of Jesus resting upon them (4:14). [4.] The Lord does not choose some sinners from among others, whether in His eternal purpose of love or in their effectual calling, because He did foresee them to make good use of their free will, for converting or sanctifying of themselves: but only because His Majesty, having all persons whom He purposed to frame unto salvation, under His all-seeing eye, did out of His free love condescend upon some in particular, while others were passed by: for those here who, according to the foreknowledge of God are chosen to salvation, are also chosen to come to the profession of it through that which the Lord's

Spirit works in them: and so there can be nothing foreseen in them to proceed from the right use of their free will which can be a motive to Him to choose them, since their sanctification is a work of His own Spirit, and they are not elected to salvation for it but through it to salvation as a means of His own working: *Elect, according to the foreknowledge of God, through sanctification of the Spirit.* [5.] When we consider the Lord in that act of choosing some to eternal life we ought to consider Him as a Father, both of Christ the Mediator and of all those whom He elects: for, though Christ did not merit electing love, in regard that love moved God to give Christ for sinners, John 3:16, yet we are allowed to conceive the Lord in that same act of appointing some to everlasting blessedness, to be also appointing His own Son to be their Redeemer, and to be the purchaser of that blessedness for them, and so to be putting on a fatherly affection toward them in Him, Eph. 1:4. That which costs us many thoughts and which we do, in a manner, break in many pieces in our conception was but one eternal act of God whose absolute perfection does not admit of such succession in His thoughts or purposes as He allows us to have in our thoughts concerning these: for, while the Apostle speaks of election according to the foreknowledge of God, he calls him *the Father.* [6.] All who are chosen to partake of that everlasting blessedness which Christ has purchased are appointed to come to the possession of it through *sanctification*, whereby their minds are enlightened to see their woeful condition by nature, Rev. 3:17,18, to see the possibility and excellency of a better estate, Eph. 1:17,18; their hearts are powerfully inclined to close with Christ, John 6:44,45, and they are enabled to forsake sin and follow after that which is well-pleasing in the sight of God, Jas. 1:27. And so the whole man is separated for the Lord's use, 2 Tim. 2:21, which is sanctification in a large sense: for, these whom the Apostle affirms here to be elected to partake of what Christ has purchased, he clearly intimates that they must come to it *through sanctification.* [7.] It is not in the pwer of man's free will, or of any creature whatsoever, to work any good motion or inclination in a sinner's heart (that is the work of the Spirit of God alone): for sanctification which comprehends all gracious qualities is here called the work of the *Spirit.* [8.] Jesus Christ our Mediator has both obeyed the Law perfectly for us that He might make up the defects of our imperfect obedience, Col. 2:10, and cast us a perfect copy, which we are bound to aim at in conformity, Heb. 12:2; and likewise has borne all that wrath which was due to all the elect for their breach of the Law, that so deserved wrath might pass over all His redeemed ones (as the destroying Angel passed by those whose doors were sprinkled with the blood of the paschal lamb, to which the Apostle's expression here alludes); for, both these, which are commonly called Christ's active and passive obedience, are here expressed by the Apostle, while he says, *Elect,* &c, *unto obedience and sprinkling of the blood of Jesus Christ.* [9.] All the elect will certainly partake of all that Christ has purchased by His doing and suffering for them: the first fruits whereof they get in time and the full harvest afterward: none of them can fall short of what they are from eternity destinated unto: for the Apostle says here, they are chosen *unto obedience, and sprinkling of the blood of Christ,* which is nothing else but to be chosen to lay hold on both by faith and at last fully to enjoy what both have merited for them. [10.] Although Christ's fulfilling of the Law and suffering for our breach thereof, which is here called His *obedience,* and *the sprinkling of His blood,* be in order first imputed to us for justification, before our sanctification, Rom. 8:30, yet our assurance and comfort of our interest in His obedience and sufferings is not had till after our sanctification, see John 14:21; for, to be elect through sanctification of the Spirit unto obedience, and sprinkling of the blood of Jesus Christ, is to be from eternity chosen to come by the way of holiness to the full participation of what Christ has purchased by His obedience and sufferings, to wit, peace and joy in the Holy Ghost here and the full enjoyment of God hereafter: both which are the purchase of His obedience and sufferings, to which we are elected: *Elect unto obedience and sprinkling.* [11.] When we consider that great work which concerns the salvation of lost sinners, we are to look upon all the Persons of the blessed Trinity as concurring therein, that so we may have the higher esteem of the work which has such agents, and may have our hearts raised to give equal glory to all the Persons: for though our election, redemption, sanctification and glorification be each of them the work of the whole Deity, and none of the Persons are to be excluded from any of these, yet the Scripture allows us to have such thoughts about the order of the Persons in working as we may have about the order of their subsistence: for here the Apostle sets forth the *Father* out of His good pleasure electing sinners to grace and glory: *the Son,* by His obedience and suffering, purchasing the same for them: and the *Spirit* by His virtue and power, working grace in them, and so preparing them for that blessedness which the Father has appointed and Christ has purchased for them: *Elect according to the foreknowledge of God the Father, through sanctification of the Spirit, unto obedience and sprinkling of the blood of Jesus Christ.*

From the salutation, learn, [1.] The ministers of Christ, while they are dealing with the Lord's people, should labour for enlarged desires after their welfare; so will they be the more serious and affectionate in dealing with them: their pains will be the more sweet to themselves, and the more acceptable to and successful with the people: for the apostles ordinarily begin their epistles with such ample expressions of their desires after the good of those to whom they wrote, as this Apostle does here: *Grace and peace be multiplied unto you.* [2.] No less than a continual increase of the proofs of God's favour and of all saving graces, together with true quietness of spirit and every blessing of God necessary for the same, is the Lord's allowance to His redeemed and sanctified ones: whatever measure of this allowance any of them have received, there is still more of it to be had: and still more of it will be given to them, except their unbelief and other sins obstruct the outletting thereof: for all this and much more the Apostle wishes to them and pronounces upon them in this salutation, *Grace and peace be multiplied unto you.* [3.] It is only those who have fled to Christ's merits and have begun to be changed by His Spirit, who can expect this comfortable allowance to be let forth to them: and those only Christ's ministers may in his Name certify of: for it is only those who are described in the former part of the verse to whom this is spoken: and this is not only a favourable wish of the Apostles, but a definitive sentence of the Spirit of God passed in their favours, that *Grace and peace* shall be *multiplied unto them.*

3. **Blessed be the God and Father of our Lord Jesus Christ, which according to his abundant mercy hath begotten us again unto a lively hope by the resurrection of Jesus Christ from the dead.**

Here the Apostle enters upon the first part of the chapter, wherein he sets forth the excellency of the state of believers in Jesus Christ, that thereby he may confirm them in the truth, comfort them under their sufferings and enforce upon them the study of holiness which is his principal scope in the whole Epistle. And this part he begins with a song of praise to God which all believers should follow in their hearts: the reasons of which song contain their privileges whereof every one proves their state to be most excellent, and that therefore they ought to be constant sufferers and holy walkers. The first reason is that they had a new spiritual life and nature communicated to them in their regeneration, whereby they were now made children of God: and this privilege is described and commended, [1.] From the Author thereof, that it is God, and the Father of such a Son as Christ, who has made us His children. [2.] From the impulsive cause moving Him so to do, to wit, nothing in us, but mercy in Him, which is commended from the plenty or abundance of it. [3.] This privilege of regeneration is commended from the effect of it, that thereby the regenerate are made to hope for those excellent things spoken of in the following words. The nature of which hope is cleared [1.] From the property or effect of it; it is lively, quickening the soul that has it. [2.] From the ground of it, which is the cause of its liveliness, to wit, that our Cautioner,[1] who died in our room is risen to apply His purchase and to possess us in it.

Hence we may learn, [1.] The way to make Christians steadfast in the truth, cheerful under their sufferings for it, and thriving in holiness, is to have their hearts brought to a praising disposition, from the consideration of their spiritual privileges and the excellency of the state of grace wherein they are, their hearts being thereby sweetly diverted from sad reflections upon their outward afflictions and strongly encouraged to hold on in the way of truth and holiness, notwithstanding of all discouragements: for the Apostle's scope being to confirm and comfort sufferers and to provoke them to the study of holiness, he labours first of all to engage their hearts to this exercise of praise, by raising this psalm before them, *Blessed be the God and Father*, &c. [2.] They are fittest to cheer up the hearts of others to spiritual joy and praise who have their own hearts kept so sensible of the excellent state of believers, because of their spiritual privileges, that they are ready to burst forth in the praises of God themselves and go before others in that exercise as they have a calling and opportunity: for the Apostle, being to comfort those heavy-hearted exiles under their sufferings and

---

[1] 'Cautioner': in Scottish law, a 'Guarantor'.

provoke them to praise, has his own heart so full that he must break forth in singing before them, *Blessed be the God and Father*, &c. [3.] Our praise or blessing of God is not any addition of blessedness to Him who is in that respect especially above all blessing and praise, Neh. 9:5, but it is only our acknowledgment of His praise-worthy perfections and of His goodness to sinners that they may fall in love with Him and join with us in the same acknowledgment: for that word which is translated *Blessing of God* in the New Testament signifies to speak well of Him. [4.] Of all the spiritual privileges bestowed upon sinners in time, which call them to joy and praise, the first and principal is their regeneration whereby they who are dead in sins and trespasses, and born heirs of God's curse, have a new life communicated to them, Eph. 2:1,3, and such heavenly qualities stamped upon their soul as makes them in some measure resemble their heavenly Father, Eph. 4:24; for the Apostle puts our regeneration for the first reason of this song, *Blessed be the God and Father of our Lord Jesus Christ, who hath begotten us again.* [5.] This change of a sinner's nature, which is made in regeneration, is the alone work of the omnipotent God, as the principal and efficient cause wherein He makes use of men as instruments in His hand, 1 Cor. 4:15, and of the Word from them as His means, Jas. 1:18, there being no more power in man naturally to work this change in himself than can be imagined in any man to have begotten himself. Therefore is it set forth here by such a word as may lead all the regenerate to consider themselves as wholly passive when first this change is made upon them: *Blessed be the God*, &c, *who hath begotten us again.* [6.] It exceedingly commends the free love of God in making this change upon sinners and may much heighten in their hearts the esteem of His work that He who has such a Son as Jesus Christ, who was and is His peer and equal, Phil. 2:6, the express image of his Person, Heb. 1:3, and His full delight, Prov. 8:30, should have vouchsafed upon such unworthy things as we are so sweet and honourable a relation to Himself, and that blessed Son of His, as is imported in this His begetting of us again! the esteem whereof the Apostle heightens in his own heart and in the hearts of the regenerate by this, that it is *the God and Father of our Lord Jesus Christ who hath begotten us again.* [7.] The Lord is not moved to bestow His grace upon sinners by any goodness which He did foresee or find in them, seeing none can give first to Him, Rom. 11:35, nor be profitable to Him, Job 22:2, who needs nothing from any, Acts 17:25, but

14

only by His own mercy which is that lovely property whereby He is strongly inclined to let out of His goodness to unworthy and miserable sinners who deserve the contrary from Him: for here *Mercy* is made the alone and sufficient motive of our regeneration, while the Apostle says, *According to his mercy he hath begotten us.* [8.] That mercy which moves the Lord to work a saving change upon any sinner is both very plentiful for the quantity of it and most excellent for the quality of it; and it must be so, there being so many provocations found and foreseen in sinners which only plentiful mercy can overcome, Isa. 48:8, and so many excellent favours to be bestowed upon the regenerate as never entered in their hearts to conceive, 1 Cor. 2:9, that it must be excellent mercy that bestows them. Therefore, that which moves the Lord to regenerate sinners is not simply called *mercy* but *abundant mercy*, which in the original signifies not only the plenty of it for quantity but also the excellency and worth of it for quality. [9.] The regenerate come not presently[1] to the possession of what Christ has purchased for them; they must be first tried whether they will glorify Him by living in the confident expectation of what He has purchased and promised, which is *hope* flowing from *faith*, and only differing from it in this, that *faith* apprehends the thing promised as if it were present, so giving it a spiritual kind of subsistence in the soul, Heb. 11:1, and *hope* makes the heart, with some measure of cheerful patience, expect that good which it looks upon as absent for the time, Rom. 8:25; for the want of possession for a time after regeneration is imported in this, that we are *begotten again unto a lively hope*. [10.] Before the Lord makes this powerful change upon sinners in regeneration they are altogether without any true and well-grounded hope of a better life than this, whatever strong and groundless presumptions thereof they may entertain: for so much is supposed in this, that we are *begotten again unto a lively hope*. [11.] All that have gotten a new life and nature from the Lord in regeneration have gotten therewith this grace of hope and so have His allowance to keep up their hearts in the expectation of all that He has promised: and though their ignorance and unbelief often mar the exercise of this grace, Lam. 3:18, yet they must again attain unto some measure of the exercise thereof, Lam. 3:24, it being a special act of the new life which is given in regeneration and is here made the immediate effect of

---

[1] 'presently': immediately.

it, as is imported in this, *He hath begotten us again unto a lively hope.*
[12.] The hope of the regenerate is a lively hope, quickening
them in the use of all means for attaining to what they hope for,
Heb. 12:28, and for keeping of themselves free of everything unsuitable for them, who are born to so great hopes, 1 John 3:3;
for it is here described from the property or effect of it: it is a
lively hope. [13.] That which keeps the hope of the regenerate in
life and exercise, and is the solid ground and cause thereof, is,
that Christ their Cautioner[1] having once died in their room is
now risen as a conqueror over all their spiritual enemies, Col.
2:15, in testimony that He is fully discharged of all their debt,
and they in Him, Rom. 1:4 and 4:25; whereby also they are
certified that they shall rise and share with Him in the possession
of what He has purchased and possesses in their name, John
14:2,3; 2 Cor. 4:14, for *the resurrection of Jesus Christ* is here made
the ground and cause of this lively hope.

**4. To an inheritance incorruptible, and undefiled, and that
fadeth not away, reserved in heaven for you.**

The second reason of that song of praise which all the regenerate
should keep up in their hearts is that they have a matchless inheritance to look for beyond time, which is both excellent in
itself and made very sure for them. The excellency of it the
Apostle sets forth by three properties of it, which prove it to
excel very far all earthly inheritances: [1.] That it has nothing in
itself which inclines it toward any decay. [2.] That it can admit of
nothing from without to stain the beauty and excellency of it.
And therefore, [3.] It remains to all eternity in its primitive and
native lustre. All which are sweetened by this, that it is safely kept
for the regenerate in a place above all hazard.

Hence, learn, [1.] That blessed state which the regenerate have
good ground to hope for is so matchless and excellent that it
cannot be set out by anything here away.[2] The best inheritance
here inclines to a decay, and is still defiled and fading one way or
other: but this inheritance is incorruptible, undefiled and fadeth
not away. Many words cannot commend it sufficiently, for here
are several, and those metaphoric and negative, to tell us that we
may more easily conceive and express what it is not, and what it

[1] See p. 13.
[2] 'here away': down here.

16

is like, than what it is. [2.] If the Lord's people would keep their hearts in a praising disposition, if they would be constant and cheerful in their adherence to the truth of Christ, notwithstanding of sufferings, they must have their hearts much taken up with the consideration of the excellency of their portion which is made sure for them beyond time. So will they undervalue afflictions by the way, 2 Cor. 4:17,18, and rejoice under them, Rom. 5:2,3. So will they despise the pleasures of sin, Heb. 11:25, and sweetly digest all pains in the duties of holiness, 2 Cor. 5:8,9, for the Apostle, to work up the hearts of those to whom he writes toward this frame, does here commend and propose to their consideration the excellency of their inheritance, that it is *incorruptible, undefiled, and that fadeth not away.* [3.] This inheritance which the regenerate are born unto and have good ground to hope for, is nothing else but the Lord Himself blessed for ever, to be enjoyed by them to all eternity: for what is here attributed to it is elsewhere in Scripture attributed to Him. He is *the Inheritance* of His people, Psa. 16:5, 6, *incorruptible*, Rom. 1:23, *undefiled*, Heb. 7:26, and *that fadeth not away*, Psa. 102:27. [4.] This heavenly inheritance of the saints does not come to them by their own purchase or procurement, but by virtue of their sonship, Rom. 8:17, which they have immediately upon their closing with Christ, John 1:12, as a thing purchased to them by their Father, Eph. 1:14, who has left it to them in legacy, John 17:24, and lives for ever to be the Executor of his own Testament, Heb. 7:25, and is so far from being merited by any of them that it falls as it were by lot, as Israel's inheritance in Canaan did, to which the Apostle here alludes, while he sets forth everlasting blessedness by this word *inheritance*, which signifies a thing come by heirship, left in legacy, and fallen by lot. [5.] This blessed state is made very sure for the regenerate, being from eternity decerned[1] to them, Matt. 25:34, secured to them in time by the promise of the faithful God, John 6:40, and now possessed by their Surety and Head in their name, Heb. 6:19,20, for the Apostle says, it is *reserved in heaven for them.*

5. Who are kept by the power of God through faith unto salvation ready to be revealed in the last time.

The third reason of the joy and constancy of suffering believers

---

[1] 'decerned': in ancient Scottish law, 'decreed by judicial sentence'.

is that their perseverance is made sure, the almighty power of God being employed as their guard and safe conduct by the way, to strengthen their faith and keep it from failing, till they come to the possession of their inheritance which is ready for them: and for the communication whereof the particular time is fixed and set.

Hence learn, [1.] The Lord has a great mind that the joy and consolation of the heirs of salvation should be strong and full, foreknowing that they are ready to apprehend much matter of fear and uncertainty: He guards them on every hand, having assured them in the former words that their excellent inheritance was above hazard of being lost; here He certifies them that they are no less sure and beyond all hazard of being lost in their way to the possession of it. An earthly inheritance may be sure enough kept for an heir, but who can secure the heir from death or other accidents, which may hinder his possessing of it? But for the regenerate, their inheritance is reserved in heaven for them, and they are *kept by the power of God for it.* [2.] Even the regenerate are not able of themselves to step one right step in the way to their inheritance, there being so many temptations and trials betwixt them and it to wrestle through, Acts 14:22, and the measure of grace received, so small in the best, Phil. 3:13; for their weakness is imported,[1] while so strong a guard is given to convey them through, *Who are kept* (it is a military word in the original and signifies to keep as in a strong garrison) *by the power of God.* [3.] The saints' perseverance does not depend upon their own free-will, or upon their right use of the grace already bestowed upon them, but upon the power of God engaged to be forthcoming for them and constantly employed in their through-bearing by enabling them to resist temptations, 2 Cor. 12:9, supporting them under their trials, Deut. 33:27, raising them up from their falls, Psa. 37:24, and lifting them over difficulties insuperable to them, Isa. 40:11, so as not one of these can finally fall away or be lost: *Who are kept by the power of God.* [4.] The principal way how this power of God works in making the saints to persevere is by giving them faith to rest upon His Word, who is faithful and able to save to the uttermost, Heb. 7:25, keeping it in life and exercise, Psa. 66:9, and answering of it with necessary supplies, John 16:24, for so says the Apostle here, the power of God keeps believers *through faith*: which is not

---

[1] 'imported': implied.

to be understood as if this power presupposed faith at first (for God's power works it, 2 Pet. 1:3, or, as if this power did not act for us, even when our faith falls from exercise, Psa. 94:18. But the meaning of it is that perseverance in grace presupposes faith, and is wrought by the means of faith in exercise, and that the power of God works most comfortable effects, when the exercise of that grace of faith is most lively, and works always for believers through faith, insofar as all the offices which this power performs for them are in answer to that faith which did receive Christ for salvation, and the through-bearing to the possession of it. [5.] It does not now appear to the saints what a blessed portion is made sure to them. If they got but a glimpse of it they would be ready to be swallowed up, Matt. 17:6, for that there is a vail now upon it is imported in this that the Apostle says, It is *ready to be revealed*. [6.] The want of the full possession of this inheritance by the saints is not because it is not ready for them (for it is designed for them, Matt. 25:44, it is brought to them, Eph. 1:14, and possessed by Christ in their name, John 14:2, who is said to prepare it, in regard His possessing of it in our nature was necessary before our bodies could come there) but because they are not yet ready for it, neither will they be ready till the full number of the elect be brought in, Rev. 6:11, and every one of them be brought to their full stature in grace, which is appointed for them in this life, Eph. 4:13; both which should be furthered by the prayers and endeavours of all that long to be in heaven: for of that inheritance, which is all one with salvation, the Apostle says *It is ready to be revealed*. [7.] It may be very comfortable to the saints to consider that the particular time when they shall be possessed in their heavenly inheritance is determined: the marriage day betwixt Christ and His bride is fixed, and will be in the time that is fittest and happiest for them: and especially to consider that that day cannot now be far off, these days of ours being the last days, so that the bodies of the saints who live now are not to sleep long in the dust: for the word here signifies that determinate point of time which is fittest for the work: and thereby the Apostle may safely be conceived to add some weight to this reason of believers' joy and constancy, to wit, that their inheritance which is made so sure for them is also ready to be revealed *in the last time*.

6. Wherein ye greatly rejoice, though now for a season (if need be) ye are in heaviness through manifold temptations.

That the Apostle may yet further provoke sad-hearted sufferers to spiritual joy and praise, wherein himself had gone before them, he here commends them as having already attained to a good measure of delight in that exercise. And withal gives two further reasons thereof: the one is, that all their hard exercises, and heaviness occasioned thereby, were but of short continuance. The other is, that both of these were necessary for them as he clears in the following words. Both which reasons prove that neither their hardships, nor heaviness flowing therefrom, should hinder their joy and constancy: and that their spiritual estate behoved to be most excellent since it could afford them such matter of joy under so sad a temporal condition.

Hence learn, [1.] None of the children of the Lord should think, because of the excellency of their spiritual estate and privileges, to be exempted from a very sad lot in the world, but so much the rather may expect to be hated by the world, John 15:19, to be assaulted by Satan, Luke 22:31, and chastened by the Lord for their trial and humiliation, Heb. 12:6; for, those who were before described to be elect, regenerate and heirs of a matchless inheritance, are here supposed to be *in heaviness through manifold temptations*. [2.] Variety of afflictions may meet together upon the dearest of God's children, there being in the best of them many corruptions to be discovered and subdued, Psa. 19:12, for which cause afflictions are sent, Isa. 27:9, and many graces are to be tried and proved, Rom. 5:3, for which trials, afflictions are as workmen, working to others' hands, Rom. 8:28; for here the heirs of the heavenly inheritance are supposed to be in *manifold temptations*: which words do signify, both many for their number and various for their kind or quality. [3.] With the manifold trials and afflictions of the godly, there come oftentimes along to them temptations to sin against God: particularly, temptations to question the love of the Lord to them because of these hardships, Isa. 49:14: Psa. 77:9; to take some sinful course for their ease or out-gate, Psa. 125:3; to weary of all duties under their trials, yea, and of life itself, Jonah 4:8, for the Spirit of the Lord makes use of one word here, and ordinarily in Scripture, to signify both the afflictions or hard exercises of the godly, and temptations, strictly so called, or solicitations to sin against God; both which, because they are not ordinarily separated, are comprehended under these words *manifold temptations*. [4.] When the people of God are exercised with variety of trials, and those accompanied with variety of temptations to sin, then heaviness of spirit seizes readily upon them; partly because they do not consider how well the love of the Lord and such a lot may stand together, Heb. 12:5, and partly, because they mind their own weakness more than the power engaged to carry them through, Isa. 51.12,13, for such is the case wherein the godly here spoken to are supposed to be, to wit, not only under manifold temptations but *in heaviness through manifold temptations*. [5.] Heaviness of spirit, occasioned by manifold temptations, and much spiritual joy, may consist together in one and the same soul; these contrary qualities are sometimes in the hearts of the godly not only in a remiss degree at the same time so as hardly they will know which of them is prevalent, Psa. 94:19, but also in their height sometimes they are successively, one consideration making them very sad and another succeeding thereto making them so glad as hardly can they keep their joy within, Psa. 30:5; for those here spoken to were both in heaviness, considering the many trials and temptations wherewith they were exercised, and yet considering the Lord's everlasting love, their fair inheritance formerly described and their advantage by their trials spoken of afterward, they did *greatly rejoice*; which words signify joy, breaking out in expressions and gestures as appears by comparing Luke 6:23 with Matt. 5:12. [6.] All the hardships of the godly and their heaviness occasioned thereby, are of very short continuance: the Lord knows their spirits are ready to fail, Isa. 57:16, and they are in hazard to put forth their hands to iniquity, Psa.125:3, and therefore he gives them many breathing times, sometimes from their troubles, sometimes from their heaviness while their troubles are continued; and sometimes gives them such sweetness inter-mixed with both as makes them think little of either, Rom. 8:18, and though their whole life, even to old age, were like Heman's, Psa. 88:15, yet being compared with eternity it is but according to this word in the text, a little *now* or a small *season*. [7.] All the temptations and heaviness that come upon any of the children of God are needful for them that thereby they may be reclaimed from their wanderings, Psa. 119:67, made like their head Christ Jesus in sufferings and temptations, Rom. 8:29, that by these they may be made partakers of His holiness, Heb. 12:10, and (as it is in the following words) that their graces may by tried and themselves fitted for glory. Therefore the Apostle says, *If need be*, they are in heaviness through manifold temptations. [8.] The short continuance and necessity of all the trials and heaviness incident to the godly should cheer up their hearts under them: for, both these are here mentioned as further reasons of that song which the Apostle began before: *Now for a season (if need be) ye are in heaviness*, &c. [9.] The experience that the Lord's people have had of any comfort or cheerfulness in His service under their former trials and heaviness should make them constant in His way and should guard their hearts against fears of future trials: for, it being the Apostle's scope to provoke to constancy and cheerfulness, he makes their own experience of former sweetness in their state an argument for that end; *Wherein ye greatly rejoice, though now for a season*, &c. [10.] Even those who for the present have as many reasons as makes them rejoice in their condition, do stand in need to have yet more represented to them: for, while the Apostle says *wherein ye greatly rejoice*, &c, he holds forth this, that they had attained to much spiritual joy from the consideration of their fair inheritance, and other privileges spoken of before; and yet here he finds it needful to present them with two further reasons of joy, to wit, that their trials and heaviness were both of short continuance and necessary for them. [11.] It is no easy matter to get the hearts of them who have much reason of spiritual joy and have attained to a good measure thereof already, kept in that frame and brought to that height in it which is possible, especially when they are under a sad condition outwardly, they being then ready to think themselves exempted from further, as impossible to be attained unto, Psa. 137:4; for after the Apostle has raised the song to them and given them several reasons of it in the preceding words, he here makes use of other reasons and takes another course to provoke them to this duty in these words, *wherein ye greatly rejoice*, &c, which may be both taken for a commendation of them, to engage them to hold on, and likewise for a command: for, the words in the original may be read in the imperative, *Wherein do ye greatly rejoice*, &c.

7. **That the trial of your faith, being much more precious than of gold that perisheth, though it be tried with fire, might be found unto praise and honour and glory at the appearing of Jesus Christ.**

The sixth reason of the song of the regenerate which proves that neither their temptations nor their heaviness should mar their joy, is taken from the spiritual advantage they have by their trials, to wit, that the grace of God in them, particularly their faith, is thereby discovered to be sound and saving, which advantage the Apostle affirms to be of more worth to them than if they had the best gold on earth: for that being never so well tried will soon perish; but faith proved to be sound by a steadfastness under trials shall be much commended and gloriously rewarded by Jesus Christ at His appearance.

Hence, learn [1.] The children of the Lord have not ordinarily so clear a proof of the reality of His grace in them, especially of their faith, as when they are under sore trials. Before these come they are often either succumbing to their own fears as if they had no faith at all to bear them through, as *David* was, Psa. 55:5, or else, presuming their faith to be much stronger than it is, as *Peter* was, Matt. 26:33,35; for the Apostle makes this the advantage of sufferings to the godly, that by them they have the trial, or as the word signifies the experiment, to wit, of the soundness of their faith, importing they had it not, at least in that measure, before. [2.] Those very exercises whereby the Lord tries and discovers to his people the soundness of their faith, ought to be more esteemed of and rejoiced in than those exercises which bring greatest gain to men of any in the world, there being so much comfort flowing in upon the soul upon the discovery of the soundness of faith: for the comparison is here between those painful exercises which men have in trying gold wherein they take great pleasure, and those painful exercises wherewith God tries and discovers the reality of the faith of his people, as the words in the original make clear, *That the trial of your faith, being much more precious than of gold that perisheth.* [3.] The smallest measure of saving faith is of more worth than the most precious thing in this world: not so much for any worth in that grace itself, as because of the worth of what it apprehends and because of the promises made to the soul endued with it; by virtue whereof it keeps them that have it from fainting under their trials, Psa. 27:13, guards their hearts from the evil of the worst of outward plagues, Psa. 91:9,10, and is such a jewel as can never be lost Rom. 11:29; for if those exercises which are for the trial of faith be more precious than those which are for trying of gold that perishes, as the Apostle here affirms, then how precious must faith itself be! [4.] So glorious shall be the reward that Christ shall bestow upon those who have been faithful to Him under trials that many words cannot express it. He shall then commend (as the word *praise* signifies) their faith before men and angels, Rev. 3:5. He shall then lift them up to high dignity, which the Scripture expresses by setting them on thrones, Rev. 3:21, and giving them crowns, 2 Tim. 4:8, and which the Apostle here calls *honour*, and shall make them share with Him of His own blessedness, John 17:22,24 which is here called *glory*. His people should consider if all this may not make up all the shame and disgrace that can be in their trials, that their faith shall be *found unto praise and honour and glory at His appearing*. [5.] Notwithstanding of all that is held forth concerning Christ in Scripture and spoken from it by His servants, to make Him known, His worth and excellency will be much hid from the best of His own till the last day, which is here called *The appearing* (or as the word signifies, the opening up of the hid things) *of Jesus Christ*. [6.] The present advantage of trials to believers, to wit the discovery of the soundness of their faith and the future reward of constancy under them, which is eternal glory, should recompence and make up in their esteem all the pain, shame and loss that can be in those trials: for this verse contains an argument to believers of joy and praise, notwithstanding of trials and heaviness occasioned thereby, to wit, that by those they should have a trial of their faith which shall be *found unto praise and honour and glory at the appearing of Jesus Christ*.

8. **Whom having not seen, ye love: in whom though now ye see him not, yet believing, ye rejoice with joy unspeakable and full of glory.**

The seventh reason of the joy and constancy of believers under their sufferings is taken from the happy effects of that faith which their hard exercises were sent to try. The first effect of it is that it made them to love Jesus Christ though they have never seen Him in the flesh. The second is that while they did exercise their faith upon Him as their Saviour, though now absent from them in regard of His bodily presence, their hearts were filled with exceeding great joy, which the Apostle describes from two properties of it. [1.] That it was such as no tongue could express either the nature or height of it, and [2.] That it was a beginning of that joy which glorified spirits have in heaven.

Hence, learn, [1.] True faith in Jesus Christ has always love to Him flowing from it, which will make the soul hate everything it knows to be contrary to His nature and will, Psa. 97.10, and will constrain the soul to set about everything it knows will please and honour Him, 2 Cor. 5:4; for here love to Christ is made the effect of that faith which after trial is found to be sound: *Whom having not seen, ye love*. [2.] That faith which has love to Christ flowing from it will bring in much joy to the soul of the believer even under sore trials and sore heaviness occasioned thereby upon the natural spirits, that faith being the grace which appropriates the chief good to the soul that has it, Canticles 2:16, and lets the soul see clearly through present afflictions to a certain and blessed outgate, 2. Cor. 4:18, and our love to Christ being a clear proof of the love of God to us, John 16:27; for here joy is made another effect of that faith which has love to Christ flowing from it: *Whom having not seen, ye love: in whom, though now ye see him not, yet believing, ye rejoice*. [3.] They who do by faith heartily embrace Christ offered to them in the Word, will love Him and joy in Him as if they had seen Him and conversed with Him bodily; it being the nature of true faith to make the thing it closes with spiritually present to the soul, Heb. 11:1. Therefore those suffering believers are here commended that they did love and rejoice in Jesus Christ though they had never seen Him as the Apostle had done, to wit, in the flesh: *Whom having not seen, ye love: in whom, though now ye see him not, yet believing, ye rejoice*. [4.] There are many who are true lovers of Jesus Christ and have now and then some good measure of spiritual joy in Him, who do not as they ought reflect upon themselves as such, and therefore do not find themselves so engaged to cheerfulness and constancy under their trials as otherwise they would; for here the Spirit of the Lord directs the Apostle to lead suffering Christians to reflect upon themselves as those who did love Christ and rejoice in Him, importing that they needed this intimation; and that by taking themselves to be such, they would be much encouraged to constancy and cheered up under their sufferings; *Whom having not seen, ye love: in whom, though now ye see him not, yet believing, ye rejoice*, &c. [5.] Whatever impediment or difficulty a believer goes over in the exercise of any grace, it will be taken much notice of by Jesus Christ, and will tend much to the believer's advantage when Christ and he meet: for the difficulty which those sufferers went over in the exercise of their love and faith is twice expressed: *Whom having not seen, ye love: in whom, though now ye see him not, yet believing, ye rejoice*, importing that the fewer sensible helps faith has beside the Word it is the more highly esteemed by Jesus Christ, and will so much the more be found to praise and honour and glory at His appearance. [6.] It is not impossible for a child of God in the midst of many trials and discouragements (having nothing that can give him comfort but the Word of the Lord) to have his heart now and then filled with such joy as hardly can be kept within doors, and such as no tongue nor words can sufficiently express; while by faith he closes with God as his Father in Christ, and views his spiritual privileges, the certainty of his perseverance and the excellency of his reward: for, upon these grounds held forth in the former words, the Apostle here affirms of these suffering and sad-hearted exiles that *believing, they did rejoice* (which is a word that signifies such joy as breaks forth in outward signs and expressions, and yet cannot be sufficiently expressed, for he adds) *with joy unspeakable*. [7.] The lively exercise of faith will sometimes give the soul that has it some tastes of the first fruits of glory, to wit, of that sweetness in communion with God which they that are in glory live upon, the believer having in his heart the well-grounded assurance of the full possession thereof, Rom. 5:2 and 8:38, and will enable the soul humbly to boast and glory over all possible difficulties, while it takes hold of that power which is engaged to carry it through (v 5) for in both these respects the Apostle affirms this joy which flows from believing, to be *full of glory*.

9. Receiving the end of your faith, even the salvation of your souls.

Here is a third effect of that faith formerly described, which is also the cause of that love and joy flowing from it; to wit, that while believers do close with Christ offered in the Gospel, they do thereby receive in the arms of their faith an undoubted right to, and some begun possession of, eternal salvation, which is here called the end of their faith; because it is one main blessing of Christ which faith is allowed to aim at in holding fast to Him, and for the obtaining whereof that grace is given.

Hence, learn, [1.] Even in this life believers may get a begun possession of life eternal. While they receive Christ upon His own terms they not only get a right to it through Him, as sure as if they were possessed of it, Eph. 2:6, but sometimes also they get foretastes of that sweetness which is in heaven, Rev. 2:17, for the

Apostle makes this a third effect of that faith which by trials is discovered to be sound, that by it believers do *receive the salvation of their souls*. [2.] Jesus Christ allows those who fly to Him by faith to eye the salvation of their souls as one prime benefit to be had by Him, and does not so hold forth Himself to be the object of saving faith, as if all that have it behoved, while they close with Him, to abstract from their own advantage by Him: for here the exercise of saving faith, which shall be found to praise at His appearing, is made to consist in a *receiving of the salvation of the soul* as one act thereof. [3.) It is not enough once to have taken hold of salvation through Christ in the promise, but as we would have true comfort along the course of our pilgrimage, we must be still renewing our grasp of Him for salvation, from the renewed sense of our lostness and hazard to perish without Him: for the Apostle speaks here of those believers who had, no question, long before closed with Christ for salvation in the promise, as yet still, or frequently at least, exercising their faith in Him for that end: *Receiving the end of your faith, the salvation of your souls.* [4.] It is not so much the habit of saving faith as the exercise thereof that brings in to the soul that true spiritual joy whereof the Apostle spoke in the words before. If the exercise of faith be, by the neglect or slighting of duty, or by the commission of any sin, interrupted, then will that joy unspeakable and full of glory be also interrupted; for this faith whence that joy, described in the former words, flows is here set out by a word in the present time, importing that when it has that effect it must be in exercise: *Receiving the end of your faith, the salvation of your souls.* [5.] While the believer is enabled to close with Christ for salvation in the promise, he begins to be victorious over all his enemies, because of his union with Him who has overcome them all, John 16:33, and gets that in hand which he should esteem a reward of all his pains in Christ's service; to wit, an undoubted right to the salvation of his soul through Christ: for the word *receiving* here, whereby the Apostle expresses the act of faith, has in it a metaphor from those wrestlers who, after the victory, are taking the prize and carrying it: and the word which is here translated the *end of faith* may be also rendered the *reward of it; receiving the end of your faith, the salvation of your souls.* [6.] Whatever a believer may lose upon his journey, seeing he is sure to come well to the end of it, and has his better part, the soul, beyond peril, he may rejoice in the midst of all sufferings by the way; for this may safely be taken for the nearest cause of that joy unspeakable and full of glory which believers have, that while they did exercise their faith, they were *receiving the end of their faith*, or the reward of it, even *the salvation of their souls*.

10. Of which salvation the prophets have enquired and searched diligently, who prophesied of the grace that should come unto you:

In this and the two following verses is contained the last reason of the joy and constancy of believers under their sufferings (which might be branched out in several arguments to that purpose), the sum whereof is that all the prophets and apostles, yea, the very angels of heaven are co-disciples and fellow-students of this way of salvation which the Gospel holds forth: and therefore it is worthy to be rejoiced in even under sufferings for it. This tenth verse holds forth how accurate and serious searchers into the nature of this salvation, as held forth in the Gospel, the prophets were, who did foretell of a more clear manifestation of the doctrine concerning it, and of a more plentiful out-letting of the graces of the Spirit upon those who live after Christ's incarnation than had been upon those who lived before: and this may be taken for an argument by itself to move those upon whom that grace is bestowed, cheerfully to adhere to the Gospel, notwithstanding of sufferings for it.

Hence, learn, [1.] The way of salvation by Jesus Christ, which is held forth in the New Testament, is no new light broken up since Christ's days in the flesh; but is the very same in substance which was known to the prophets under the Old Testament, and by them made known to the church then. Although the doctrine of salvation be now clearer and the gifts and graces of the Spirit more plentifully dispensed, since the price of redemption is actually paid, for which God gave out upon trust grace and glory to the elect before; yet the way of salvation then, and now, is one and the same for substance: for of that salvation which believers in Christ do by faith now under the Gospel receive, the Apostle here speaks: *Of which salvation the prophets have enquired*, &c. [2.] So sweet and ravishing a study is that way of salvation through Christ incarnate that the more knowledge thereof any attain to, they will still be the more and more inquisitive and diligent after a further measure of it; so that those can know nothing of Christ savingly who satisfy themselves with any measure of the knowledge of Him that they have already attained to: for even the prophets after some insight in that way, partly by immediate revelation and partly by their former diligence, were not taken off from the painful use of ordinary means; such as reading, meditation, prayer and careful prying into the meaning of those manifold types which held forth that way of salvation through the Messiah to come and the benefits which the redeemed have by Him; but did renew and double their diligence, as is imported by the several words here to one purpose; *Of which salvation the prophets have enquired, and searched diligently.* [3.] All that deliver the mind of God to His people ought to be affectionate and serious students of it themselves, that so they may make the truths they are to deliver their own and have their hearts affected therewith. Psa. 45:1. So may they expect it shall be more blest to take impression and have effects upon the hearers: for the words here, expressing the prophets' pains in the study of that way of salvation through Christ, do import that never did hunters with greater eagerness and delight pursue their game, nor those that dig in the earth where they know some rich treasure is to be had more seriously apply themselves to that exercise, than the prophets did insist upon this study: *Of which salvation the prophets have enquired and searched diligently, who prophesied before.* [4.] The prime subject both of the Old and New Testament, whereupon all the ministers of Christ should insist with His people, is the free grace of God, manifested in giving Christ for sinners, in His powerful drawing of their hearts to close with Him, for pardoning grace and for renewing of their natures by inherent grace; and so obliging and enabling them to walk worthy of that grace of God: for the sum of the prophets' work (in which the apostles concur, as the following words make clear) was *to prophesy of the grace that should come unto us.* [5.] Although this grace was made known, and communicated to them who lived before Christ's incarnation, Acts 10:43, yet it is in a special manner come to those who live after in regard of a clearer manifestation of the doctrine of God's grace, 2 Cor. 3:18, a more plentiful communication of the gifts and graces of His spirit, Acts 2:16, and that both of these are extended to some of all nations, Col. 3:11. In which respects it is here called *the grace come unto us.*

11. **Searching what, or what manner of time the Spirit of Christ which was in them did signify, when it testified beforehand the sufferings of Christ, and the glory that should follow.**

The Apostle clears yet further the prophets' pains in the study of that way of salvation through Christ incarnate, showing that they were exceeding desirous and diligent to have known the particular time of His coming in the flesh, and to have known more clearly than they did, how happy those times behoved to be, whereof the Spirit of Christ (who was even then in an extraordinary way present with them) did mean, when He moved them to describe, so long beforehand, the humiliation or sufferings of the Messiah, and His exaltation, or the glorious effects that were to follow upon His sufferings, to Himself and His redeemed ones: therefore they who lived after His incarnation ought cheerfully and constantly to adhere to the Gospel, notwithstanding of all their sufferings.

Hence learn, [1.] It is the way which the Lord usually keeps with the dearest of His servants to let out His mind to them by little and little, to make plain some things to them and keep up other things from them that He may humble them, quicken them to diligence, and keep up correspondence between Himself and them; for though it was made clear to the prophets that Christ was to be incarnate, that much grace should be in His days and more blessed times than any they had seen: and however, all of them had some intimation of the time of His incarnation by *Jacob's* prophecy, Gen. 49.10, and those of them who lived after the Captivity by *Daniel's* prophecy, Dan. 9:24, yet they were kept dark concerning the particular time when He should come, and the distinct quality of His times, what form of worship and way of administration of Gospel ordinances there should be then. Therefore are they here set forth, *Searching what, or what manner of time the Spirit of Christ which was in them did signify* &c. [2.] The Holy Spirit is a Person subsisting, distinct from the Father and the Son, proceeding from both, John 15:26, and true God, equal to both, to whom future events are known as if they were actually existing: for, here He is called the Spirit of Christ, and is said to *testify beforehand the sufferings of Christ*. [3.] Jesus Christ, the second Person of the Trinity, has been before His incarnation actually exercising the office of mediatorship, revealing to the church in all ages the way of salvation through His sufferings: for, it was the Spirit of the Son of God that dwelt in the prophets and made known to them those things concerning the Mediator whereof they did prophesy: *The Spirit of Christ in them testified beforehand.* [4.] The chief things which the Spirit of Christ manifested to the prophets and wherewith their prime study was taken up, were the sufferings of the Mediator, and the glory that should follow thereupon to Him and His redeemed ones; it being the end of all the discoveries of sin and threatenings of wrath that are in the Law, to point out the necessity of His satisfaction, Rom. 8:3, and the very substance and signification of all the types and sacrifices to point forth His sufferings and the glorious effects thereof, Heb. 10:1; for the Apostle comprises the substance of that which the Spirit of Christ in the prophets did signify to them and testify to the church by them in these two: *The sufferings of Christ* and *the glory that should follow.* [5.] This method was kept with Christ the Head, and none of His members should expect to have it changed with them, that He was first to suffer and then glory was to follow. So that the Jews have no warrant from any thing in the prophets to expect a Messiah in worldly glory without suffering: for this is the sum of all that the prophets spoke of the Messiah at the direction of His Spirit in them. *They testified beforehand of the sufferings of Christ and the glory that should follow.*

12. **Unto whom it was revealed, that not unto themselves but unto us they did minister the things which are now reported unto you by them that have preached the Gospel unto you, with the Holy Ghost sent down from heaven, which things the angels desire to look into.**

That the Apostle may yet further commend the truths of the Gospel as worthy to be rejoiced in and suffered for, and may prove the state of believers now to be in some respects more excellent than that of the ancient prophets, he shows, [1.] What success the prophets had of their pains; although they got not the very thing they did so much desire, which was not only to have known the time of Christ's coming in the flesh, but to have lived to see it, as is clear by comparing the former verse with Luke 10:24. Yet the Lord condescended to give them such an answer of their pains as might quiet their hearts, to wit, that they themselves were not to see the temporal accomplishment of their own prophecies. That was reserved for them who were to live after Christ's incarnation. [2.] He shows that what the prophets had foretold was now much cleared to the Christian church by the apostles who were for that end endued with an extraordinary measure of the Holy Spirit sent down upon them in the day of Pentecost. And [3.] He affirms that this way of salva-

31

tion through Christ already incarnate, as it is now cleared and administered under the Gospel, is so ravishing a subject that it takes up the delight and study of the angels in heaven to pry in upon it. Every one of which infers that conclusion which is to be understood as the Apostle's scope, that therefore believers now ought cheerfully to adhere to the truths of the Gospel whatever they may suffer for so doing.

Hence learn, [1.] Although the Lord does not always answer the approved pains of His servants with desired satisfaction in the particular that they aim at, yet it is not His way to leave them without such an answer and fruit of their pains as shall be more for His honour, their true good and the good of others also, than if they had received that satisfaction which they so much desired: for, though the prophets (who were approved in their search after the time of Christ's manifestation in the flesh, there being somewhat concerning it revealed, Gen. 49:10, Dan. 9:24, and there being nowhere a discharge of enquiry after that time, as there is after the time of Christ's second coming. Matt. 24:36, 1 Thess. 5:1:) got not their desired satisfaction either by seeing or knowing particularly the time of Christ's incarnation, yet they were not left without an answer from their Master, but had as much of His mind manifested to them as might quiet their minds; *Unto whom it was revealed, that not unto themselves, but unto us they did minister.* [2.] It ought to be no discouragement to Christ's servants that He puts them to much pains in His service for the good of others, withholding from them in the meantime that measure of satisfaction which He minds to bestow upon others by their pains; it being a sufficient encouragement to any of His servants or people to know that He honours them to serve Him acceptably, and that He will make up all their present loss when He and they meet; for, to the prophets, who were very laborious and assiduous as the bees who make sweet honey for others and taste but sparingly of it themselves, *It was revealed* (as a sufficient reward of all their pains) *that not unto themselves, but unto us they did minister.* [3.] Although the fruit of Christ's death has ever been, since the beginning of the world, forthcoming for the salvation and comfort of the elect, Rev. 13:8, yet the advantage of those who live after His incarnation is, in some respects, greater than theirs who lived before: and that (besides other reasons) because the truth of things revealed then is now more evident to those who may compare prophecies with their accomplishment: for it is here set down as some piece of disadvantage to the prophets that *not unto themselves, but unto us they did minister the things.* [4.] There is a complete harmony between the Scriptures of the Old and New Testaments whatever seeming contradiction may be apprehended by blind minds to be between them, for the Apostle affirms here that the prophets did minister the same things *which are now reported by them that have preached the Gospel.* [5.] To make the truth lovely to us and to confirm us in adhering to it under sufferings, it is necessary that the Spirit of Jesus be acknowledged to be with the messenger, making known to him the truth and enabling him to deliver it: although the way of the Spirit's presence with and assistance of extraordinary messengers, was different from His way with ordinary ministers. Yet, if it was necessary to be acknowledged in order to people's profiting by the one, it is much more necessary for their profiting by the other. Therefore to make the doctrine of the Gospel lovely to people, and to confirm them in adhering to it, notwithstanding of sufferings, the Apostle says that the same things which the Spirit of Christ did signify to the prophets were reported by them that preached the Gospel to them, *with the Holy Ghost sent down from heaven.* [6.] Although the glorified angels can have no such desires as have any painful unsatisfaction with them, seeing they live in the blessed vision and constant fruition of God, Matt. 18:10, yet so excellent and ravishing a mystery is this plot of the salvation of lost sinners through Christ incarnate which the Gospel manifests, that they are no less humble and accurate students of it, and no less seriously taken up with the contemplation of the way of God's reconciling Himself to sinners, and keeping familiar correspondence with them in the man Christ, than if they had such desires; as is imported in this word in the original which has in it an allusion to the type of the two cherubim that were upon the Ark looking down into the Mercy-seat; *which things the angels desire to look into.* [7.) The more attesters of the truths of the Gospel we have, the more worthy those have been and the more taken up with the study thereof, the more we are obliged to delight and adhere to the same, notwithstanding of all sufferings: if we slight so great a salvation, or faint in our adherence to the Gospel revealing it because of any possible sufferings from men, great must our judgment be. Many witnesses may be brought forth against us in the day of the Lord, even this cloud of witnesses, all the prophets and apostles and the angels of Heaven who have with such harmony and earnestness delighted in this study: for this is the force of the

Apostle's principal argument in this and the two preceding verses which might be branched out in many pertinent arguments to press cheerful suffering for the truth of the Gospel, that the prophets were such serious and painful students thereof; the apostles also have agreed with them, and these same things also *the angels desire to look into.*

13. Wherefore gird up the loins of your mind, be sober, and hope to the end for the grace that is to be brought unto you at the revelation of Jesus Christ;

In this second part of the chapter the Apostle draws from his former doctrine concerning the excellent state and rich privileges of believers several exhortations to the study of holiness and presses the same by several motives. The first exhortation is that they would draw up their affections (which are here called the loins of the mind because they follow the motions of the understanding) from things below and unite them together upon Jesus Christ, and their spiritual and eternal privileges spoken of before. The second is that they would study sobriety; which is not only to keep themselves free of unlawful pleasures, but mainly to meddle sparingly with lawful delights. The third is that they would live constantly in the believing expectation of that full manifestation of God's favour and that perfection in holiness which Christ will bring with Him to His own at His last appearance. And all these the Apostle presses by the consideration of those privileges of believers formerly mentioned as the first motive, comprehensive of many others.

Hence learn, [1.] The consideration of our spiritual privileges by Jesus Christ should stir us up to the study of holiness; our diligence in that study being the means of our perseverance and that which clears our right to take the comfort of those privileges, 2 Pet. 1:10,11. So that whatever matter of joy and praise believers have, it should be turned by them in motives to the duties of holiness; and therefore they can have no true comfort in their spiritual privileges who are by the apprehension of them cast over in security and not quickened to their duty: for the Apostle (having in the former part of the chapter held forth many grounds of joy and praise to believers under all their sufferings, from their election, regeneration, their right to the heavenly inheritance, the certainty of their perseverance and other privileges) teaches them here to turn all these into motives to holiness, while he infers from them these and the following exhortations, *Wherefore gird up the loins of your mind, be sober*, &c. [2.] Till the heirs of glory be possessed of their inheritance they should still think with themselves that much of their way and work and many difficulties are yet between them and the possession thereof, that so they may be kept from security and defection and may be still fitting themselves for their journey, and their warfare: for, this ancient custom of trussing up long garments, whence the word here is borrowed, was especially used when they were to journey, or run a race, 1 Kings 18:46; 2 Kings 4:29, or when they were to fight, Isa. 8:9: *Gird up the loins of your mind.* [3.] The affections of the children of the Lord are oftentimes low and scattered, partly while they are sinking under sinful discouragement, Psa. 42:5, and partly while they are divided and spent upon base and sinful objects, Psa. 119:36,37, both which, as main hindrances of Christians in their course toward their heavenly inheritance, are set out in this exhortation to be their too ordinary temper: *Gird up the loins of your mind.* [4.] It should be the great study of those who mind their spiritual journey and warfare to get their affections elevated above things earthly, united together upon Jesus Christ (see Col. 3:1, Psa. 86: 11) and taken up with their privileges by Him, and the duties their privileges calls them to; otherwise they can no more make progress in their Christian course than a man whose garments are about his feet can run or fight: *wherefore gird up the loins of your mind.* [5.] They that would keep up their affections from discouragement or settling upon things earthly, should labour to have their minds upward, the notions and discourses thereof (as the word here translated *the mind* signifies) taken up with things spiritual and heavenly, because the affections do follow and depend upon the motions of the mind or understanding; for which cause, they are here called the *loins of the mind.* Therefore the Apostle, having in the former part laboured to draw up their minds to the contemplation of their spiritual and eternal privileges, he here exhorts to draw up and unite upon these their affections: *Gird up the loins of your mind.* [6.] They that would make progress in their journey toward their heavenly inheritance must study sobriety, which consists in the composing of the rage and excess of carnal passions and perturbations, Luke 8:35, in the entertaining and expressing a mean esteem of our selves and a high esteem of the least good in others, Rom. 12:3, in a prudent wariness to meddle with or vent our opinion of things above our reach or calling, Act 26:25, in a spare meddling with all sensible delights, though lawful in themselves; the excess whereof no less indisposes Christians for spiritual performances than excess of meat or drink does a man for his work or journey, Luke 21:34, and in a holy and strict watchfulness (as the word in the original also signifies) lest we offend in any of these ways: for, as all the rest of the exhortations here are given to fit believers for their journey toward their fair inheritance formerly described, so is this, *Be sober*. [7.] Even those for whom the heavenly inheritance is made sure and who have attained to some comfortable measure of assurance that they shall possess it, have need to be stirred up to the study of perseverance in grace and holiness; especially to keep their hearts still up in the confident expectation of that blessedness which faith closes with in the promise, which is the exercise of the grace of hope; and to live so as they may never mar that confidence, whether by security or discouragement, knowing that when we lose our confidence we do therewith lose our strength for all duties, Lam. 3:18, for even those for whom the heavenly inheritance is made sure (v 4), whose perseverance is also sure (v 5), and whose comfort in the believing of both is very great (v 6), are here exhorted *to hope to the end*. [8.] That which strengthens the believers' hope of glory, and keeps it in life and exercise, is the believing consideration of that complete ransom paid by Christ for them that fly to Him, His undertaking to cause them to persevere, and their own frequent reflecting upon the evidences of His grace in themselves: for, upon these grounds held forth in the former part of the chapter, does the Apostle infer this exhortation, *Wherefore gird up*, &c. *and hope to the end*. [9.] The largest manifestations of the favour of God and the highest degree of holiness which any attain to in time is but small, being compared with that measure of both which believers have good ground to hope for when Christ and they shall meet: for these who had a good measure of both are here exhorted to look for a further: *Hope to the end, for the grace that is to be brought*. [10.] Christ is now under a veil to believers, his bodily presence being necessarily withdrawn from them, John 16:7, and his spiritual glory but seen in a glass darkly by them who could not endure a clear sight of either; but at his second coming the veil shall be taken off and we made able to behold and enjoy Him visibly, conversant with us in our flesh for ever: for that day is here called *the revelation of Christ*.

CHAPTER 1 : VERSE 14

14. As obedient children, not fashioning yourselves according to the former lusts in your ignorance:

Here is the second motive to the study of holiness, taken from that sweet privilege of adoption: by the consideration whereof, the Apostle excites them as children to give themselves up to their Father's obedience, and to keep themselves free of the slavery of their lusts, wherein they had lived before they knew Christ savingly.

Hence learn, [1.] Although the best that ever lived have reason to judge themselves unworthy to be in the rank of servants to the Lord, Matt. 3:11, yet it pleases Him to advance the meanest that receive Christ by faith to the dignity and privileges of His children: for the Apostle designs[1] all believers, even the meanest, by this style, *Obedient children.* [2.] Whenever the children of the Lord consider their dignity of sonship they should be thereby strongly moved to the study of obedience to their Father: which consists in a sincere endeavour after conformity to all his commands, without exception of any, Psa. 119:6, in their kindly submission to all his corrections, Heb. 12:5, and both these out of love to Him, as now become their Father in Christ. So shall their sonship be clearly evidenced to them when they devote themselves wholly to their Father's obedience and go about every part of it, *as obedient children.* [3.] The faith of this blessed relation to God as our Father in Christ is that frame of spirit wherewith we should labour to go about every duty of new obedience; so will we be confident that our infirmities shall be pitied, and our weak endeavours to obey accepted, Psa. 103:13. Also our wants shall be supplied as shall be necessary, Matt. 6:32, for as these words contain a motive to obedience, taken from our adoption, so they hold forth the right manner of children going about every duty, to wit, *As obedient children* in obedience and out of love to their Father.[4.] Before that saving change which the Lord makes upon sinners in regeneration, they are not only void of the saving knowledge of God in Christ, but (as the word here signifies) they are also incapable and without a mind to know anything of that sort: for this is one part and the first part of that misery wherein these who are now children of God are supposed to have been; *in ignorance.* [5.] Ignorance is the fountain and root of profanity and of folks

---

[1] 'designs': designates, indicates.

37

serving of their lusts: they who know not the terror and sweetness of the Lord can never be deterred nor drawn from delighting in the slavery of their sins: for the Apostle makes their ignorance the rise of their profanity, while he dehorts[1] them from *fashioning themselves according to their former lusts, in ignorance.* [6.] Not only are the unregenerate in ignorance and therefore slaves to their lusts, but they are voluntary slaves, giving themselves wholly away to the satisfaction of their sinful desires, and shaping or moulding (as the word here signifies) their endeavours and undertakings according to the sinful motions of their corrupt nature: for so were those once who are now children, not only living in ignorance and following their lusts, but *fashioning themselves according to their lusts.* [7.] It is necessary for the children of the Lord to have a clear representation of the woeful case wherein they were before Christ changed them, that they may be kept still humble and careful to testify their thankfulness to Him for making a change upon them in all the duties of new obedience whereby He is honoured: for, while the Apostle is pressing these duties, he gives this clear representation of that woeful condition wherein they had been formerly, *fashioning themselves according to their former lusts, in their ignorance.* [8.] Although there be no hazard that any of the regenerate shall ever lose their new nature which is the seed of God abiding in them, 1 John 3:9, yet because their former lusts are but in part subdued and therefore old love to them is soon kindled, there is a great hazard that they should become for their present disposition and carriage very like unto what they were before they got a new nature: the consideration whereof should stir them up to diligence and progress in the study of mortification: for this hazard is insinuated by the Apostle while he presses upon the regenerate that they should not *fashion themselves according to their former lusts, in their ignorance.* [9.] Diligence in new obedience flowing from the faith and sense of our spiritual privileges, especially of our adoption, is that which keeps the children of the Lord from the wonted slavery of their lusts: for these words may be taken as a remedy against the prevailing of them: *As obedient children, not fashioning yourselves according to the former lusts, in your ignorance.*

---

[1] 'dehorts': dissuades.

15. But as he which hath called you is holy, so be ye holy in all manner of conversation;

16. Because it is written, Be ye holy; for I am holy.

The apostle, having in the former verse pressed the study of holiness negatively, from that great privilege of adoption, here presses the same positively by two further motives. The one is, that since the Lord has vouchsafed to call them from an estate of sin and wrath to a state of holiness and happiness, they ought therefore to walk answerably to their holy calling. The other is, that there should be a conformity between the holy Lord and all His children, and therefore holiness, which is His property, ought to be studied by them, and manifested in all the particular passages of their Christian course. And this last argument the Apostle confirms from the Scripture, whereof though there be no particular place here cited, yet the substance of the words is to be found in several places, Lev. 11:44, 19:2 and 20:7, Matt. 5:17.

Hence learn, [1.] They that would prove themselves to be truly holy and so to be the children of the Lord, must not satisfy themselves with the negative part of holiness, which consists in abstinence from what is unsuitable to the relation of children; but they must also labour for the positive part of it, which consists in some measure of conformity to their heavenly Father in His holiness: for after the Apostle has pressed that study negatively, that they should not conform themselves to their former lusts, in their ignorance, he urges here the positive part thereof, *But as he which hath called you is holy, so be ye holy.* [2.] They who have found the Lord powerfully calling them from that estate of sin and wrath wherein they are naturally, to a blessed condition of grace and happiness, should think themselves thereby strongly obliged to the study of holiness whereby Christians in heart and practice are alienated and drawn from things earthly, and are set apart for the use of their Lord. So do they evidence to themselves their effectual calling, 2 Pet. 1:10, for as a motive to the study of holiness the Apostle here suggests to believers their calling: *But as he which hath called you is holy, so be ye holy.* [3.] Although it be altogether impossible for any man or angel to be conformed in holiness to God who is essentially immutable and infinitely holy, 1 Sam. 2:2, yet there is no absolute unerring pattern lower than the Holy One to be set before the eyes of the children of the Lord who ought not to make the holiest on earth a sufficient copy to them, but being still ashamed of their defects in holiness and unsatisfied with their present measure thereof, must still be aiming at a nearer conformity with Christ the Lord and daily making use of Him who is their sanctification, 1 Cor. 1:30, to cover their defects and to sanctify them more fully: for this is the example and pattern of that holiness to which all the called children of God should aspire: *As he who hath called you is holy, so be ye holy.* [4.] Although internal holiness be mainly lovely to the Lord, Psa. 51:6, and the external without it be loathsome to Him, Matt. 23:27, yet none should satisfy themselves with that holiness which they imagine to have within, but should labour to manifest holiness in their external conversation by showing themselves in their visible actings mindful and respective of all the commands of God, Lev. 20:7,8, Psa. 119:6, whereby they glorify Him before others and evidence themselves to have true holiness, John 15:8; for this conformity to our Father in holiness must be manifested *in the conversation.*[1] [5.] There is no part of a Christian's conversation which ought not to savour of holiness and true piety; not only his religious, but even his common and civil actions, ought to be done in the Lord and for His glory, 1 Cor. 10:31. And under all the various dispensations of God with him, he ought still to prove himself a hater of sin and a lover of what the Lord approves, which is the thing here pressed, *to be holy in all manner of conversation.* [6.] The strictest of moral precepts in the Old Testament are binding to believers under the New. The substance of all of them (which is, that reasonable creatures should love their Maker and their fellow-creatures) is of perpetual equity, obliging both angels and men, and nothing being required of us, in any of them, to be done by virtue of our own strength, or that we may be justified thereby, but only what the regenerate are enabled to aim at and to attain to such a measure of, as through Christ shall be accepted, as if they had attained to what is required, Col. 2:10, for here one of the strictest of moral precepts that are in the Old Testament is pressed upon believers: *As he who hath called you is holy, so be ye holy; for it is written, be ye holy; for I am holy.* [7.] The ministers of Jesus Christ ought to have His Word so richly dwelling in them that they may be able to confirm what they deliver to the Lord's people from clear and

---

[1] 'conversation': manner of life.

express testimonies thereof, especially when they press such truths as natural hearts are most averse from: for, even this extraordinary minister, the Apostle, whom people had less reason to suspect than any ordinary minister, while he presses this high pitch of holiness, to wit, the study of conformity to the Holy One, he thus confirms his doctrine by Scripture: *Because it is written, be ye holy; for I am holy.* [8.] Although it be the duty of ministers sometimes to point out to people the particular place of Scripture whereby they do confirm their doctrine, Acts 13:33, yet ought the Lord's people to be so well acquainted with the written Word that upon the hearing of any sentence of it, they may acknowledge it to be the Lord's mind, so that there may be no necessity for ministers to spend time and burden people's memories with multiplied citations for every truth they deliver; especially where the words of Scripture are remarkable and frequently to be found; for so the Apostle, citing this remarkable Scripture which is frequently to be found in the Old Testament, does not name any particular place, but only says *It is written, Be ye holy for I am holy.*

17. **And if ye call on the Father, who without respect of persons judgeth according to every man's work, pass the time of your sojourning here in fear:**

Follows the fifth and sixth motives to the study of holiness. The one is, that even those who take the Lord for their Father and themselves for His children will find Him an exact and impartial Judge of them and all their actions. The other is, that His children are but strangers and sojourners and so living in the midst of many hazards and temptations; both which should move them to study holiness whereof this is a special part to carry along in their hearts, throughout their pilgrimage, some fear of offending their heavenly Father, who is to be their Judge.

Hence learn, [1.] The more acquaintance with the Lord and confidence of His fatherly affection Christians attain to, the more are they obliged to the study of holiness; and particularly to walk in fear of offending Him who will be sanctified in all that draw nigh to Him, Lev. 10:3, and will have every one that names Him their own God and Father to depart from iniquity, 2 Tim. 2:19; for so does the Apostle reason here: *If ye call on the Father* (or if ye name him Father) *pass the time of your sojourning in fear.* [2.] As those who may call God their Father will not lack their own pressing necessities, which will put them to cry to Him as men do in greatest extremities (as the word here signifies), so under the greatest of these, they should still maintain the faith of that standing relation between Him and them, and deal with Him in earnestness and confidence of His help, as with a Father, as is imported in this, *If ye call on the Father.* [3.] While we take up the Lord under this sweet relation of a Father to us in Christ, which may beget in our hearts familiarity with Him and confidence of obtaining necessary help from Him, we ought also to cherish other considerations of Him and look upon Him as standing in other relations to us, especially that of a Judge, that so our hearts may be kept in awe and fear of offending Him, and our homeliness may not mar our reverence: for the Apostle holds forth both these relations between the Lord and his children to be jointly considered by them: *If ye call on the Father who without respect of persons judgeth.* [4.] The Lord is both an impartial Judge who cannot be biased either with the expectation of any benefit or terrified by the apprehension of any hazard from creatures, Job 35:7,8, and likewise so exact in judging that neither person nor action can escape his judgment: for *without respect of persons he judgeth according to every man's work*, says the Apostle. [5.] There will be no exercise of mercy (as it is taken for the pardoning of sin not formerly pardoned) at the last reckoning: those that are in Christ shall be judged according to His obedience and works which will be reckoned theirs, Phil. 3:9, and their good works done in His strength only remembered, Rev. 14:13. As for those who never fled to Him, they shall be judged according to the strictest rigour of the law of works, Rom. 2:6,8,9 for the Apostle looks mainly to the last judgment while he says *He judgeth every man according to his works.* [6.] The children of the Lord are pilgrims and strangers in this world and should esteem themselves to be such, Heb. 11:13, and therefore should live in fear of snares and hazards as the Apostle here presses, never imitating the fashions of this world, Rom. 12:2, satisfying themselves with such sober entertainment as God's providence brings to their hand upon their journey, Heb. 13:5, and still hastening toward their country, Luke 12:35, for so much does the Apostle import while he thus expresses our condition here, *The time of our sojourning.* [7.] Although they that are fled to Christ ought never to fear any hazard from flesh which may discourage them in the way of their duty, Matt. 10:28, nor yet eternal wrath, further than to stir them up to renew their flight to Him, and to engage them to His service, who has delivered them from it, Luke 1:74, Rom. 8:1, yet such a fear of offending their Father (flowing from the consideration of His excellency, Jer. 10:6,7, and of His goodness, Hos. 3:5, as makes them watchful against temptations, considering their own weakness, 1 Cor. 10:12, and quickens them to their duty, Heb. 12:28) should be carried along in their hearts through their whole time, and cherished by the consideration of those relations they have to God as a Father and a Judge: *If ye call on the Father, who without respect of persons judgeth,* &c. *pass the time of your sojourning here in fear.*

18. **Forasmuch as ye know that ye were not redeemed with corruptible things, as silver and gold, from your vain conversation received by tradition from your fathers;**
19. **But with the precious blood of Christ, as of a Lamb without blemish and without spot:**

Here is the seventh motive to the study of holiness taken from that great privilege of our redemption which is here described: [1.] From the price thereof; and this the Apostle expresses negatively, that it was not so base as the best of corruptible things; such as have sometimes ransomed the greatest of men from outward bondage, 2 Kings 18:14,15, and positively, that it was the meritorious blood of the innocent Son of God who was typified by the Paschal Lamb which behoved to be without blemish, Exod. 12:5. [2.] This work of redemption is described from the effect of it toward the Christian church and believers in it, to wit, that they were thereby delivered from that legal dispensation which was altogether unprofitable, as the observance thereof had been pressed upon them by many of their fathers; and from every other sinful course wherein they had been hardened by their fathers' example and precepts. So the sum of this argument is, that since they themselves did take it for granted that they were bought with so excellent a price from so woeful a condition, they ought therefore to live to the honour of their Redeemer in the study of holiness.

Hence learn [1.] All that are redeemed by Jesus Christ were once slaves and in bondage to Satan, 2 Tim. 2:26, to their own lusts, Tit. 3:3, and so under subjection to the wrath of God, Eph. 2:3, for *redemption* supposes captivity and bondage. [2.] There could be no freedom of sinners from this bondage but by the paying of a price to offended justice; God's mercy could not be bestowed upon any sinners (the covenant of works being once made) but with the safety and satisfaction of His justice, Rom. 3:25,26, which could not have been except the price had been paid which justice required; for *redemption* supposes also the paying of a price. [3.] Believers in Jesus Christ are by Him brought to a state of liberty and freedom, not from their obedience to His holy Law, Luke 1:74, but from any right Satan had over them before their believing in Him, Col. 2:15, from the curse of the Law, Gal. 3:13, and from the dominion and slavery of sin, Tit. 2:14. And the whole church under the New Testament is by Him delivered from the yoke of Mosaical ceremonies, Gal. 5:1, for this privilege of *redemption* imports a state of freedom and liberty. [4.] Not even the most excellent of corruptible things, which are most valued among men, could be sufficient to be the price of redemption for sinners, one soul being of more worth than all things of that sort, Psa. 49:7,8. Therefore the Apostle expresses the price of redemption negatively: *Not with corruptible things, as silver and gold.* [5.] It is not impossible for sinners to know themselves to be of the number of them that are redeemed by Jesus Christ, there being clear marks of such given in Scripture, Tit. 2:14, and the Spirit promised that they may know the things that are freely bestowed upon them, 1 Cor. 2:12; for the Apostle supposes this while he says *Forasmuch as ye know that ye were redeemed,* &c. [6.] The more confident Christians be that they are of the number of the redeemed ones by Christ, the more should they be moved to study holiness for the honour of their Redeemer, considering that the study thereof is the very end of their redemption, Luke 1:74, and the evidence thereof, both to themselves and to others, Isa. 62:12, for this is brought in here by the Apostle as an argument to the study of holiness, and particularly to pass the time of our sojourning here in fear, *Forasmuch as ye know that ye were redeemed,* &c. [7.] The ordinary way how the redeemed of the Lord attain to the knowledge of their redemption is by discerning in themselves a real and gracious change made upon their heart and life by virtue of Christ's death: for the Apostle supposes that those who knew themselves to be redeemed behoved also to know that they were liberated from their *vain conversation.* [8.] So long as men are not changed in their heart and life by the application of the merit of that price which Christ paid, all that they can do whether in religious performances or in their ordinary practices is altogether vain and such as can bring no true comfort or profit to themselves or honour to Jesus Christ: for so the Apostle designs[1] the way wherein the redeemed walked before their regeneration, calling it *a vain conversation*: which may comprehend both their religious and common performances. [9.] Although there be both a proneness in fathers to transmit to their children that wickedness wherein their fathers have rooted and hardened them, and in children to receive and transmit the same to their offspring again, yet neither is the example nor precepts of fathers a sufficient warrant to their posterity for any practice whatsoever: for the Apostle imports that those to whom he writes had received from their fathers what they had received from theirs before, although it was vain: and reckons it a great advantage that they were now delivered from that *vain conversation*, although it was *received by tradition from their fathers*. [10.] No less could be a sufficient ransom for lost sinners than the blood of Jesus Christ. The favours to be purchased for them, to make them eternally blessed, being of infinite value, and the sentence of everlasting death being passed upon all *Adam's* posterity, either all behoved to die, or one worth all the rest; and such an one had never been found if God had not given His Son to be a man, that so man might be redeemed *with the precious blood of Christ*. [11.] The blood of Jesus Christ considering the excellency of His Person, the greatness and freedom of His love in shedding it for such as we are, and the worth of the favours merited by it to believers, such as the favour of God and eternal life, ought to be in high esteem with all the redeemed: for to work this in their hearts the Apostle thus commends it, *The precious blood of Christ*. [12.] It behoved Him who was to be our Redeemer to be altogether free of the defilement of sin for which He was to satisfy in the behalf of others; as being the truth and signification of the Paschal Lamb, to which the Apostle here relates; and other spotless sacrifices which typified Him under the Law that so as man He might be completely lovely and acceptable to God and be a perfect pattern of holiness to all His redeemed ones: therefore, the Apostle thus commends Him *as a Lamb without blemish, and without spot*.

20. Who verily was foreordained before the foundation of the world, but was manifest in these last times for you,

[1] See page 37.

To the end there may be yet a higher esteem of the Redeemer wrought in the hearts of the redeemed and that they may be the more engaged to the study of holiness, that so He may be honoured by them, the Apostle goes on to describe Him further. [1.] That He was from eternity appointed by the Father to be the Saviour of sinners, and [2.] That He was now more clearly manifested after His incarnation than He had been before; both which make up the eighth motive to the study of holiness, that seeing Christ had been from eternity designed[1] Mediator, and now more clearly than ever manifested with a special respect to the good of those lost sheep of the house of *Israel* to whom the Apostle writes, therefore they were bound to live to His honour in the study of holiness.

Hence learn, [1.] Whenever we attain to any serious thoughts of that great business of our redemption by Christ incarnate and crucified, we should not suffer our hearts to be soon diverted from them, but should labour to dwell upon them and to search out more and more considerations of that sweet subject, every one of them being worthy to take up our affections and to engage us to the study of holiness. For the Apostle in the former words, having fallen upon the mentioning of our redemption as a motive to holiness, he does in this and the following verse run out in expressing the thoughts he had of the Lord's everlasting purpose about that work; of the glory that Christ now possesses in our nature and of the Father's intention in exalting Him, *who verily was foreordained before the foundation of the world*. [2.] Our Mediator was from all eternity designed[1] to the office of Mediatorship in that everlasting covenant of redemption wherein the Father gave the elect to His Son, Psa. 2:8, and appointed Him to assume human nature, therein to suffer for their redemption, Heb. 10:5; and Christ accordingly undertook to satisfy His will, Psa. 40:7,8. So that we who have Christ offered to us in the Gospel are invited to feed upon those dainties that were prepared for us from all eternity. And who are we that the thoughts of God should have been so long since taken up about us while He appointed His own Son for us, *who verily was foreordained before the foundation of the world?* [3.] Although Christ was made known immediately after the Fall, Gen. 3:15, and ever since has been sufficiently manifested for the salvation of the elect in all ages, Acts 10:43, yet there was a more clear manifesta-

---

[1] 'designed': see page 37.

tion of Him reserved for the time after His incarnation, the more to heighten the esteem of that great mystery of His incarnation, in the hearts of all His people. Therefore the Apostle speaks of Him here as more clearly held forth to the church than before: *But now made manifest in these last times for you.* [4.] The more clearly Christ be held forth in any time, the more strongly are they that live in that time, and have that clearness, obliged to live to His honour in the study of holiness, considering that the more unanswerable men's walking be to the light they have, the greater will their condemnation be, John 3:19 and 15:22. They that live since the incarnation of Christ and the clearer outbreaking of the light of the Gospel which reveals Him, should think the Lord has had a special respect to them and has in a peculiar manner designed Christ for them and manifested Him to them that they may be more eminent in holiness and thankfulness to Him, for to this end the Apostle speaks thus of Christ: *Manifested in these last times for you.* [5.] Although experience has proved that there was a considerable part of time to be after Christ's incarnation, yet all that is but the last time in regard it is to be much shorter than the time that was before: and because after that time, though there be a continual increase of knowledge and grace to be expected, Ezek. 47:1 &c., yet there is no more change of that way of worship and ordinances which Christ settled before He left the world, Matt. 28:18,19,20; for which cause, among others, the times after Christ's incarnation are here called *The last times*.

21. **Who by him do believe in God, that raised him up from the dead, and gave him glory; that your faith and hope might be in God.**

Having commended Christ the Redeemer, he describes those for whose sakes He was appointed and manifested, to wit, those who do by faith flee to God through Him; and that they may be the more encouraged so to do, he leads them to consider the Father as one fully satisfied with the ransom paid for sinners by Jesus Christ, seeing after the payment of it He has exalted and glorified Him for this very end, that the faith of sinners may safely and comfortably rest upon God as now pacified toward all that flee to Him through Christ; which purpose contains the ninth argument to the study of holiness. That since the Father has exalted and glorified our Cautioner[1] in our nature for this very end, that we may confidently draw near to Him as to our own reconciled God, we ought therefore to live to the honour of the Father and the Son in the study of holiness.

Hence learn, [1.] Whenever the ministers of Christ hold forth the ransom paid by Christ for sinners and the benefits purchased thereby to them, they ought also to design[2] and describe the persons who may appropriate the same to themselves: and ought not to propose that which is peculiar to some (John 10:15) as common to all. So shall the few that have right to apply the benefits of His redemption be the more sure and comforted, and others shall not be disappointed: for so does the Apostle here, while having described Christ the Redeemer and set forth some of the benefits of His redemption, he comes next to describe what manner of persons they are who may comfort themselves in that redemption purchased by Him, even those *who by him do believe in God*. [2.] Although our faith may close with any one of the blessed Persons of the Trinity, providing we do not divide in our thoughts the Divine Essence which is One in all the Three, 1 John 5:7, yet God the Father (considered as the fountain of the Deity to whom we come through the Second Person, clothed with our flesh, being helped by the Holy Spirit, the Third Person) is that full and most satisfying object with which saving faith closes when it acts most distinctly: for, such an object is here proposed with which the faith of the redeemed closes, to wit, the whole Godhead in the Father apprehended as ours, by the Son incarnate, through the help of the Spirit, as the next verse compared with this makes clear. [3.] There is no closing with God as ours but by the Mediator Christ, in whom God trysts with sinners, who has merited God's favour to them, the power to believe the same; and actually works that faith in them, *who by him do believe in God*. [4.] Although Jesus Christ being the same God, equal with the Father, Phil. 2:6, did by His own proper virtue, raise Himself from the dead, John 2:19 and 10:18, yet to assure us of the Father's full satisfaction with the price paid by our Cautioner[1] and because the power of all the Three Persons is one, and the actions ascribed to any of them, in reference to the creatures, are common to all, His raising from the dead and exaltation is here (as frequently elsewhere in Scrip-

[1] See page 13.
[2] See page 37.

ture, Eph. 1:20, Phil. 2:9) attributed to the Father, *who raised him from the dead and gave him glory.* [5.] God's justice is fully satisfied in the behalf of all that flee to Him through Jesus Christ, because their Cautioner[1] is liberated; and glory is ensured to all such, their Head being already possessed in it: for, in testimony that His satisfaction for the elect is accepted, *God hath raised him from the dead, and,* as a sure pledge that His members shall be glorified, *he hath given him glory, that your faith and hope might be in God.*

22. Seeing ye have purified your souls in obeying the truth through the Spirit unto unfeigned love of the brethren, see that ye love one another with a pure heart fervently:

The tenth motive to press upon believers the study of holiness is taken from the former progress they had made therein: whence the Apostle infers an exhortation to that particular duty of holiness, to wit, love to the saints. The sum of both is, that since by the power of Christ's Spirit enabling them to obey the Gospel, they had had their heart corruptions so far purged out as to attain unto some sincere affection to the rest of the Lord's people, therefore they should study to grow in grace, specially in love to the saints: and that they should labour to have such love to them as flows from a sincere desire of their good; and by the effects of it proves itself to be such.

Hence learn, [1.] The fairer beginnings and further progress any have already made in the way of holiness, they should find themselves the more strongly obliged to hold on in that way lest they lose the fruit of their former pains, 2 John 8, and prove more dishonourable to God and offensive to others than if they had never entered or made such progress in that way, 2 Pet. 2:22, for the Apostle here makes former progress in holiness a motive to further progress therein: *Seeing you have purified your souls,* &c., *see that ye love,* &c. [2.] As all those whom the Lord has savingly enlightened and renewed will discern in their souls many filthy and unclean roots, besides any that have broken out; so their great work should be to have their souls purged from those, knowing that from the polluted fountain of the heart flows all the pollution of the life, Matt. 15:19, and that except the heart be in some measure cleansed, all the purity of the outside is loathsome to God, Matt. 23:27; for, the Apostle thus describes

[1] See page 13.

the regenerate, that they *have purified their souls*. [3.] Although it be the alone work of God as the principal efficient cause to cleanse and purify the souls of His people, both from the guilt and dominion of sin, Ezek. 36:25, yet His people who are merely passive in the first infusion of grace, Eph. 2:1, are thereafter made by Him active instruments in the carrying on of that work of mortification, by employing Christ's virtue for subduing and fighting in His strength against their corruptions; as is imported in this, *Ye have purified your souls*. [4.] The Lord's means of purging the souls of His people from the love and power of sin which is naturally in them, is their obedience to His truth: which consists not only in their aiming at conformity to those precepts which enjoin purity and holiness, such as that is (v 15), but principally in their embracing by faith and making use of the promises of the new Covenant, wherein the Lord undertakes to work this purity, Ezek. 36:25,26,27. This is the chief part of that obedience to the truth which purifies souls: for, says the Apostle, *Ye have purified your souls, in obeying the truth*. [5.] This obedience to the truth which purifies the souls of believers cannot be attained unto by our own natural strength or the use of the fittest means of grace, without the special working of the Spirit of Jesus who clears to sinners the nature of that purity which is pleasing to God and powerfully works the same in them: for, so the Apostle affirms of those believers that they had purified their souls in obeying the truth, *through the Spirit*. [6.] One special part of this work of purging the souls of believers consists in the subduing of those filthy roots which are in their hearts, contrary to that grace of love to the rest of the Lord's people such as pride, self-love and the like: for this is here made their aim in purifying their souls that they might attain *unto unfeigned love of the brethren*, importing that their pains were much bent to purge out those evils which are contrary to that grace. [7.] Believers have need to be seriously pressed to exercise and grow in these graces and duties whereof they have already attained to some approved measure: for upon those who had already purified their souls unto unfeigned love of the brethren, the Apostle presses this, *See that ye love one another*. [8.] It is not every sort of love to the saints of God that evidences mortification and the indwelling of Christ's Spirit; but such only as is without dissimulation or hypocrisy, which is *unfeigned love* such as flows from holy principles, to wit, respect to the command of Christ and not from respect to our own credit or advantage only; from desire of the true good of others and not from love to ourselves which is *Love out of a pure heart*; and such as breaks forth in real proofs and is continued toward others notwithstanding of provocations from them, which is *To love one another fervently*.

23. Being born again, not of corruptible seed, but of incorruptible, by the Word of God, which liveth and abideth for ever.

The eleventh motive whereby the Apostle presses upon believers the study of holiness (especially that branch of it which he was last upon, to wit, love to the saints) is taken from the excellency of their spiritual original: the sum whereof is that since they had a new life and nature in their regeneration, wrought in them not by so fading a cause or principle as that which is the instrument of producing their natural substance, but by the Word of God which in the effects it has upon the regenerate lives and abides for ever. Therefore the excellency of their new nature and permanency of their spiritual estate should move them to walk suitably unto it, and particularly to live in love with the rest of their Father's children.

Hence learn, [1.] Every true believer in Jesus Christ is in some measure acquainted with a new and second birth which is that work of God with sinners whereby there is a new spiritual life and nature communicated to them, Eph. 2:1, and they are brought through some pangs and straits arising from the sight of their own sinfulness and fear of deserved wrath, Acts 2:37, out of their darkness and bondage (which is natural to them and is resembled by the state of the child before the birth) into a state of light and knowledge of God in Christ, 2 Cor. 4:6, and freedom from the slavery of sin and subjection to wrath, Rom. 8:2, and whereby also they are made in some measure to resemble their heavenly Father and are inclined to obey Him and to love Him and all His children, 1 John 5:1. For this the Apostle makes a description of true believers that they are *born again*. [2.] Our life and nature that we have by virtue of this second birth or regeneration is far more excellent than what we have by the first: our natural estate is subject to corruption and will shortly be dissolved; but our spiritual estate can never fade: for though all have immortal souls that are not corruptible, yet the natural life and state of all shall be dissolved, and the eternal being of those who are unacquainted with regeneration and a second birth will be but an eternal corruption, or perishing, which should make all long to be acquainted with regeneration. For to lead us to esteem the one above the other the Apostle commends the one above the other from the difference of their seeds: *Not of corruptible seed, but of incorruptible.* [3.] Although the Word, separated from the working of the Spirit, can do nothing to the regenerating of a sinner, John 3:5, yet the Word is the ordinary instrument of the Spirit, who makes use of all the principal parts of it in that work; of the Law, to put the sinner in some straits of the second birth through fear of deserved wrath; and of the Gospel to revive the soul and liberate it from those fears; and of the Law again to direct the regenerate how to walk suitably to their estate: for the Apostle explains what that incorruptible seed is, of which we are born again, to wit, *The Word of God.* [4.] Although there be no life either formally or by way of efficiency in the letter or sound of the words of Scripture; and though that Word passes with the speaking as any other words do, yet in regard of the effects which through the operation of the Spirit it has upon sinners, such as fear and terror upon the believing of the threatenings, Acts 2:37, comfort under crosses and quickening for duties upon the believing of the promises, Psa. 119:50, it is as the Apostle here calls it, *A Word that liveth.* And in regard of the execution of eternal wrath upon them that reject it and of the performance of those everlasting blessings which are promised in it to them that receive and obey it, it is *a Word that abideth for ever.* [5.] They who do profess and esteem themselves to be of the number of those who are born again should, by the consideration of their second birth, be strongly moved to the study of holiness for the honour of their Father; and especially to live in love with the rest of their Father's children: for, the Apostle brings this as a further argument to the study of holiness (and particularly to the study of that branch of it which he had pressed in the former words concerning mutual love amongst professors) that they were *born again, not of corruptible seed, but of incorruptible, by the Word of God*, &c.

24. **For all flesh is as grass, and all the glory of man as the flower of grass: the grass withereth, and the flower thereof falleth away:**

25. **But the Word of the Lord endureth for ever. And this is the Word which by the Gospel is preached unto you.**

The last motive whereby the Apostle presses upon believers the

study of holiness and constancy under sufferings is taken from a
further commendation of the excellency of their spiritual estate,
which the Apostle sets out by comparing the same with the best
estate of men naturally considered, with all their ornaments
wherein they use to glory which is (according to the Scripture,
Isa. 40:6) like unto withering grass and fading flowers. In the
application of which comparison the Apostle insists upon his
former commendation of the Word (which is the seed whereby
believers are begotten) from the perpetuity of it, to wit, in the
effects thereof upon them, which might easily lead them to judge
of their state accordingly, and applies this commendation of the
Word to that doctrine which was preached to them by himself or
others of the Lord's servants. All which strongly presses his
scope that therefore they should live holily and suffer cheerfully
as became those who were in so excellent an estate.

Hence learn, [1.] Although it be much in the thoughts and
desires of natural men that they might have a perpetual enjoyment of this life and the comforts of it, Psa. 49:11, yet themselves
and all that they can glory in, is frail and fading, like the grass
and flowers of the grass; whereupon they should read their
frailty and mortality and so be stirred up to provide for a better
life and a more enduring substance than what they have here:
for, *all flesh is as grass and all the glory of man as the flower of grass.* [2.]
Though every common gift of God wherein men use to glory,
whether riches, wisdom, strength, beauty or the like be fading as
the grass and flowers thereof, yet because men's credit or glory
before the world is that wherein they use to glory most, and of
the perpetuating whereof they are most strongly desirous, Psa.
49:11, the Lord has put a special fadingness and vanity upon
that, and will have it as easily blasted as any other thing wherein
men glory: for, though *the glory of man* here spoken of may be
taken largely as comprehending everything for which men lift
up themselves and wherein they use to glory (as the word is used,
Matt. 4:8), yet it seems especially to point out that honour and
credit which men affect to have before the world; in which
signification it is used, 1 Thess. 2:6, the property whereof the
Lord pronounces to be fadingness or withering: *And all the glory
of man as the flower of grass.* [3] Though this be a plain truth taught
by daily experience and commonly acknowledged, that our
natural estate with all the ornaments thereof is frail and fading,
yet it is not easy to make this truth take due impression upon the
hearts of men who are naturally unwilling to admit thoughts of a

change, Amos 6:2. Therefore the Spirit of God bears it in upon men's minds under the same similitude in very many places of Scripture, Job 14:2, Psa. 103:15, Isa. 40:6, Jas. 1:10 and here by many expressions: *all flesh is as grass, and all the glory of man as the flower of grass, the grass withereth, and the flower thereof falleth away.* [4.] The believing consideration of this frailty and fadingness of men's natural estate and earthly contentments, should heighten in their hearts the esteem of that spiritual and better estate whereunto by receiving the Gospel they may be advanced; and should be to them a powerful motive to the study of holiness which will abide when other things fade, 1 John 3:9, and especially to the study of mutual love among themselves (those earthly things for which usually they contend, Gen. 13:8, and particularly their credit, the love whereof is often the greatest occasion of strife among them, Luke 22:24 being so fading and uncertain); for as a commendation of the state of the regenerate, or motive to the study of holiness and particularly of brotherly love, is this here brought in. *All flesh is as grass, and all the glory of man as the flower of grass: the grass withereth, and the flower thereof falleth away: but the Word of the Lord endureth for ever.* [5.] Whatever can be spoken to the commendation of the Word serves also for the commendation of them who have by faith received it and are regenerated by it. That which is the seed and principle of their spiritual being, their charter and right to all their privileges and inheritance, being excellent and worthy, their state must needs be such likewise: for it is clear the Apostle's purpose here is to commend the state of the regenerate as far more excellent than the best natural state; and this he esteems to be sufficiently done by commending the Word from the perpetuity of it in opposition to the frail state of men naturally considered, *All flesh is as grass,* &c. *But the Word of the Lord endureth for ever.* [6.] They who have received a new spiritual life and so are entered in a new state by their receiving of the Word, ought to fix in their hearts by frequent meditations the perpetuity of that *Word* in the accomplishment of the good things promised therein which shall endure to them for all eternity, that so they may the better see and be the more affected with their own blessedness: for the Apostle having commended the *Word* from this property of it before, repeats it here again, *The Word of the Lord endureth for ever.* [7.] As Christ's own worth and excellency is best seen when He is compared with other things which may seem to have worth in them, Canticles 2:3, so the worth of our spiritual estate is best seen and most esteemed of by us when we compare it with the frailty and fecklessness of the best state on earth beside: for to heighten believers' esteem of the one, he compares it with the other: *All flesh is as grass* &c. *but the Word of the Lord* (and consequently their state who are begotten again by the Word) *endureth for ever.* [8.] Whatever good esteem the Lord's people have of the Word of God in general, they ought to have the same of the particular messages that are brought to them from or according to that word by the Lord's servants who are sent to them: and ought not to content themselves with a high esteem of the written Word or of the preaching thereof in the general, in the mean time having a slender esteem of those portions of truth which God carves out to them by the messengers whom He sends to them: for the Apostle leads those to whom he writes to look upon that commendation of the *Word*, which Isaiah had given out before him as agreeing to the *Word* written, and preached to them by himself, and others of the Lord's servants in that time: *And this is the Word which by the Gospel is preached unto you.* [9.] Although the precepts and threatenings of the Word have their own efficiency as instruments in God's hands to prepare the soul for the new life by breaking and humbling of it, Acts 2:37, yet it is mainly the Gospel or the glad tidings (as the Word signifies) of free salvation through Jesus Christ to all lost sinners who get grace to receive the offer thereof, whereby a new life is conveyed to and increased in the soul and whereby it is brought into that excellent state of regeneration; for the Apostle applies the commendation of the Word which is the seed of regeneration mainly to the Gospel: *And this is the Word, which by the Gospel is preached unto you.*

CHAPTER TWO

In this chapter the Apostle goes on to press such duties of holiness as are most suitable for that excellent state of the regenerate described in the former. In the first part of it he exhorts to growth and progress in such duties of holiness as concern all Christians in whatever relation they stand in the world, as namely, the study of mortification (v 1), a hearty in-drinking of the doctrine of the Gospel, because their so doing is the means of their spiritual growth (v 2). It is the way to prove that they had experimentally tasted of the sweetness of Christ's grace (v 3) and because by their daily use-making of Christ offered in the Gospel, they should find an increase of spiritual life and fitness for every duty (vv 4,5) and that, because the Scripture witnesses Him to be given with the Father's goodwill for a solid foundation of salvation and comfort to every soul that flies to Him (v 6). Whence the Apostle infers that Christ cannot but be very dear to believers and that He shall not be the less glorious because many slight Him; who, by their so doing shall only ruin themselves and prove themselves reprobates (vv 7,8). But as for those whom He hath so highly honoured that they might be forthcoming for his praise who had made so remarkable a change upon them (vv 9,10), their great study ought to be to keep up the battle against their inward lusts (v 11) and to walk so as the most wicked among whom they converse may be allured to fall in love with Christianity (v 12).

In the second part of the chapter the Apostle presses such duties as are suitable for Christians considered under some of their special relations. And first he exhorts them, as subjects under heathen rulers, to respect every form of lawful government, whether in the person of the supreme or inferior magistrate; and this he presses by many arguments. Firstly, because they should thereby evidence their respect to God's command. Secondly, because magistrates are appointed of God for so good ends as he expresses (vv 13,14). Thirdly, they should thereby silence their slanderers (v 15). Fourthly, because otherwise they should abuse their Christian liberty to licen-

56

tiousness (v 16). And fifthly, because other unquestionable duties did necessarily infer this (v 17).

The Apostle also exhorts them as servants under heathen, persecuting masters, in which case many Christians then were, to carry themselves dutifully toward such masters and patiently under wrongs from them, whether they were of the worse or better sort (v 18), and this the Apostle presses to the end of the chapter by several reasons. Firstly, because they might expect a gracious reward from God if they were put to unjust sufferings from men for respect to His commands (v 19). Secondly, because it would be a disgrace for Christianity if Christians did deserve hard usage from heathens for their miscarriage (v 20). Thirdly, because they were obliged to patience under the cross by their calling. Fourthly, because Christ had suffered harder things for them. Fifthly, because He had cast them a sweet copy of the right way of suffering (v 21). Sixthly, because Christ was a most innocent sufferer (v 22). Seventhly, because He was the most patient. And eighthly, the most confident under greatest wrongs that ever was (v 23). Ninthly, because by His death He has purchased reconciliation with God. And, tenthly, healing to all his people's wounds, especially for His cause (v 24). Eleventhly, since they who were once in the way to perdition were now brought to a state of safety by Him (v 25). Therefore they ought patiently to suffer wrongs in following their duty to Him: the pressing whereof is the Apostle's scope.

1. Wherefore laying aside all malice, and all guile, and hypocrisies, and envies, and all evil speakings,

The Apostle's scope in the first part of this chapter being to press upon all Christians the study of progress and growth in holiness, as appears by the second and fifth verses, in order to this, he stirs them up to the battle against their unmortified corruptions, giving instances of such as are most contrary to that love of the regenerate one toward another which he had pressed before as an evidence of their regeneration (1:22) and to that hearty receiving of the Word which he presses in the following verse, as the principal means of their growth in grace, not excluding other evils not here mentioned, but leading them by these to the knowledge of all the rest, that are unbecoming a regenerate state.

Doctrine, [1.] There remains in the children of the Lord not only after their regeneration, but even after some progress in mortification, many strong corruptions and filthy frames of spirit which are left to humble them, Rom. 7:24, and to stir them up to earnest employment of Jesus Christ, both for mercy and power to subdue them, 2 Cor. 12:8; for upon those whom the Apostle supposed to be not only born again (1:23), but to have attained to a good degree of mortification (1:22), he here presses that they should *lay aside malice, and guile and hypocrisy*, &c. [2.] Our corruptions ought to be renounced with detestation, as things very noisome to be no longer kept, Isa. 30:22, and with a purpose never to meddle with them again, Hos. 14:8, for there is a metaphor in the words, taken from a man putting off an old suit of clothes full of filth and vermin which would be both hurtful and disgraceful to be longer worn; *Wherefore laying aside all malice*, &c. [3.] Even the children of the Lord are ready to cleave very close to their unmortified corruptions, to forget the necessity of a further degree of mortification than what they have already attained to, and to entertain their corruptions as if they were necessary for them, yea, and to account them their very ornaments: for, the metaphor in the words is taken from a man that is unwilling to shed his garments which, though they be old and full of filth and vermin, yet he keeps them close to him as his necessary ornaments: *lay aside all malice*, &c. [4.] Our regeneration and former progress in mortification should be so far from making us indulgent to our lusts, remaining yet unmortified, that the more clear we be concerning the one, and the further advanced in the other, the more are we obliged to set[1] against the remaining power of those unmortified corruptions, we having now stronger obligations to fight against them, greater strength for that effect and being more ready to dishonour God by their prevailing than formerly: for upon those whom the Apostle supposed to be born again, to know themselves redeemed ones and to have purified their souls, (in the former chapter) he presses here for the study of mortification with a *Wherefore, laying aside*, &c. [5.] Our new birth is mainly evidenced to us by our opposition to and victory over those corruptions which stir in us, contrary to that love and duty which we owe to our brethren, the rest of the regenerate ones; our victory over these being the kindly effect of our victory in some measure

---

[1] 'set': contend.

over our ignorance of God, atheism and unbelief, and such other sins as are more directly against the first table, 1 John 3:2,3; for all the particular evils here named are such as relate mainly to our neighbour as contrary to that love and duty which we owe to him; and the mortification of them is here pressed as that which should evidence our regeneration, as appears by comparing the 23rd verse of the former chapter with this and the verse following: *Being born again*, &c. *Wherefore, laying aside all malice*, &c, *as new born babes*, &c. [6.] Not only is the actual hurting of our neighbour an evil, unbecoming the regenerate ones, but the very intention of the heart to harm him is such an evil also, and therefore to be mortified, for intention to hurt our neighbour is the first evil which the Apostle here dissuades from; *laying aside malice*, &c, [7.] The Lord takes notice of folks' cunning conveyances, of their plots and practices, which tend to the prejudice of others; those being more dangerous to the party and more grievous when discovered or felt in their effects, than more open injuries, Psa. 55:11,12,13, for that artificial way of hurting others which hides the hurt intended from the party is the next evil the Apostle exhorts to be laid aside, as is clear from the signification of the original word, *guile*. [8.] As hypocrisy in the matters of God, whereby Christians draw near Him with their lips while their hearts are far from Him, Matt. 15:7,8 and give out themselves to be much for Him when they are nothing so, 2 Tim. 3:5, is an evil very detestable to Him, Matt. 23:25, so hypocrisy in dealing with others, whereby men in their words and carriage behave themselves with seeming respect and love, in the meantime aiming at the disgrace and hurt of others, Psa. 55:21, is a guilt unbecoming the regenerate which they should study to mortify as they desire to prove themselves such: for, of both these sorts of hypocrisies may this third evil be understood which the Apostle exhorts to be laid aside; *And hypocrisies*. [9.] To be grieved and vexed at the good of others, their excellencies or preference before ourselves, as it is a frame of spirit natural to all, Gal. 5:21, and incident to the regenerate, Jas. 4:5, so it is an evil very detestable to God, Tit. 3:3, and hurtful to the person in whom it is, Prov. 14:30, and therefore to be opposed and mortified as most unbecoming the regenerate who should rejoice in the welfare one of another as if it were their own, 1 Cor. 12:26, for this is the fourth particular which the Apostle here exhorts to mortify; *and envies*: which word signifies an evil, wasting them that have it with grief at others' welfare. [10.]

Speaking evil of others is the fruit that grows upon malice, envy and other inward evils of that kind which are clearly betrayed to be prevalent in the heart, when there is in the tongue much reviling, backbiting, contradicting and other sorts of evil speakings, whereby the reputation of our neighbour is hurt: for, as this is here the last in order so it may be safely looked upon as the effect or ordinary consequent of the former; *laying aside all malice and guile and envies and evil speakings.* [11.] However, there may be some one sin to which the heart of the regenerate is more inclined than to others, against which one they should mainly bend their strength, Psa. 18:23. Yet as they desire to prove themselves regenerate they ought to oppose and mortify all sin, considering that they are weak before every temptation, Gal. 6:1,3, and that the root and branch of every sin is hateful to God and contrary to His holy Law, as is clear by Christ's exposition of it, Matt. 5 and 6; for the Apostle puts the note of universality to some of these evils and puts the rest in the plural number; *laying aside all malice and guile and hypocrisies,* &c. [12.] There are degrees of the strength of unmortified corruption and several ways how it vents itself; so that when one branch of it is cut off, and one way how it prevails is stopped, there are yet many other branches of that same sin to be searched out and fought against: for the first two evils here named have an *all* with them, importing that, when one branch or degree of malice and guile is laid aside, there may be yet much of them behind unmortified. And the rest of the evils here named are in the plural number, importing that there are many sorts and kinds of *envies and hypocrisies and evil speakings* to be mortified in every Christian; *Wherefore lay aside all malice and all guile and hypocrisies and envies and evil speakings.* [13.] The right order which believers should keep in the mortifying of sin is to begin with the inward roots thereof that are in their hearts, so shall they the more easily curb the sins of the outward man: for in this order the Apostle presses this study upon the regenerate, that they should first *lay aside malice and guile,* &c, and then *evil speakings.* [14.] There is no right receiving of the Word so as souls may grow by it till first they set about the mortifying and putting off of such filthy frames of spirit as are here named: the truth must be received in love both to Christ and all His people, to which the evils here named are contrary: for the laying aside of them is here pressed as a means towards the duty held forth in the following verse: *Wherefore laying aside all malice* &c. *desire the sincere milk of the Word.*

2. As newborn babes' desire the sincere milk of the Word that ye may grow thereby.

The Apostle, having dissuaded from those evils which are great hindrances to the right receiving of the Gospel, here, in the next place, exhorts the regenerate to labour for such a sharp edge upon their appetite after the truths of the Gospel by which they were begotten and must be nourished, as lively infants have after the milk of the mothers' breasts. And this exhortation the Apostle bears in by three motives in this verse, taken from the nature and effects of the truths of the Gospel. [1.] That those truths are the *sincere milk*, that is, most pure truths, without any mixture of falsehood or error. [2.] That they are full of spiritual reason and so suited to the sanctified understandings of men and women; for the original may be rendered *that rational milk*. [3.] That the greedy indrinking of them will prove a principal means of spiritual growth and progress in grace and comfort.

Hence learn, [1.] the truths of the Gospel are to the truly regenerate what the milk of the breasts is to the young infant, those being no less necessary and fitted for the cherishing and entertaining[1] of their spiritual life, no less refreshing and strengthening through God's blessing to them than this is to the newborn babe: for however the first principles, or grounds of religion, which used to be held forth in a catechism are, for their plainness and fitness for the weak, called *milk*, as contra-distinguished from more profound truths which have the name of strong meat, Heb. 5:13,14, yet, for the causes formerly mentioned, the whole Word is here called *milk*, to be much thirsted-after by all the regenerate: *As newborn babes, desire the sincere milk of the Word*. [2.] The desire of a truly regenerate person after the Word will in some measure resemble that desire after the breasts which is in newborn babes: for, as the best thing on earth beside the breasts cannot be satisfactory to a lively infant, as it is most grieved for the want thereof, most unwilling to shed with it, and most delighted to have it of any other thing, so is it with the regenerate in reference to the Word as is imported in this exhortation. *As newborn babes' desire the sincere milk of the Word*. [3.] This desire of the regenerate after the Word ought to extend itself to all the parts thereof, every one of these having influence upon their spiritual growth. The discovering and threatening part of it

---

[1] 'entertaining': sustaining.

should serve them as a glass wherein to see their defects and spots, Rom. 3:20, that so they may be chased to Christ, Rom. 10:4, the promises thereof being the channel through which life, strength and transforming virtue to make them resemble their Lord is conveyed to them, 2 Pet. 1:4, and the precepts and directions thereof serving as a lamp to direct them in their Christian course, Psa. 119:105; for here the Word indefinitely, without restriction to one part of it more than another, is by the Apostle held forth as the object of this desire of the regenerate: *desire the sincere milk of the Word.* [4.] This desire of the Word formerly described is a clear evidence of regeneration and a new pasture; no sooner is a sinner born again by the virtue of the Spirit working with the Word, but as soon is there a kindly appetite after the Word wrought in the sinner's heart, even as the infant presently after the birth evidences some inclination and desire after the breasts: for the Apostle, having asserted their new birth (1:23), here puts them to evidence it: *As newborn babes, desire the sincere milk of the Word.* [5.] There is nothing in the Word of the Lord to deceive any that get grace to receive it by faith and walk by it, there being no mixture of error with the truths therein delivered, or of falsehood either in the promises, threatenings or predictions thereof: and therefore ministers in handling of it should keep it free of the mixture of their own inventions and passions; and people should love it and rest upon it because it is the sincere milk of the Word, or as the original is, the Word without guile or mixture of anything that deceives. [6.] Although natural reason of itself, except it be elevated above itself and enlightened by the Lord, cannot comprehend the truths revealed in the Gospel, nor look upon them as reasonable, 1 Cor. 1:18,23 and 2:14, yet all of them are most reasonable in themselves and cannot but be acknowledged to be such by all that have the use of sanctified reason, when they consider what subjection and credit we owe to Him of whom we have our being; when they compare His precepts and commands with His promises of furniture[1] for obedience, and of a gracious reward thereof; and when they consider how justice and mercy are agreed. Righteousness and peace do kiss each other in that way of salvation which is devised through Christ incarnate; and neither these truths nor any other in Scripture, are contrary to pure natural reason, though some of them be far above the

---

[1] 'furniture': provision, equipment.

reach of it: for this text may be translated (as the like word is, Rom. 12:1) *desire that rational and sincere milk.* [7.] There are none of the children of the Lord so far advanced in knowledge, grace or holiness as that they ought to be satisfied with their measure, but ought still to aspire toward a further degree of growth, both downward in humility, 2 Sam. 6:22, and stability, Col. 2:7, and abroad in public-mindedness, showing itself in real endeavours after the salvation and comfort of others, Hos. 14:5,6,7, and upward in joy and praise, Psa. 71:14, for upon those who were already far advanced in grace (1:22,23) is growth here pressed: *desire the sincere milk of the Word, that ye may grow.* [8.] According to the strength of our desires after and greedy in-drinking of the Word by application and use-making thereof, so will be our growth in grace and holiness. They cannot but be under a great decay in both who have lost their appetite after the Gospel: for this desire after the Word is here pressed by the Apostle as a means of growth: *desire the sincere milk, that ye may grow thereby.*

3. If so be ye have tasted that the Lord is gracious.

The fourth motive to sharpen their appetite after the Word is that if they did greedily drink it in, that they might grow by it, their so doing should prove to them the reality of any experience they seemed to themselves to have of the graciousness or sweetness of the Lord to them: of which, whosoever gets a taste they cannot but thirst earnestly after more of it through the Word; and they who do not so thirst cannot conclude they have tasted thereof. And therefore an eager appetite after the Word is to be laboured for.

Hence learn, [1.] The Lord Jesus Christ, whom believers seek and serve, has in Him everything that may be useful and sweet for them, and a strong desire in His heart to let out the same to them; whereof He has given abundant proof in providing such a remedy for lost sinners as Himself to die for them, Tit. 3:4 &c, in His daily pardoning of their daily failings, Isa. 55:7, in His succouring of them under their extremities, Heb. 2:18, and in His waiting for the fittest opportunity for proving Himself to be such a one to them, Isa. 50:8, for all these and much more are in this attribute of His, as the Scriptures cited, which express the effects of His graciousness, do make clear: and therefore it cannot but be sweet to all that ever *have tasted how gracious the Lord is.* [2.] Although all that are in the world do in some sense taste of the goodness of God, Psa. 145:9, yet only His own elect and regenerate ones taste of His graciousness as it is manifested in the forementioned effects thereof: for it is only the regenerate who are presumed here to have *tasted how gracious the Lord is*. [3.] Although the way of believers' partaking and feeling of this graciousness or sweetness of the Lord be spiritual, arising in their hearts from their exercising of their faith in God as favourable to them through Christ, Rom. 5:1,2, yet it is no less real and certain than that which is by any of the outward senses closing with and delighting in their proper objects. Therefore as it is elsewhere in Scripture set forth by smelling, Psa. 45:8, and by seeing, Isa. 45:22, so here (as also Psa. 34:8) by tasting: *If so be ye have tasted how gracious the Lord is*. [4.] All that believers get of Christ in this life is, in comparison of that full enjoyment of Him which they shall have in the life to come, but a part, a sparing measure to sharpen appetite after more: for so it is here called *a tasting how gracious the Lord is*. [5.] That which proves our tastes of Christ's sweetness to be kindly, and proper to the regenerate, is that thereby our inward and beloved lusts are weakened and we are made to lay them aside and to loathe them, and our desires after the Word are more sharpened; by which the sweet feelings of the regenerate are differenced from those which hypocrites may have, which have no such concomitants, Heb. 6:4, for, by considering the connexion of this verse with the former two, it appears the Apostle has pressed mortification of sin and desire after the Word for growth, as things which could not but be in them, if so be they had *tasted how gracious the Lord is*. [6.) All those tastes of the graciousness and sweetness of Christ which the saints may expect in this life are to be looked for in and through the Word: for while he makes their former tastes of that kind an argument to sharpen their desires after the Word, he clearly imports that both their former tastes of that sort had been through the Word and that more of these tastes were to be found in the same way and no way else: *desire the sincere milk*, &c, *if so be ye have tasted that the Lord is gracious*: and so would desire to taste more of that sort. [7.] All the former experiences we have had of the graciousness and sweetness of Christ should sharpen and put an edge upon our desires after more of that sort, and after the Word through which those experiences are conveyed: for to quicken their appetite after the Word through which the Lord's people taste of His sweetness, he mentions their former tastes here: *If so be ye have tasted that the Lord is gracious*.

4. **To whom coming, as unto a living stone, disallowed indeed of men, but chosen of God, and precious,**
5. **Ye also as lively stones, are built up a spiritual house, an holy priesthood, to offer up spiritual sacrifices, acceptable to God by Jesus Christ.**

Here is the fifth motive to the hearty receiving of the Word, taken from the great advantage of daily closing with Jesus Christ offered therein: and this advantage the Apostle sets forth in several branches; as first, that Christ should prove Himself living; and secondly, a solid foundation to such as by faith build themselves upon Him. Thirdly, that however the most part of men reject Him as unworthy to be their choice, yet is He the Father's choice, and as our Mediator, in high esteem with Him and therefore worthy to be our choice, and daily to be made use of, v 4. Fourthly, that they who do close with Him, as the Gospel offers Him, shall be made in some measure to conform to Him in spiritual life and stability. Fifthly, that their union with Christ and the rest of the saints should be growing more and more straight. Sixthly, that so they should be made fit for entertaining communion with Himself, dwelling in them by His Spirit as in His spiritual temple. And seventhly, that by their so doing they should prove themselves to be a people consecrated to the Lord (as the priests were of old) to offer up their prayers, praises, and other parts of their worship, which Christ, to whom they are daily coming, makes well-pleasing to the Father (v 5).

From v 4 learn, [1.] With how much greater desire we do receive the truths of the Gospel, by so much the more do we come nearer to Jesus Christ offered therein, to enjoy a comfortable communion with Him and to partake of the benefits purchased by Him: for if we observe the current of the Apostle's speech we may see that instead of showing the advantages of receiving the Gospel, he shows the advantages of closing with Jesus Christ offered therein, importing these two to be one: *To whom coming, as unto a living stone.* [2.] It is not enough that sinners once come to Christ for life, and close with Him as the Word offers Him to them; but they must make a trade and a life of coming to Him, daily renewing and strengthening the acts of their faith in Him, for pardon and furniture[1] for everything they have to do, there being much distance still remaining between

[1] See page 62.

Him and the best while they are here, 2 Cor. 5:9, Psa. 73:28, and still a nearer communion with Him attainable, Philip. 3:13, for coming to Christ, which in Scripture is believing in Him, John 6:35, is here pressed upon those who had believed in Him before, and that by such a word in the present time as signifies the continuance and renewing of the acts of faith: *To whom coming,* &c. [3.] There is no growth in grace or holiness, nor in ability to oppose our corruptions, except we be thus coming frequently to Jesus Christ in whom the fulness of grace is, Col. 1:19, and who is both our righteousness and our strength for all we have to do, Isa. 45:24; for this coming to Christ here pressed may be looked upon as the means of growth in mortification and every grace, as is clear by comparing this, *to whom coming* &c., with what goes before and follows after. [4.] All that come to Jesus Christ shall find Him a solid foundation to rest upon, able to bear them and all their burdens, constant in His love to them and in the fulfilling of all His undertakings; and as such He is daily to be closed with: for, for these and the like causes, He is here set forth as the object of faith under the similitude of *a stone*. [5.] Christ is a living foundation for sinners to build themselves upon, having life in Himself essentially, John 5:26, and communicating life spiritual and eternal to every soul that closes with Him, 1 John 5:12, for so also is He here proposed as the object of saving faith, *to whom coming, as unto a living stone.* [6.] Felt deadness should not keep any soul back from Jesus Christ who sees need of life from Him and hazard of eternal death without Him, it being impossible to attain to spiritual or eternal life but by closing with Him, John 6:51; for *coming to Him, as to a living stone* imports that the desire of life should draw souls to Him that do find much spiritual deadness and fear death eternal; *to whom coming, as to a living stone.* [7.] There is not another rock or foundation stone whereupon the Church or any true member thereof can be built but Jesus Christ Himself. The prophets and apostles are only called the foundation, Eph. 2:20, in so far as they hold out in their doctrine this living foundation: and this Apostle, by that Rock, whereupon Christ said He would build His Church, Matt. 16:18, did not understand himself or his successors (though never so faithful ministers) but Jesus Christ Himself, whom he had a little before confessed to be this living stone: and therefore he thus holds Him forth here: *To whom coming, as unto a living stone.* [8.] Though Christ be a solid and living foundation for sinners to rest upon, yet is He rejected by the most part of men as unworthy to be their choice, He having little outward glory to draw hearts toward Him, Isa. 53:2, and all men being naturally blind concerning His spiritual excellency, 2 Cor. 4:4, and their own need of Him, Rev. 3:17, and there being but a very few in comparison of the rest, that are given to Him to be saved by Him, John 12:39. Therefore is it that He is *disallowed indeed of men.* [9.] The rejecting of Christ by others should be so far from discouraging His own to close with Him and make use of Him, that by the contrary it should move them to a more hearty and frequent closing with Him, being confident that He shall deal the better with them that they are not hindered or discouraged by the example of rejecters from closing with Him: for, even this may be also looked upon as having the strength of an argument to move those who have hitherto been strangers to Christ to come now to Him; and those who are near to come yet nearer, that He is *disallowed indeed of men.* [10.] Christ is disallowed when he is not fled to and made use of, for that life and rest and other advantages to be had in Him; for in opposition to believers coming to Him and use-making of Him, He is said to be *disallowed indeed of men.* [11.] Jesus Christ, not only as He is God but as He is our Mediator, is and has been from eternity, Prov. 8:30, the Father's choice and delight in highest esteem with Him; which is evidenced by the Father's giving all things into His hand for our good, Matt. 11:27, and all for that very end that He may be honourable in our esteem, John 5:23, by His hearing of Him as our intercessor in all His petitions, John 11:42, and hearing all our lawful desires for His sake, John 16:23, and by the unspeakable terror which He will manifest against rejecters of Him beyond what other sinners shall find, Heb. 10:28,29. All which do prove that as our Mediator He is most dear and precious to the Father; and worthy is He to be so, there being none in heaven or in earth fit for that work of redemption but He, Rev. 5:4,5. Therefore is He *chosen of God and precious.* [12.] The Father's high esteem of and delighting in the Mediator, Christ, should move sinners to come to Him, to choose Him for their portion and to delight in Him, being confident that their so doing cannot but be well-pleasing to the Father, who has chosen Him that He may welcome sinners, and has fitted Him to be all things to them that may contribute for their blessedness, 1 Cor. 1:30, for this is a motive of coming to Him, that He is *chosen of God and precious.*

From v 5 learn, [1.] Christ's way of engaging the hearts of His own to a daily use-making of Him is by proposing to them in His Word the sweet advantages and rich privileges which they shall have by their so doing: with the consideration whereof He allows them to move their own hearts to perseverance in that exercise: for this verse contains a bundle of advantages and privileges that souls have by daily use-making of Christ, branched out to move them thereunto, to wit, that by their coming to Him, as to a living stone, *they also as lively stones are built up a spiritual house*, &c. [2.] Every renewed act of faith closing with Christ, as the Scripture holds Him forth, draws from Christ some new increase of spiritual life, whereby the soul is made more sensible of sin, has more appetite after Christ and His truth and more activity in duties that may honour Him; all which are effects of spiritual life and resemblances between it and the natural life: for this is here made a prevailing motive to that coming to Christ which is recommended to sinners in the former verse, that they who did so should be made lively stones, which must be understood of an increase of spiritual life, it being spoken to them who are supposed before to have been born again. [3.] Even as believers are holden throng[1] in daily employing and use-making of Christ, so do they make progress in grace and holiness. So do they also become solid and fixed in their understanding of the truth, that they may not be carried about with every wind of doctrine, constant in their love to Christ and in their believing of His love to them and established in their walking like unto His truths: for in opposition to the un-settledness of mis-believers and of them who do not live in the daily employing of Christ, but rest upon their measures received, those that are daily coming to Him are here said to be *lively stones, built up*, &c, importing, beside their progress, a state of stability and fixedness, which they attain to by their so doing. [4.] The lively and frequent exercise of faith draws virtue from Christ to make the believer resemble Him in those com-municable perfections of His wherewith the Scripture holds Him forth adorned and to be closed with by sinners, so that under whatsoever consideration of Christ held forth in Scrip-ture sinners do close with Him, they are thereby in some measure changed to some likeness with Him in that considera-tion. If the unclean soul close with Him offered under the con-sideration of a fountain, it becomes in some measure like Him

---

[1] 'holden throng': associated.

in purity and holiness. If the dead sinner receive Him offered as life, he becomes to live like Him. If the unstable soul come to Him as the foundation-stone, it grows stable as a stone. And so of every consideration under which Christ offered in the Word is closed with: for, He being before proposed under the consideration of a living stone, as the object of faith to be closed with, the Apostle here affirms that they who did so close with Him should find that by their so doing they *also as lively stones should be built up.* [5.] Those souls who may expect that the Lord will keep communion with them and dwell familiarly in them as in His house, must labour to be made spiritual in their minds, enlightened and elevated to discern things spiritual, which the natural man cannot do, 1 Cor. 2:14,15, Prov. 8:12, in their affections humbled in the sense of their unworthiness and sinfulness, Isa. 57:17, confident of their acceptation with God through Christ, Heb. 6:3, cheerful in Him as reconciled to them, Psa. 22:3, loathing sin and loving holiness, 2 Cor. 6:16, &c., and all persons that are holy, 1 John 4:16. All which, the Scriptures cited make clear to be of a spiritual frame, which is to be studied by all those who may expect the Lord to dwell in them as in His house: for believers, in order to their enjoying of fellowship with Christ, are here said to *be built up a spiritual house.* [6.] The more heartily and frequently sinners flee to and make use of Jesus Christ as the Gospel offers Him, the more fit are they to be an habitation for Him to dwell in, and the more familiarly will He converse with them; and that, because the only way to attain to and grow in a spiritual frame which makes sinners a fit habitation for the Lord to dwell in, is to be daily flying to and making use of Jesus Christ who gives the Spirit for working of that frame, 2 Cor. 3:18; for believers by coming to Him (v 4) are here said to be *built up a spiritual house.* [7.] Near union with Jesus Christ and daily use-making of Him by faith is the best way to make the saints one among themselves: the division, difference of judgment and alienation of affection among them proves one or other, or all of them, to be at a distance from Him: for while the Apostle says *To whom coming, &c., ye are built up a spiritual house,* he imports that believers by their closing with and use-making of Jesus Christ, are as closely united one of them to another as the stones of a building are. [8.] Every particular believer should esteem himself a part of the church universal which makes up one house to God, 1 Tim. 3:15, and so should seek the good thereof, Psa. 122:9, and sympathise with the sufferings of the whole, or any member thereof, 1 Cor. 12:25,26, seeing *they are built up* (to wit, in the universal church with the rest of the members thereof) *a spiritual house.* [9.] Although the most eminent believers may not take upon them any part of the ministerial office without a lawful and orderly calling thereunto, Rom. 10:15, Heb. 5:4, yet all professors of Christianity do in some respects resemble the priests under the Law in so far as they are separated by the Lord from all the rest of the world; and true believers among them do receive that unction from the Lord, to wit, His Holy Spirit, 1 John 2:20, which was signified by that oil wherewith the Priests were anointed, Exod. 28:41, and have their service accepted, while others are rejected, Prov. 15:8, in which respects they are here called *An holy priesthood.* [10.] Although internal or real holiness be not the necessary qualification which makes one a member of the visible church, Acts 8:13, John 15:2, yet is it the duty of all to study that holiness, and the mark of all the true and lively members of the church to be endued therewith: therefore they are here called *A holy priesthood.* [11.] The great employment of believers in Jesus Christ is to offer sacrifices to God, not typical (which are now abolished by Christ, Heb. 10:1, &c.), nor expiatory (which Christ alone has once offered, never to be repeated, Heb. 7:27) but *gratulatory*, in testimony of their thankfulness to Him for that sacrifice of Himself for them; such as the sacrifice of themselves for His service, Rom. 12:1, their penitent and humble supplications, Psa. 51:17 and 141:2, their praises, Heb. 13:15, and their charity to His saints, Phil. 4:18. These and the like are they to offer, who are *a holy priesthood to offer up spiritual sacrifices.* [12.] Whatever sacrifices of this sort believers offer up to God they must be spiritual, done from a spiritual principle, a new nature, Ezek. 36:26,27, upon spiritual furniture,[1] the strength of Christ, Phil. 4:13, and for a spiritual end, the glory of Christ, 1 Cor. 10:31, in which and the like respects they are here called *spiritual sacrifices.* [13.] Such spiritual sacrifices as believers offer up to God are well-pleasing to Him, not for any worth that is in them, Isa. 6:6, or advantage they can be to Him, Psa. 16:2, Acts 17:25, but because they are presented to God by Jesus Christ, who takes away the iniquity of their holy things, Exod. 28:38, and perfumes their service with the incense of his merits, Rev. 8:3. Therefore are their sacrifices *acceptable to God by Jesus Christ.*

---

[1] See page 62.

6. Wherefore also it is contained in the scripture, Behold, I lay in Sion a chief corner-stone, elect, precious: and he that believeth on him shall not be confounded.

The Apostle confirms his former doctrine concerning the usefulness and excellency of Jesus Christ for the church and believers in Him, by a testimony of Scripture which (though no particular place be here cited) is to be found, Isa. 28:16. And withal, he adds two further arguments to move them to that hearty receiving of the Gospel and use-making of Christ offered in it which he has pressed in the former words: the one is that we have Jesus Christ who is the Father's choice and highly esteemed by Him, with the Father's great good will laid in the church as the foundation and chief corner-stone thereof, for every soul to flee to and rest upon. The other is that whosoever betake themselves to Him by faith shall never need to be ashamed of their so doing.

Hence learn, [1.] The ministers of Christ ought to have the written Word so richly dwelling in them that they may be able to confirm every truth they deliver from that Word; and the Lord's people ought to be so well acquainted with the same, that though ministers do not spend time to cite particularly every chapter and verse where every passage they bring forth is to be found, they may, notwithstanding, upon the hearing of it faithfully and for the substance repeated to them acknowledge and receive the same for the Lord's mind: for even the Apostle here, as frequently elsewhere, confirms his doctrine by Scripture; and yet, supposing those to whom he writes well acquainted at least with the letter thereof, he does not condescend upon the particular place, judging it sufficient to say, *Wherefore it is contained in the Scripture, Behold I lay,* &c. [2.] True faith can have solid footing nowhere but upon the written Word of God, nor should any of the Lord's people be satisfied with the most pleasant notions about Christ Jesus till they see them grounded upon and drawn from that Word. Therefore the Apostle, having in the former words commended Christ as the object of saving faith, here repeats again the same commendation of Him from the Old Testament, that so faith might rest safely upon Him as such a one; *Wherefore it is contained in the Scripture, Behold, I lay in Sion a chief corner-stone,* &c. [3.] Jesus Christ and He alone is that to the church and to every soul that flees to Him, which the chief corner-stone, whether the lowest or the highest, is to the building. He is the stone first laid, in regard He was and behoved to be actually exercising His mediatory office before any sinner could attain to union or communion with God, Col. 1:18. He is the stone laid lower than any of the rest in His humiliation, Psa. 22:6. He bears the weight of the whole church and of every believing soul, Heb. 1:3. He is more curiously wrought than any of the rest of the stones of the building (as the chief corner stone used to be), and engraven by the art of His Father adorning Him with all perfections suitable for the necessities of poor sinners, Zech. 3:9. He is the bond whereby most-differing nations, such as *Jews and Gentiles*, are united in one building, Eph. 2:16, as the foundation corner-stone knits the two side walls of the building together; He is the perfection of the whole, in whom the building and every lively stone thereof is complete, Col. 2:10, as the highest corner-stone, and as that also He is the glory and ornament of all the building, Isa. 22:24. In all which things, He is resembled by that, whereby the Spirit of the Lord here sets Him forth to our capacity, *The chief corner-stone*. [4.] We have this great blessing, Christ for the chief corner-stone of this spiritual building, with the Father's great good will, who has laid Him, firstly, in His eternal counsel or decree, as the word used by Isaiah (28:16) and here translated *to lay* signifies, Psa. 2:2; secondly, in His actual exhibition of Him to the church as Mediator (first, in the promise of Him, Gen. 3:15, and next visibly in our flesh; for so this word is also used, to signify the publishing or execution of things formerly decreed, 2 Chron. 9:23, Prov. 3:19); and thirdly, in His exalting of Him when He had perfected the work of redemption, so much of it as concerned Him to do in the state of his humiliation: for, so this same word (used in Psa. 8:2) is translated, Matt. 21:16, to perfect a work; in all which respects the Father lays Christ the foundation or chief corner-stone in the church; and calls all to behold what pleasure He has in so doing: *Behold, I lay in Sion a chief corner-stone*. [5.] The Father's condescendency to give His own blessed Son for the above-mentioned uses to His church and believers in Him, which this similitude here made use of holds forth, is worthy of our most serious consideration; and Christ, this chief corner-stone, is much to be admired as differing from all other corner-stones, He being one stone who is both the lowest and highest of the building, Phil. 2:6,7, who has immediate connexion with the least stone or meanest believer as well as with the greatest or most eminent, whether prophets, apostles or even the virgin *Mary*, John 17:20,21. He communicates an influence of life and growth to every stone laid upon Him, Eph. 2:21, and never suffers any that are built upon Him to fall totally and finally off Him, John 10:28. In all which respects we are here called to admire Jesus Christ and to give our most serious attention and consideration to the Father in giving Him by this word, which serves both to draw attention and admiration; *Behold, I lay in Sion a chief corner-stone* &c. [6.] Though Christ be God's gift to the whole church made up of Jews and Gentiles, Eph. 2:14, which often has the name of Sion in Scripture, Obad. 17, yet with a special reference to the church of the Jews who first had that name, He is said to be laid in Sion, being first preached publicly and held forth in promises, sacrifices and types to them, Psa. 147:19,20, being come of them according to the flesh, Rom. 9:5, and first offered to them after His incarnation, Matt. 10:5,6, from whom the news of Him is come to the rest of the world, Micah 4:2, and by whom Christ shall yet have a great part of His public glory in the world. Hos. 3:5, Rom. 11:12,15. All of which should make us pity their present case and pray for their conversion: for with a special eye to them is this spoken, *Behold, I lay in Sion a chief corner-stone* &c. [7.] Christ's fitness for this great work of our redemption as evidenced by the Father's choosing of Him for it, from among all others, as the word *elect* signifies, and by His high esteem of Him as our Mediator, should strongly draw the hearts of sinners in to Him and move them to dwell upon the thoughts of His worth and of the Father's esteem of Him, as He is the receiver of all that come to God through Him: for the Apostle, having commended Christ before, from these two epithets, that He is *chosen of God* and *precious*, as motives to draw sinners in to Him, repeats them here again as delighting to write and think of so sweet a subject as Christ: *Elect, precious.* [8.] That which builds sinners upon Christ, this chief corner-stone, is that grace of believing which, according to the signification of the word in the Hebrew when the Apostle translates this text, is the fixedness or stayedness (as this same word is translated, Exod. 17:12) of the soul in the expectation of salvation through Christ offered in the Gospel; and whereby the soul is fed and nourished upon Him as its necessary food, which is also in the signification of the word in that language: for the Apostle, instead of insisting further upon the metaphor of a building, which would have required him to say, he that is built upon Him

73

shall not be ashamed, speaks properly, expounding what it is to be built upon Him, to wit, to close with Him by faith: *He that believeth on Him shall not be ashamed.* [9.] Patient waiting on God, in the use of His means for the performance of His promises, without such hasting to a delivery as makes us faint or fret under the delay thereof, or the use of unlawful means for attaining to it, is the kindly effect of saving faith, and that which keeps off shame and confusion, which such hastiness occasions to the Lord's people: for the Apostle translating these words of Isaiah, *He that believeth shall not make haste,* expresses the effect of not hasting in the aforesaid sense to be this, *He that believeth on Him shall not be confounded.*

7. **Unto you therefore which believe, he is precious: but unto them which be disobedient, the stone which the builders disallowed, the same is made the head of the corner,**
8. **And a stone of stumbling, and a rock of offence, even to them which stumble at the Word, being disobedient, whereunto also they were appointed.**

The Apostle, having commended Christ, that sinners might be moved to make use of Him as the Gospel offers Him, here holds forth the dignity and disposition of all that believe in Him; as also the disposition and judgment of all that reject Him, that so none might stumble or be discouraged when they see Him rejected by so many. As for believers, Christ is an honour to them and they have a high esteem of Him: both which readings, the original words in the beginning of the seventh verse will bear. And as for others, who will not be persuaded to believe and obey the Gospel, that stone, Jesus Christ the Mediator, whom the rulers of His time set at nought, is exalted by the Father (according to the Psalmist's word, Psa. 118:22, which the Apostle here rehearses) to be the glorious Head of the church and believers, and a terror to all whose blind and carnal hearts do still find out something in the Gospel whence they take occasion to reject Christ, and refuse to take on his yoke. Thereby they do but ruin themselves, as a mad man that dashes himself against a stone in his way, or foolish mariners that run their ship against a rock, which are the similitudes here made use of, taken out of Isa. 8:14, and so do prove themselves to be reprobates. Which purpose contains three further motives to press that hearty receiving of the Word and use-making of Christ offered in it which the Apostle has recommended in the former words: every one of which motives serves to guard against the offence that might arise from wicked men's rejecting of Christ. The first is, that Christ Jesus is an honour to all that believe in Him. The second is, that His glory is nothing diminished by others' rejecting of Him (v 7). And the third is, that they who continue so to do will but run themselves upon that ruin to which they have been from eternity appointed for the rejecting of an offered Saviour (v 8).

From v 7 learn, [1.] Christ is the true honour of all that truly believe in Him. He is a great credit to all His poor kindred who are honoured by Him, not only to serve Him but to be served by Him, Matt. 20:28, and by His best servants, Heb. 1:14, to be made sons of God, John 1:12, to have a marriage-relation to Him, 2 Cor. 11:2, to be heirs and co-heirs of glory with Him, Rom. 8:17; and it does not yet appear, but we shall know it afterward, how much is in this word which in the original is in the abstract and runs thus, *Christ is an honour to you that believe.* [2.] Jesus Christ is most dear and precious to all that truly believe in Him, He being their life, Col. 3:4, their light, John 1:4, their wisdom, 1 Cor. 1:30, their food, John 6.56, their raiment, Rom. 13:14, and everything to them which is most necessary; and consequently most precious to the children of men: and therefore He cannot but be in so high esteem with them that the very thoughts of Him, Psa. 139:17, His ordinances, Isa. 58:13, His people, Psa. 16.3, must be precious and excellent to them; and their most precious things in this world cannot be dear to them for His sake, Acts 20:24, but must be dung and loss, that they may gain Him, Phil. 3:8. And this esteem of Christ, wherever it is in any real measure, is a clear mark of true and saving faith; for so much is expressed in our translation of the word, *Unto you that believe He is precious.* [3.] It is our clear up-taking of Christ in His excellency and usefulness for sinners, as the Word reveals Him, and some experimental feeling upon our closing with Him, that He is such a One to us, which begets this precious esteem of Him in the hearts of believers: we can never esteem of Him till we know how excellent a One He is, and taste in some measure how gracious He is: for, of those whom the Apostle supposes to know Christ in some measure as He is formerly described (vv 6,7), and to have tasted how gracious he is (v 3), He affirms here, *Unto you therefore which believe He is precious.* [4.] They who do not believe in and esteem highly of Jesus Christ are not only guilty of neglecting and slighting of Him (the hazard whereof is unspeakable, Heb. 2:3), but they are also guilty of high rebellion and disobedience to God, it being one of His greatest and most peremptory commands to believe in His Son, 1 John 3:23, and to honour Him, John 5:23, without obedience to which it is not possible to give any acceptable obedience to any other of His commands, Heb. 11:6. There is no midst between these two. Men must either believe in Christ and have a precious esteem of Him, or be disobedient and rebellious, as the word signifies. Therefore the Apostle thus expresses that disposition in opposition to believing and a precious esteem of Christ: *them which be disobedient*. [5.] Although Jesus Christ in His dealing with souls has the strongest reasons upon His side that ever were used with any, Prov. 8:5 &c. and great variety of most alluring motives to gain souls to His obedience, Matt. 11:20, &c, yet there are a great many who are so addicted to their own will and lusts, Jer. 2:25, that they will not suffer themselves to be persuaded by Him, or to admit that He should reform their hearts and lives: for this description of the wicked designs[1] persons that have been by strong reasons and alluring motives dealt with, but have shown themselves averse from all yielding or persuasion: *but unto them which be disobedient*. [6.] Those whom God has placed in authority in or over His church (and who are obliged to Christ for their place and power more than others, not only to build themselves by faith upon Him but to employ their wit and power to draw many others in to Him, and one of them to work to another's hand, like so many builders in the advancement of His work) are too often found opposers of His work, and rejecters of Himself as if He were unworthy to be laid as a stone in their building, or that His interest should be minded in their designs: for, those who were in authority in Christ's time are designed[1] by this name of builders, to which they should have been answerable, but it was not so: *Christ was the stone which the builders disallowed*. [7.] The higher any be set in eminency of power or place above others, the more does the Lord resent and take notice of their rejecting of Him and opposing of His work: for though many of the common people among the Jews did reject Christ, for which they bear their judgment, Matt. 23:38, yet this guilt is mainly charged upon the rulers: *The stone which the builders disallowed*. [8.] Christ our Mediator will not be the less

[1] See page 37.

honourable, nor will His glory be any whit diminished, that many and those the chief among men do reject Him and slight Him, but rather, *that* will tend to His greater glory, the Father taking occasion by their so doing to let out the more of His grace and love to His own church and people that embrace Him: and to illustrate His justice the more in the ruin of rejecters of Him; for, while Christ is disallowed of the builders, what comes of Him? For the comfort and glory of His church, *He becomes the head of the corner*; and for the terror and ruin of His enemies, *a stone of stumbling*, &c.

From v 8 learn, [1.] Although there be nothing in Christ to make any stumble or offend at Him, Jer. 2:5, but everything that might draw the desire and delight of all toward Him, Psa. 45:2, Hag. 2:7, yet through reason of men's blindness and ignorance of His worth and excellency, Luke 19:42, of their own hazard by rejecting of him, Luke 23:34, their violent prosecution of their lusts, Jer. 8:6, and malice against any that would hinder them in their pursuit, Act 13:45, and such other things as are resembled by the causes of men's stumbling in their way, they do take occasion from the meanness and simplicity of Christ Himself in regard of His outward condition in His estate of humiliation, Isa. 53:3; Matt. 13:55,56,57, and of His followers, John 7:48,49, and ordinances, 1 Cor. 1:23,26, from the unlikelihood of the way of salvation through His death and imputed righteousness to carnal reason, Rom. 9:32,33; John 6:61, the contrariety that is in corrupt affections to the precepts of the Gospel, Matt. 5:29, and from the many crosses that ordinarily attend his followers, Matt. 26:31, not only to halt and sit up[1] in the study of believing in Him and obedience to His Gospel, but by reason of their malice and opposition to dash themselves against Him and His will; for in the forementioned sense *He is a stone of stumbling and a rock of offence to them that stumble at the Word.* [2.] Christ Jesus is not more properly the cause of sinners rejecting of Him and ruining of themselves by their so doing, than a stone in the way of some blind, furious or drunken traveller, whereupon he might rest himself to help him in his journey, is the cause of his breaking his neck upon it; or a rock in the sea is the cause of desperate mariners' shipwreck; for from these is the similitude here taken, while Christ is said to be to misbelievers and rejecters of him, *a stone of stumbling and a rock of offence.* [3.] Those who will not suffer

---

[1] 'sit up': seems to be used in the sense of 'sitting in judgment on (another)'.

themselves to be persuaded to receive the gracious offers made
in the Gospel but will run violently on in their own sinful ways
against the directions thereof, and instead of subjection to it are
the more incensed by it; these are they who stumble and offend
at Jesus Christ; and by their so doing will hurt themselves, not
Him, as the man does who stumbles at a stone in his way; for
here the Apostle describes those to whom it is that Christ is a
stone of stumbling and a rock of offence: *Even to them that stumble
at the Word, being disobedient.* [4.] Although the elect may for a
long time before their conversion stumble at Jesus Christ and
oppose him, Acts 9:1, and after conversion may for a time under
the fit of a temptation do the same, Matt. 26:31, yet none will
continue so to do but those who have been from eternity
ordained for condemnation in God's spotless decree, which
infuses no evil in men, Jas. 1:13, seeing they sin with no less
freedom and delight than if there were not a decree concerning
their reprobation, Acts 4:27,28, and are not damned because of a
decree, 2 Thess. 2:12, but either because of their sinning against
nature's light, Rom. 1:21 and 2:12, or for their wilful slighting
of an offered Saviour, John 3:20. The continuance in such sin is
the clearest proof and evidence of reprobation of any in the
world, for the everlasting ruin and condemnation of souls
ordained from eternity to the same for their wilful slighting of
Jesus Christ is referred to in the last words of this verse as being
thereby most clearly evidenced: *They stumble at the Word, being
disobedient, whereunto also they were appointed.*

9. **But ye are a chosen generation, a royal priesthood, an holy
   nation, a peculiar people; that ye should shew forth the
   praises of him who hath called you out of darkness into his
   marvellous light.**

After the description of the woeful state of them that slight
Christ, the Apostle returns again to illustrate further the
excellency of the state of true believers, to whom these
honourable titles which the Lord vouchsafed of old upon the
visible church of the *Jews*, Exod. 19:6 and Deut. 7:6,7 (and so
may yet in some sense be safely applied to all visible professors)
do most fully and truly agree: for, speaking to all the *Hebrews*
who were professors of Christianity, he affirms: Firstly, they

were wailed[1] out from among the rest of the world: which is true of all of them insofar as they were made members of the Christian church; and of some of them in a more special way, insofar as they were made objects of his special grace and love; and so they were *a chosen generation*. Secondly, they did partake of the benefits of Christ's kingly and priestly office and did in some respects resemble Him in the exercise of both, insofar as all of them were professed and some of them true subjects of Christ, the King of the church. All of them were by profession, and some of them in effectual calling, separated from the world for His service; and had spiritual privileges answerable to those of kings and priests; and so were a *royal priesthood*. Thirdly, they were all of them federally holy and some of them endued with true sanctification; and so were a *holy nation*. Fourthly, all of them who did externally subject themselves to Christ, were owned by Him as His propriety and prime interest, in comparison of the rest of the world; and true believers among them as His elect and redeemed ones; and so were *a peculiar people*. And all for this end, that they might in their practice commend and express His properties to His praise, who had called all of them externally, and some of them effectually, out of the state of sin and wrath to a state of favour and happiness: which purpose contains two further arguments to press a hearty receiving of the Gospel, and daily use-making of Christ offered in it, in order to their spiritual growth. The one is taken from the excellency of their present estate in the several fore-mentioned particulars: the other, from that wonderful change which God had made upon them from so woeful to so blessed a condition.

Hence learn, [1.] It is very safe and suitable to Scripture language to give to the whole visible church and all the professors within the same these styles and compellations,[2] which do only agree in their full and best signification to true believers. Suppose the most part within the visible church void of saving grace, yet in respect of the rest of the world and by virtue of that covenant which is between the Lord and her and all her members (Deut. 26:17 &c. and 29:10 &c.), all professors may in some sense have all the styles that are here in the text and others like them, for though these styles be most truly verified in believers, yet did the Lord of old give them to the whole church of the *Jews*: and the Apostle here gives them indefinitely to all the

---

[1] See page 8.
[2] 'compellations': appellations, styles of address.

nation of the Jews who were professors of Christ, to whom he writes, though with a special eye to those who were true believers among them: *ye are a chosen generation*, &c. [2.] So excellent is that state whereunto sinners are advanced by believing in Jesus Christ, that the sharpest sighted in the world, the longer they look upon it, will still see more and more of the excellency and privileges thereof. The discovery whereof to the Lord's people, especially while they are under affliction, should much take up the heart and pains of all the ministers of Christ, it being his people's prime comfort under all their crosses, and their chief motive to all their duties, that they are in so excellent a spiritual state: for, after the Apostle has largely described it in the former chapter, and spoken much of it in the former part of this, he comes yet again upon the branching out of it here: *But ye are a chosen generation, a royal priesthood*, &c. All which styles do most truly agree to true believers. [3.] They who do by faith choose Jesus Christ for their portion, who entertain in their hearts a high esteem of Him and make use of Him daily for growth in grace and holiness, they have the characters and marks of such as have been from eternity elected of God, and in time effectually called, there being no other ordinary way to evidence the latter to us but by the former, 2 Pet. 1:10, for of election and effectual calling in reference to true believers, may this be understood which here the Apostle affirms of those to whom he said before, that Christ was precious: *But ye are a chosen generation.* [4.] As that dignity whereunto sinners are advanced by flying to Jesus Christ does, in a spiritual sense, resemble that of the priests under the Law (as was cleared in the tenth doctrine upon the fifth verse) so are they also thereby brought unto a kingly dignity; and in a spiritual sense they only are truly royal, having a new nature in some measure resembling the divine, 2 Pet. 1:4, being co-heirs with Jesus Christ, Rom. 8:17, of a kingdom that cannot be shaken, Heb. 12:28, and more than conquerors over all their spiritual enemies, Rom. 8:37. In all which, and the like respects, they are *a royal priesthood*. [5.] Our union with Jesus not only obliges us to keep a distance from the disposition and profane fashions of the men whose portion is in this earth, and to consecrate ourselves wholly for the Lord's use in the study of holiness, but likewise it does really make believers a *holy people*. Insofar as He is daily made use of by faith, their hearts are purged from the love of their lusts, Acts 15:9, and they are made to exercise other graces and duties of holiness wherein He is honoured, Gal. 5:6, for this third branch of the commendation of their excellent state includes both their duty and their privilege. They are *a holy nation*. [6.] As all the people on earth are the Lord's, they being all the works of His hand, and under the disposal of His providence, Acts 17:26; and all the members of the church visible are His in a more peculiar way than others, Amos 3:2; so believers in Jesus Christ are in a most special way His propriety and peculiar interest, whom He has purchased to Himself at a dear rate, Acts 20:28, and made new again by a second creation, Eph. 2:10, in whom He delights, Zeph. 3:17, and whom also He will maintain and never forsake, Psa. 94:14, for this is the fourth branch of the dignity of His people which does in some sense agree to the whole company of professors, and most truly to true believers, that they are a *peculiar people*. [7.] That which is the Lord's end in bestowing all these privileges upon believers, and which they should make the great end and business of their life, is that they may show forth the praises of the Lord by numbering out (as the Hebrew word, Isa. 43:21, which the Apostle here translates, signifies) to the Lord Himself His blessed perfections or virtues (as the word here rendered *praises* is in the original), or rather by their prudent and seasonable commending to others His properties, such as His wisdom, power, terror, sweetness, faithfulness, manifested in His dealing, Psa. 145:4, &c, 10, &c, that so others may be stirred up to serve Him and praise Him; but especially by their expressing and holding forth in their practice some resemblance of His properties to His praise, Phil. 2:15,16, by their prudent and wise carriage, declaring to on-lookers that He is most wise by whose counsel they are guided; by their hazarding upon affliction rather than sin; demonstrating His terror to be above the terror of flesh; and by their patience and cheerfulness under crosses and trials, proclaiming to discerning beholders that His power is great that sustains them, and His consolations sweet that do refresh their hearts under such afflictions and make up the bitterness of them – all this is here set down as the end of all the fore-mentioned privileges and the compend of believers' duty, *that they should shew forth the praises of Him*. [8.] Even the elect, before conversion, are living in gross ignorance of their own miserable condition and the remedy thereof, Eph. 5:8, in the slavery of their lusts, Rom. 13:12. They are under a state of wrath as well as others, Eph. 2:3, and so without any true comfort, Eph. 2:12. All which in Scripture is frequently set out by this word *darkness*, whereby the Apostle expresses the state of the elect before conversion. [9.] Conversion brings sinners into a state of *light* which comprehends some clear knowledge of their own misery, Rev. 3:18, and the remedy thereof, 2 Cor. 4:6, a new and spiritual life communicated to them whereby they are enabled to close with Christ and cleave unto Him, John 8:12, to walk in holiness of life, Matt. 5:16, their living in His favour, Psa. 89:15, their having a right to glory, Col. 1:12, and His allowance to rejoice and comfort themselves in their blessed estate, Rom. 5:2. All which are set forth in Scripture by this word, whereby the Apostle expresses the excellent state of converted ones, *who are called out of darkness into his light.* [10.] The blessed estate of true converts is much to be admired by them, considering the Lord's wonderful condescendency in plucking them out of so woeful a condition as they were in before; His marvellous loving kindness in possessing them of such excellent privileges as they have in their new state; and giving them an undoubted right to so matchless an inheritance, as cannot but surpass the power of their understanding to comprehend, and so make them wonder at their own happiness which is here called *marvellous light.* [11.] The way how the Lord brings His own out of the state of nature which is here called *darkness*, into the state of grace, which is called *light*, is by His calling of them by the Gospel, 2 Thess. 2:14, opening their hearts to receive it by the power of His Spirit coming along with it, Acts 16:14, and so powerfully changing them into His own image, 2 Cor. 3:18, *Who hath called us out of darkness into His marvellous light.* [12.] Those upon whom the Lord has wrought this blessed change ought frequently to reflect upon their former woeful state, that they may be kept humble, 1 Cor. 15:9, and compassionate to others who are yet in the like, Tit. 3:2,3, and likewise upon their present blessed condition, that they may be provoked to praise and to the study of holiness, 1 Tim. 1:16,17, for which and the like causes the change of believers from the one state to the other is here represented to their thoughts that *they might shew forth the praises of Him, who hath called them out of darkness into his marvellous light.*

10. Which in time past were not a people, but are now the people of God: which had not obtained mercy, but now have obtained mercy.

Here is a further description of that happy change wrought

upon these Christian *Hebrews* to whom the Apostle writes, to wit, that they, who before their embracing of the Gospel had not been owned nor dealt with by the Lord as His peculiar people in covenant with Him, neither yet had enjoyed any of His special mercies, were now made His in a more special way than others; and had saving and special mercies offered to all of them and bestowed upon some of them, so that Hosea's prophecy (chap. 2 v 23) concerning the restoring of the Jewish nation after their rejection for a time, had now a begun accomplishment in them; especially in those of them who had felt the fore-mentioned remarkable change, whereby they should be moved to live to the praise of Him that made it.

Hence learn, [1.] When the Lord speaks to His church in one age, or to some particular persons in it, He does often speak also to His church in after ages, and to all the rest of His people who are to live afterward. See Mark 13:37 and Heb. 13:5 compared with Josh. 1:5, and therefore it is the duty of all His people to mark how far promises, made long since to the church, or particular believers in it, have their accomplishment toward themselves; that so they, finding what was long since spoken to others made good to them, may be the more affected with that ancient and constant love of God whose thoughts have been upon them for good, while He was speaking to others who lived many ages before them; for the Apostle cites and applies this Scripture, spoken by Hosea to the people in his time, as now verified upon these Christian *Hebrews* to whom he writes, *Which in time past were not a people*, &c. [2.] They that would delight in showing forth the praises of God and have their hearts engaged to the study of holiness, must learn to dwell upon the thoughts of their woeful case, wherein they were before conversion; and upon the blessed state whereunto, through God's mercy, they are advanced; and often to compare the one with the other that so they may be the more affected with the change and engaged to study His honour that made it: for after the Apostle had in the former verse represented this to their thoughts, as a motive to holiness, he here insists upon and represents the same again by a new enlargement of it (which is mainly verified in true converts), *Who in time past were not a people, but are now the people of God*, &c.

Although the elect be the Lord's people from eternity in regard of His purpose of grace toward them, Psa. 90:1, 2 Tim. 1:9, yet in regard of any actual manifestation of special love to them, or of His complacency in them as carrying His image, they are not His people; but remain slaves to Satan, Eph. 2:2, and to their own lusts, Tit. 3:3, until such time as by His power, put forth with the preaching of the Law, their woeful case be discovered to them, Luke 1:17, and by the same power, coming along with the preaching of the Gospel, they be made willing to accept the offer of reconciliation through Jesus Christ, Psa. 110:3, and thereby also be fitted for the duties of new obedience for the honour of Christ, Isa. 43:21. All which, as the places cited prove, are marks of them whom He does in a special way own for His people: for of the chosen generation the Apostle thus speaks in reference to their state before and after conversion; *Which in time past were not a people, but are now the people of God.* [4.] though there be not a sinner in the world who has not many mercies of God freely bestowed upon him, Psa. 145:9, and many deserved strokes kept off him, Rom. 2:3, yet even the elect before their conversion have not obtained that special mercy whereby their sins are actually pardoned, Acts 3:19, and whereby the Lord has complacency in them, Ezek. 16:8, and so they cannot be justified actually from eternity: for only of true converts is the Apostle's speech here principally to be understood, while he says that *in time past* (to wit, before their conversion) *they had not obtained mercy.* [5.] The closing of sinners by faith with Jesus Christ as the Gospel offers Him to them brings them to a most sweet and excellent state, namely, to be owned and dealt with by the Lord as His people in a most special manner, whom He will never forsake, Psa. 94:14, and to obtain mercy of Him for pardoning their daily sinfulness, Mic. 7:18, for pitying and supplying as is fitting all their necessities, as the word here translated *to obtain mercy* signifies; and for bearing them through all the straits of their life, Psa. 23:6, and at last crowning them with glory, 2 Tim. 1:18. All which is comprehended under this, *that they are now the people of God, and have now obtained mercy.* [6.] Of all miseries that can be expressed, to live in an unconverted state under unpardoned sin, is the greatest. And of all privileges in this world, to be brought out of that state and to obtain mercy is the greatest, and the most engaging to the study of holiness; for the one is here held forth as the depth of misery, and the other as the height of happiness; and the change from the one to the other as one of the strongest engagements to duty, lying upon those *who in time past were not a people, but are now the people of God; who had not obtained mercy, but now have obtained mercy.*

11. Dearly beloved, I beseech you as strangers and pilgrims, abstain from fleshly lusts, which war against the soul;

The Apostle repeats and enlarges that which he pressed in the first verse of this chapter, in order to their spiritual growth, to wit, that they should keep up the battle against their inward unmortified lusts; and this is pressed by three arguments. The first is taken from Christ's affection and the Apostle's towards them, as being dearly beloved of both. The second, from their hard lot in the world, that they were strangers and pilgrims; which was verified in a special way of these scattered *Hebrews* to whom he writes. And the third is from the hazard of the prevailing of these lusts which is no less than the eternal ruin of the soul.

Hence learn, [1.] There remains, even in those who are far advanced in mortification such swarms of sinful motions and strong inclinations to evils yet in a great part unmortified in them; and so prone are they to give way to them and to fall slack in the battle against them, that they have great need of exhortation upon exhortation, and of one motive upon the back of another to stir them up to that exercise; for, even these whom the Apostle supposed to have made some progress in mortification (Chap 1 v 22), and whom he had exhorted to further progress therein, in the first verse of this chapter, he here again exhorts very earnestly to the same by several arguments: *Dearly beloved, I beseech you abstain from fleshly lusts*, &c. [2.] True mortification of sin consists not only in abstinence from the outward acts thereof, but in the weakening of the root and power of sin within, and the inclinations and desires of the soul after the acting thereof, which are here called *fleshly lusts*; in regard they tend to the gratifying and pleasing of the flesh, and are acted by the outward man, *abstain from fleshly lusts*. [3.] The best way for believers to fit themselves for the showing forth of the praises of God in their practice is to set about the mortifying of those motions and inclinations to sin that remain in their heart, these being the cause of all the out-breakings which dishonour God in their conversation, Jas. 4:1; for this exhortation may safely be taken as the means of attaining to that which is the great end of Christians' calling, expressed in the former verse. That they may show forth his praise they must *abstain from fleshly lusts*. [4.] The love of the Lord, manifested toward sinners, should be a very strong argument to move them to fight against these lusts which dishonour Him, and mar the sense of his love and the further manifestation thereof. For this style, *Dearly beloved*, may be taken as an argument to the duty pressed, and understood mainly of the love of God to his people: because the Apostle Paul (Rom: 9:25), citing the place which this Apostle cited immediately before, finds in it this style in reference to God: and therefore this Apostle may be conceived to make use of it here in the same sense, as a motive to the study of mortification. *Dearly beloved, abstain*, &c. [5.] Those who press people to the mortifying of their beloved lusts had need not only to entertain much love to them in their hearts, that so they may deal earnestly with them, but likewise by some prudent expressions of their love to them insinuate themselves upon their affections, that so the stirring of their passions (which are ready to rise when unmortified corruptions are touched, both in good, 2 Chron. 16:10, and bad, Matt. 14:4,5) may be prevented. Therefore the Apostle breathes forth his affection to this people, which may be safely taken to be also comprehended in this compellation,[1] as following after Christ and moving the Apostle to much earnestness, *Dearly beloved, I beseech you, abstain*, &c. [6.] As it may be the lot of those who in regard of their right to the covenant of grace and the benefits thereof are no more strangers and foreigners, but fellow-citizens of the saints and of the household of God, to be separated from their native country, as these Christian *Hebrews* were, to whom this is spoken: So, whatever their condition in the world be, they ought to esteem and confess themselves (as the best of God's saints have done, Heb. 11:13) *strangers and pilgrims*, who are absent from their own country, 2 Cor. 5:6, and may expect hard usage in their way, Gen. 31:15, who ought to lay aside everything that may hinder them in their journey, Heb. 12:1, and have their hearts still homeward, Heb. 11:16. They should take little pleasure in the delights that offer themselves in the course of their pilgrimage, Gen. 23:4, and esteem it a great honour to get leave to do any piece of service to God, while they are upon their journey, 1 Chron. 29:15. They should count much of any merciful providence they meet with, Ruth 2:10, and make their case an argument to God for his pity and kindness, Psa. 119:19, and a motive to themselves to abstain from every thing that may hinder them in the journey homeward: for this is brought in by the Apostle as an argument to all the duties of holiness, and especially to the study of mortification, that they

[1] See page 79.

were *strangers and pilgrims*. [7.] The inward motions of unmortified corruptions which are in the godly do not only fight against the welfare of their bodies, Prov. 14:30, against that light and knowledge of God which is in their understandings, Rom. 7:23, and against the graces and motions of God's Spirit which are in their hearts, Gal. 5:17, but likewise against the everlasting well-being of their souls, so that these corruptions cannot be given way to, except we would (so far as in us lies) run the hazard of the loss of our souls: for this is here a third motive to the mortifying of these lusts, *that they war against the soul*. [8.] The Lord allows Christians to stir up their hearts to the study of the mortification of their corruptions, by the consideration of the hazard that cannot but follow upon their prevailing, which is no less than the wounding of their souls by every advantage their corruptions do get; and the eternal loss and ruin of their souls by the continual prevailing of them, as is imported also in this motive to the mortification of those fleshly lusts: *They war against the soul*.

12. **Having your conversation honest among the Gentiles: that, whereas they speak against you as evil doers, they may by your good works, which they shall behold, glorify God in the day of visitation.**

In this verse the Apostle presses the effect of his former exhortation and withal prescribes a special means of showing forth the praises of God, to wit, that Christians should labour to express holiness in their outward conversation: and this he bears in by two arguments. The first is, that their lot was to converse among the enemies of the Gospel and such as would be glad to find occasion from their miscarriage to slander them as evil doers. The second is, that their holy walking among such might prove a blessed means not only to stop the mouths of their slanderous enemies, but likewise to bring about their conversion and consequently bring much glory to God when it should please him to visit them with his saving grace.

Hence learn, [1.] In so far as the power of sin is weakened in the heart, there will be a beauty and loveliness upon the outward conversation; which if it be defiled with out-breakings, clearly evidences the power and prevalency of unmortified lusts in the heart: for as a necessary consequent or effect of the former exhortation to abstain from fleshly lusts, the Apostle brings in this, *having your conversation[1] honest*. [2.] It is not so much by a fair profession or good expressions that Christians show forth the praises of God, as by an *honest conversation[1]*, made beautiful and lovely (as the word here translated *honest* signifies) to onlookers by the right ordering of all the parts of it in duties to God and men, Psa. 50:23, by the manifesting of wisdom and meekness therein jointly, Jas. 3:13, and especially by the faithful discharge of the duties of their particular callings and relations, 1 Thess. 4:11,12; Tit. 2:9,10. For the way of the Apostle's bringing in this exhortation gives ground to take this as a means of attaining to what he had pressed before, to wit, their showing forth of the praises of God, mentioned (v 9), *having your conversation honest*, &c. [3.] The more wicked the society be, with whom it is the believers' lot to converse, the more should they be stirred up to the study of an honest conversation, for the conviction or gaining of such: for by this that these Christian *Hebrews* were among heathens (whom many professors of Christianity resemble, in living like heathens without respect to the Law of God, Rom. 2:14, pursuing strongly their idols, as heathens do, 1 Cor. 12:2, and being unacquainted with the privileges and duties of the covenant of grace, as heathens are, Eph. 2:11, and ready to persecute all that run not their course, 1 Pet. 4:3; all which – the Scriptures cited – make characters of[2] heathens) the Apostle persuades them to study holiness of life: *having your conversation honest among the Gentiles*. [4.] Those of whom the world is unworthy are often represented to the world as unworthy to live in it by those whose dishonest ways are reproved by their honest conversation: for it is here supposed to be the lot of the chosen generation, the royal priesthood, &c., to be *spoken against as evil doers*. [5.] It is one of the characters of them that are without God in the world to be enemies to and slanderers of those who will not run with them to the same excess of riot: for it is here a description of the heathens that they speak against those who are of an honest conversation, *as evil doers*. [6]. The best way for Christians to stop the mouths of their slanderers is by an honest conversation: without which, any other means they can use will readily prove ineffectual for maintaining their reputation: for here the Apostle prescribes to Christians the study of a holy walking, as a means to put their very enemies upon an exercise

[1] 'conversation': see page 40.
[2] 'make characters of': that is, characterize (heathens).

inconsistent with slandering of the godly: *having your conversation honest among the Gentiles: that, whereas they speak against you as evil doers, they may by your good works which they shall behold, glorify God.* [7.] Although the Word, accompanied with the powerful blessing of God, be the principal means of sinners' conversion, Rom. 10:15,17, yet the Lord may make use of the very carriage and visible acting of His people (such as their equity in their dealings, even with their enemies; their patient bearing of injuries from them and continuing to express love and respect to them notwithstanding thereof) to allure wicked men to fall in love with His way and to give Him glory that ever sent them such a means and blessed it to them, for their reclaiming from the way of perdition: for here, an *honest conversation* is pressed as a means of gaining the enemies of Christ and His people *to glorify God in the day of visitation.* [8.] Neither the best use of natural power of freewill that unrenewed man may attain unto, nor all the pains that the godly can take upon them, will be sufficient to bring about that glorious work of their conversion whereby the Lord is so much glorified till He be pleased to visit them with His power, Psa. 110:3, and with His love, to make the change, Ezek. 16:8, for here, as a necessary prerequisite for the gaining of sinners to glorify God, the Apostle supposes that there must be a *day of visitation* whereby must be understood a visitation in special mercy, in regard it gains sinners to *glorify God.* [9.] It is not any glory to ourselves from men that should be our motive to an honest walking among them; but that we may thereby bring some glory to God from them: which being honestly aimed at by us shall bring sufficient glory to us along with it, 1 Sam. 2:30, for this is here made the principal motive to an honest walking, that thereby others might be moved to *glorify God in the day of visitation.* [10.] The children of the Lord should not lose their hopes nor quit their endeavours of gaining the greatest enemies to God or themselves, among whom they live, considering how soon and easily the Lord can make a change upon them: for the Apostle would have them looking upon those that were heathens, and speaking against them as evil doers, as such whom God might visit in mercy, and in whose conversion they might be made instrumental: *having your conversation honest amongst the Gentiles: that, whereas they speak against you as evil doers, they may by your good works, which they shall behold, glorify God in the day of visitation.*

13. **Submit yourselves to every ordinance of man for the Lord's sake: whether it be to the king, as supreme;**
14. **Or unto Governors, as unto them that are sent by him for the punishment of evil doers and for the praise of them that do well.**

In this second part of the chapter the Apostle exhorts to those particular duties whereby Christians do show forth the praises of God and commend religion in their several relations. And his first exhortation in order to these ends is, that they should carry themselves with respect and submission to any form of lawful government established in the several countries where they were scattered, whether the same were exercised by the supreme magistrate or by the inferior: which several forms of civil government he calls a human ordinance; mainly because the Lord has not determined in His Word what particular kind of government every place in the world should have, whether monarchy or some other form; but has left the determination thereof to human prudence walking by the general rules of His Word. And this exhortation the Apostle infers upon the former, wherewith the first part of the chapter is closed, as a special means of gaining wicked men to glorify God; and presses the same by two reasons. The first is taken from the respect which Christians owe to the command of God, who is the Author of magistracy. The second is taken from the good ends for which magistracy is ordained, to wit, 1, for the punishing and suppressing of wickedness and 2, for the promoting and encouraging of piety and virtue.

Hence learn, [1.] The Lord is graciously pleased to call for respect at the hands of His people, toward those who carry no respect to Him, that thereby he may either gain such to his obedience or heap coals of fire upon their heads: for He is here calling for submission and obedience unto heathen magistrates at the hands of His people, *Submit yourselves to every ordinance of man*. [2.] Although civil magistracy be a divine ordinance in regard it is of God's appointment, Prov. 8:15, yet it is here called *a human ordinance* in regard it is mainly exercised about human affairs, and for the good of human society as such, in regard the particular forms thereof are left to be determined by men, as was touched upon in the Exposition, and in some cases may be altered by them. In all which respects it differs from that spiritual government which Christ has established in His house, this being wholly about spiritual affairs, 2 Cor. 10:8, the particular form thereof determined by Jesus Christ in His Word, and never to be altered in any place of the world, Eph. 4:11,12,13; for civil government for the fore-mentioned respects, as also to difference it from the ecclesiastic, is here called an *ordinance of man.* [3.] Not only private Christians, but also the public ministers of Christ and all ranks of professors of His Name are bound to give submission and obedience in things lawful, to lawful magistrates, though they prove enemies to religion, under whose dominion God's providence has cast their lot: which submission consists in a reverent esteem of the persons of magistrates because of their office, Eccles. 10:20, in the maintaining of their authority and respect before others, especially their subjects, Exod. 22:28, in giving of our worldly substance for that end, Rom. 13:7, in our earnestness with God in prayer for his blessing upon their government, 1 Tim. 2:1,2, and in suffering patiently, and with due respect to their persons and office, what they do unjustly inflict for disobedience to their unlawful commands, Acts 23:5: for this exhortation is given both to the officers and members of the church, scattered through these nations who had only heathen kings and governors, *Submit yourselves to every ordinance of man.* [4.] This dutiful and submissive carriage of Christians towards wicked magistrates is a special means of commending religion to the profane, and gaining of them to glorify God, who use most unjustly to represent Christ's subjects as enemies to civil magistrates, Acts 24:5; for this exhortation may be conceived to be pressed as a special means of attaining to that honest conversation among the Gentiles, who spoke against Christians as evil doers, especially in the matter of their loyalty, whereunto the Apostle did exhort in the former verse; *Submit yourselves to every ordinance of man.* [5.] It is agreeable to the mind of God that there be a plurality of magistrates set over every country or incorporation of people, it being impossible for any one, or a few, by reason of the imperfection of their wit and strength, to administer justice aright to many, Exod. 18:18,21, which ought to be brought near to poor people, to prevent their toil and expenses so far as may be, 1 Sam. 7:16. And likewise that there be some order among these magistrates; some of them in greater eminency and power than others: for so the Apostle supposes here, while he mentions many magistrates and some of them more eminent than others; *whether it be to the king as supreme or unto governors.* [6.] Although the supreme magistrate may be a prime instrument in appointing and protecting inferior magistrates in the exercise of their office, 2 Chron. 19:5, in which respect the inferior may be said to be sent by him, to wit, the supreme; yet are the Lord's people no less straitly bound to obey and submit to the inferior, acting in his station, than to the supreme acting in his, the one kind being essentially judges, and in God's place, to the people as well as the other, 2 Chron. 19:6, Prov. 8:15, for the Apostle presses equally and upon the same grounds submission to both, *whether it be to the king as supreme, or unto governors, as unto them that are sent by him.* [7.] This submission and obedience which Christians owe to lawful magistrates ought to flow from their respect to God's command enjoining the same; and from love to Him who has established that order among men, and would have His people commending religion to heathen or profane magistrates by their respect to His ordinance in the persons of such; so that whosoever have not a hearty respect to God and His commands, and love to Him and His honour, lack the principle of true loyalty to magistrates, whose great care therefore should be to advance true piety and respect to God and His commands in the hearts of their subjects, as they love to find true loyalty in them to themselves: for this is here made the principle or motive of Christians' subjection to magistracy, *Submit,* &c, *for the Lord's sake.* [8.] Magistrates should be so far from giving toleration, let be encouragement, to any wicked doers under their power, whether godless and profane livers, Psa. 101:4,5,7,8, or heretics and false teachers, though never so seemingly pious, who are no less evil doers than the other, Phil. 3:2, that they should esteem it the great end of their advancement to their office, and a principal part of their duty, to restrain and punish all such: for, this is here made one end of magistracy, comprehending one chief part of the duty of magistrates: *for the punishment of evil doers.* [9.] It is the duty of magistrates to put most honour upon, and give most encouragement and respect to, those that live most subject to the will of Christ, those being the best friends of magistrates; and the disgracing or wronging of them, being in a special way resented by Christ, the Supreme Magistrate: for this is another end of their office and branch of their duty, that they are *for the praise of them that do well.*

15. For so is the will of God, that with well doing, ye may put to silence the ignorance of foolish men:

The Apostle repeats in substance his first argument, whereby he pressed upon professors of Christianity subjection to lawful magistrates, to wit, that this was now plainly revealed to be the will of Him who is above all magistrates. And withal he adds a third, that Christians' respective[1] carriage toward magistrates should prove an effectual means of confuting the calumnies of unreasonable men; who, being enraged against the Lord's people, did represent them as enemies to civil government, that so they might raise persecution against them.

Hence learn, [1.] It is not so much the fear of hazard for neglect of duty, or the apprehension of advantage by the performance of it, as the consideration of the will of the Lord, which should be the prime and most prevalent motive of Christians to their duty; considering that His will (though never so far above our natural reason and contrary to our natural inclination) is the rule of righteousness, Rom. 12:2, in our obedience whereof our welfare consists, Mark 3:35; for the Apostle having suggested this before, v 13, as a motive to this same duty, holds it forth here again more expressly; for, *so is the will of God*. [2.] Disaffection to civil government and magistracy is an old slander which has been ordinarily given in against the godly by wicked men, who hate to the death those who, by their holy walking, do reprove and shame their profanity; and therefore labour to engage those in power against them, as their enemies, Prov. 29:10. For, as it was ordinarily charged upon the servants and people of God of old, Jer. 37:13, Ezra 4:12,13, so the Apostle, prescribing a way to these Christian *Hebrews* how to silence such slanders, imports that it was in his time the ordinary trial of the godly to whom he writes, *That with well doing ye may put to silence*, &c. [3.] Although it be fitting sometimes for the Lord's people to use verbal apologies for their own clearing, and other lawful means of defence against false aspersions, Acts 24:10 &c., 25:8, yet a holy and Christian carriage is the most powerful means (though it be more seldom made use of than any) to confute the calumnies of wicked men; and to bind up their mouths (were they never so enraged) from speaking against the godly: for the Apostle having recommended this means for this

---

[1] 'respective': respectful.

end before (v 12) prescribes it here again, importing the fitness of it for the end for which he presses it, and likewise some un-willingness in people to make use of it; *that with well doing ye may put to silence* (in which word, there is a metaphor taken from the putting of a muzzle upon the mouth of some wild beast, or mad dog, such as the malicious slanderers of God's people are) *the ig-norance of foolish men*. [4.] The ground of wicked men's malice which vents itself against the godly in slanders and in mis-representations of them, especially to men in power, is that they are grossly ignorant, to wit, of the terror of that God who resents the least wrong done to His servants as done to Himself, Zech. 2:8, and of the due subordination of men in authority to Him, by reason whereof His people may disobey their sinful commands without any wrong to their office, or disrespect to their persons, Acts 4:19, for here the Apostle leads the Lord's people to take the malicious calumnies of wicked men for the language of their ignorance, that so they might rather pity and pray for them, than study to requite them, as their Lord did upon the same consideration, Luke 23:34, while he thus directs: *with well doing put to silence the ignorance of foolish men*. [5.] They who employ their wit to make the Lord's people odious, and bring them under hazard from those that are in power over them, although they may have as much use of it as may get them the ear and favour of them that are in power, and may prevail by their calumnies to bring trouble upon the godly; yet are they really and in God's esteem, mad and demented, as the word here signifies, seeing by their so doing they run the hazard of the wrath of Him who is a jealous and a terrible God against His people's enemies, Isa. 49:14,17. For the Apostle's scope and strain here imports that malicious slanders of the godly, given in to those in authority, had such acceptance and weight with them as to occasion the rise of persecution from them against the godly: and yet those who gave in these slanders are here represented by the Spirit of God *as ignorant and foolish men*.

16. As free, and not using your liberty for a cloak of maliciousness, but as the servants of God.

In answer to an objection which has been in the hearts of some professors against that subjection which the Apostle had pressed upon them to civil magistrates, to wit, that their Christian liberty did exempt them from it, especially when those magistrates were wicked and pagans, he brings in a fourth argument to press the same. The sum whereof is that however believers be brought by Jesus Christ to a state of true and spiritual freedom, yet the Lord does not allow them to make their Christian liberty a pretence or veil to cover any wickedness; and consequently, not that wickedness of despising and rejecting His ordinance of magistracy; but on the contrary, enjoins them all to use their liberty, purchased by Christ, wholly as an engagement and motive to His service.

Hence learn, [1.] Believers in Jesus Christ are by Him advanced to a state of true liberty and freedom which does not consist in a liberty to sin against God, which is Satan's slavery, 2 Tim. 2:26, nor in freedom from the sweet yoke of His service, whether it be in attending His ordinances to which He has tied us till His second coming, Matt. 28:19,20, 1 Cor. 11:26, or the duties we owe to others of His people, Gal. 5:13. But it does consist in our freedom from the Law as a covenant of works, by which we are not to seek justification or salvation, Gal. 3:18, Rom. 3:21,22. We are free from the guilt of sin, Tit. 2:14, from the dominion thereof, Rom. 6:22, and the curse due thereunto, Rom. 8:1,2, and from the yoke of mosaical ceremonies, Gal. 5:1; and especially in this are we free, that we are honoured and enabled to do God acceptable service, Psa. 119:45. In all which respects believers are presupposed truly free according to the Apostle's concession here: *As free.* [2.] Even Christ's redeemed ones have as much corruption remaining unmortified in their hearts after regeneration as makes them in hazard, not only to commit wickedness and excuse the same; but to make the privileges they have through Christ and particularly their Christian liberty, a cloak to hide it, as if sin were no sin in them, or as if Christ had purchased to them liberty to sin: for so much is imported in the Apostle's dissuading Christians here not only from refusing subjection to magistrates, but from defending the same and using their liberty as a cloak of that wickedness: *As free, and not using your liberty for a cloak of maliciousness.* [3.] When Christians shake off any duty pressed in the moral Law, under a pretence that their Christian liberty gives them warrant so to do, they are then come to such a height of wickedness as has much of malice in it; especially against any that would oppose them in that course and such as will spread to more and more wickedness: for the Apostle here sets forth Christians defending their exemption from obedience to magistrates with the pretext of their

Christian liberty by such a word as comprehends in the significa-tion of it, all wickedness; and points especially at that particular sin of malice or envy: *Not using your liberty for a cloak of maliciousness.* [4.] These iniquities which are unjustly charged upon all the godly by wicked men may be justly charged by the godly themselves upon their own hearts, as inclinable to those iniquities which do break forth in some: for the Apostle, having in the former verse called them ignorant and foolish men, who did slander all professors of Christianity, as enemies to magistracy, here warns all to beware to make their Christian liberty a cloak of it, while he says, *Not using your liberty as a cloak of maliciousness.* [5.] The right use which believers ought to make of that liberty which Christ has purchased for them is to be thereby the more strictly engaged to His service; our serving of Him being a great part of true Christian liberty, Psa. 119:45, and one great end of God's giving a Redeemer for us, Luke 1:74, for here the Apostle discovers wherein the right use of Christian liberty consists, to wit, that Christians who are truly free, should carry themselves *as the servants of God.*

17. Honour all men. Love the brotherhood. Fear God. Honour the King.

The fifth argument, whereby the Apostle presses upon all Christians due subjection to civil magistrates, is taken from the necessary connexion that is between this and other un-questionable duties, of which the Apostle gives three instances, every one whereof does in some sort infer the equity of this duty which was questioned by some of them. The first is, that some respect is due to all men, and therefore much more to magistrates. The second is, that Christian society should be very dear to all the Lord's people; and consequently they ought to respect magistrates under whose power and protection they do enjoy the same. The third is, that they should stand in awe to offend God and therefore should give that honour to magistrates which he had so straitly enjoined by the Apostle before, and here presses again in the close of this verse.

Hence learn, [1.] While the ministers of Christ are earnestly pressing some one special duty upon the Lord's people they ought also jointly to press such other duties as are to be joined therewith in their practice, and may be helpful toward the per-formance of that, lest by insisting much in the pressing of one duty, without mentioning of others, which ought to be carried along therewith, the Lord's people may receive such impression of the necessity of that one, as may make them forgetful of others, not only equally necessary with that one, but also subservient toward the performance of it: for while the Apostle is earnestly pressing subjection to magistrates by many reasons he intermixes a bundle of other duties which are necessary to be joined in practice with that; and being made conscience of, will fit them for the performance of it: *Honour all men. Love the brotherhood. Fear God.* And so, *Honour the King.* [2.] It is a prevailing way of dealing with the Lord's people (which Christ's ministers should study) to bear in upon them duties more questionable, against which they may have some prejudice, as necessary concomitants or effects of other duties which they do less question and will more easily subject themselves to, that from the acknowledged equity of the one they may be brought to yield to the other, which has necessary connexion therewith: even as it is a most convincing way of reasoning upon any subject, to make use of premises easily assented to, for gaining assent to some questionable conclusion, which is the Apostle's way here: for while he presses the duty of subjection to civil magistrates from which some professors of Christianity did apprehend themselves exempted by their Christian liberty, he presses upon them such other unquestionable duties as did infer that subjection by the force of good consequence; if they found themselves bound to honour all men, to love the brotherhood, to fear God, then they could not but find themselves bound also to *honour the King.* [3.] Although there be some so grossly and avowedly wicked that they ought to be condemned and esteemed vile by the Lord's people in comparison of others, Psa. 15:4, yet there is no man to whom the children of the Lord do not owe some respect; considering that all men do partake of some excellency from God, Acts 17:25 &c., and carry some resemblance of His image, Jas. 3:9, and that the best may know more to be loathed in themselves than they can do in the worst, Phil. 2:3, and that the worst, for ought we know, may be within the compass of God's election, 1 Cor. 7:16; for which causes we ought to give them some signs of our respect, that so we may keep ourselves in the better capacity of doing good to their souls: *Honour all men.* [4.] It is not only the duty of every Christian to give a special measure of love and respect to the persons of other Christians, beyond what they give to any other men, Psa.

16:3, and to evidence the same by their sympathy with and supply of one another under their necessities, Gal. 6:10, but also to love the society one of another, both in the exercise of public ordinances to which Christ has promised His special presence, Matt. 18:20, and in the more private duties of mutual edification, which are very pleasant to the Lord, Mal. 3:16, and profitable to themselves, Heb. 3:12,13; for the Apostle having exhorted to honour all men, subjoins this as a further degree of respect, not only to the saints themselves, but as the word signifies, to their society: *love the brotherhood.* [5.] It should be the great care of the children of God to carry along in the discharge of every duty, the fear of God in their hearts: which is a frame of spirit that He works in all that are in covenant with Him, Jer. 32:40, whereby they hate every known sin, Prov. 8:13, and in obedience to Him aim at every commanded duty, especially those of their particular relations, 2 Chron. 19:7, and is entertained by the believing consideration of the terror of the Lord, Psa. 119:119,120, His excellency, John 13:31, His goodness, Hos. 3:5, and His proneness to pardon sin, Psa. 130:4. All which is comprehended under this duty, which seasons all the rest here pressed: *Fear God.* [6.] There is a special measure of honour and respect due by the Lord's people to those whom God has set in lawful authority over them, beyond what is due to any others on earth, by reason of their place, wherein they resemble the majesty of God to His people, Psa. 82:6; for the Apostle having exhorted in the beginning of this verse to honour all men, as if that honour which is due to all were not sufficient for magistrates, he closes the verse with this, *Honour the King.* [7.] The Lord's people are so to honour magistrates as that they forget not the fear of the Lord and the duties comprehended under it, in the first place: without which no duty can be faithfully discharged to any man, Luke 18:2, for this is not only the order of the words here, but of the purpose itself: *Fear God, Honour the King.* [8.] These duties against which the hearts of the godly have some prejudice, and the neglect whereof proves most offensive to the profane, had need to be frequently and earnestly pressed upon the Lord's people; for this duty was unpleasant to many professors, and the profane, apprehending it to be so to all, were incensed against Christians: therefore the Apostle having pressed it before, v 14, renews his exhortation to it here again, *Honour the King.*

18. Servants, be subject to your masters with all fear; not only to the good and gentle, but also to the froward.

The second exhortation to the study of holiness for showing forth the praises of God is directed to Christian servants, in which rank the greatest number of believers then were, who seem to have been in hazard under pretence of their Christian liberty, not only to shake off subjection to magistrates (as was shown before) but to their particular masters (the most part whereof were also at that time heathens) to whom the Apostle presses Christian servants to give subjection and obedience, with all fear, to wit, of offending God or their masters; and that not only to the better and more equitable sort of them, but even to the more austere and inhuman.

Hence learn, [1.] As the children of the Lord, in the meanest and hardest condition wherein His providence casts them, may be instrumental in bringing some glory to Him; so He is especially glorified by them in their conscionable discharge of the particular duties of that relation wherein they are fixed: for the Apostle (having shown the end of all believers' privileges to be that they might show forth the praises of God, v 9) holds forth this to persecuted Christian servants as one principal way of showing forth His praises: *Servants, be subject to your masters.* [2.] One wrong principle being admitted in the minds of Christians concerning the matters of God may be the occasion and rise of manifold disorders in their practice; for it is clear from the former purpose that the mistake of Christians concerning the nature of their Christian liberty did make them apprehend themselves exempted from subjection to magistracy; and by this exhortation immediately subjoined, compared with 1 Cor. 7:20,21,22, it appears that the same mistake has prevailed to make servants apprehend exemption from subjection to their heathen masters, which makes the Apostle find it necessary to press them to this duty: *Servants, be subject to your masters.* [3.] Although there be some of the great ones of the earth given by the Father to Christ the Mediator, who will therefore receive Him and subject themselves to Him, Psa. 72:10, yet the most part of His subjects and servants are of the poorest and meanest in the world, whom He chooses, to commend the freedom of His grace and the condescendency of His love, which often lights upon the servant and passes by the master: for it would seem there have not been many magistrates or masters in those nations where these believing *Hebrews* to whom the Apostle writes were scattered, who have been fit to be spoken to, which makes the Apostle omit them and speak to their subjects in the former words, and to their servants here: *Servants, be subject to your masters.* [4.] Christian liberty does not exempt Christian servants from subjection to their masters though they were heathens, but does consist with obeying all their lawful commands heartily, and as service to God, Col. 3:22,23, in giving due respect to their persons as being placed above them, as the word here signifies: for this is here pressed upon the chosen generation, and such as were truly free by Jesus Christ: *Servants, be subject to your masters.* [5.] Not only the immediate acts of God's worship and service should be gone about with much fear and reverence to Him in the heart, Psa.2:11, but even these outward duties which we owe to men should be seasoned therewith, that so Christians, even while they are employed in most common duties, may be in the fear of the Lord all the day long, Prov. 23:17, for this is the qualification of that subjection which Christian servants owe to their masters: *Be subject with all fear.* [6.] It may be the lot of the Lord's dearest people, not only to be in the rank of servants, which is a part of their likeness to their Lord for His outward state in the flesh, Phil. 2:7, but likewise to be by divine providence put to serve heathens, and the worst of heathens, that so the Lord may make them instrumental to do good to some of these, 2 Kings 5:2,3, or convince them that God is with their servants, Gen. 31:44, for here the Apostle supposes some of the chosen generation and the peculiar people to be servants to heathens, and to froward and perverse heathens. [7.] Although all that are without the saving knowledge of God in Christ be in a like damnable and cursed estate, Eph. 2:3, yet there may be amongst them much difference of disposition, some of them being of a more bountiful and liberal temper, as the word here rendered *good* may signify, Matt. 20:15, and less rigid in exacting all that in strict justice they might, as the word translated *gentle* imports; others of them more perverse and harder to have dealing with, according to the signification of this word *froward*; which difference mainly flows from the Lord's various dispensation of the gifts of nature, and His common influences for improving the same, according to His sovereign pleasure: for here among wicked and heathen masters there are some good and equitable or moderate, to wit, in comparison of some others of them, and there are others who are more perverse or froward. [8.] The wickedness of those to whom in God's providence Christians are tied by any relation does not exempt them from making conscience of the duties of that relation toward those to whom they are tied, the ground of our duty not being the qualification of the person to whom we owe it, but the command of God obliging us to it: *Servants, be subject to your masters with all fear, not only to the good and gentle, but also to the froward.*

19. **For this is thankworthy, if a man for conscience toward God endure grief, suffering wrongfully.**
20. **For what glory is it, if, when ye be buffeted for your faults, ye shall take it patiently? but if, when ye do well, and suffer for it, ye take it patiently, this is acceptable with God.**

From this point to the end of the chapter the Apostle brings many arguments to press upon Christian servants – dutifulness to their pagan masters and patient suffering of injuries from them in following their duty to Christ. The first is, that if, out of respect to Christ's command and glory, they did hold on in their duty, notwithstanding of hardest sufferings, He should graciously reward their so doing as acceptable service to Him (v 19). The second is, that it would be a great disgrace for Christians to deserve, by their miscarriage, hard usage from heathens; but if they were faithful in their duty and patient under sufferings for it, they might be sure of God's approbation (v 20).

Hence learn, [1.] Although neither our doing nor our suffering can merit any thing at God's hand, it being wholly His grace (as the first expression, v 19, may be rendered from the original) that enables us for both, Phil. 1:29, yet when His grace has in some measure enabled us for both, He is pleased to esteem thereof as if it were worthy of thanks from Him; and graciously to reward it with a further increase of grace and ability to do and suffer, Matt. 25:29, with begun peace and consolation in the heart under sufferings for duty to Him, 2 Cor. 1:5, as earnest of the full reward which His grace is to bestow at last, Rev. 3:4,5, which ought to be a sufficient encouragement to the godly in their duty against all their sufferings from men, for which end it is held forth here: for *This is thankworthy* or (as the original may be rendered) *this is grace.* [2.] God not so much respects the sufferings of professors, even for truth and duty (seeing hypocrites may attain thereunto, 1 Cor. 13:3) as He looks to the principle and manner of their sufferings, whether they suffer because of their former engagements by profession or otherwise, and because they desire to carry a name and esteem of religious persons to the end with them: or whether they suffer out of conscience toward God, that is, in obedience to Him, who commands them to choose affliction rather than sin, and from a desire to please and honour Him, by bearing testimony to His truth by suffering: for this suffering and this only is reckoned thankworthy, *if a man for conscience toward God endure grief, suffering wrongfully.* [3.] Although the Lord sometimes keeps heaviness and grief off the spirits of his people under such sufferings as are very heavy and grievous in themselves, Acts 16:25, yet at other times He sees it fitting not only to exercise them with hard and unjust sufferings from men, but likewise with many sad weights upon their spirits under these sufferings, arising partly from the sight of God's dishonour by their enemies, Psa. 4:2,3, and partly from the fear of their own miscarriage under their trials, John 14:1, together with their mis-belief of the promise of their through-bearing and out-gate, Psa. 116:11, both which exercises together are sometimes necessary for the godly, that they may be completely denied to their own strength and courage, and may be taught to depend on God for their through-bearing, 2 Cor. 1:8,9. And therefore both exercises ought to be patiently submitted to by them, in so far as they are for their trial and advantage, even as they would expect a reward from God: for *this is thank-worthy, if a man for conscience toward God, endure grief, suffering wrongfully.* [4.] Although it be the mark of hypocrites to do all duties of religion for respect to their own credit and glory before men, Matt. 23:5, yet the Lord allows His own people to have so much respect to their own credit, especially before the profane, as may provoke them to a tender and holy walking, and to eschew everything that may disgrace them, and their holy profession: for this is here made an argument to duty and patient sufferings of wrongs, that if they neglected duty, and so were put to suffer for their miscarriage, that would be no glory, but rather a disgrace to them and their profession; *for what glory is it if, when ye be buffeted for your faults, ye shall take it patiently?* [5.] As it has pleased the Lord for the good of human society to leave in the minds even of heathens some knowledge of what is contrary to His will, Rom. 2:14,15, and some inclination to punish the same, Acts 28:4, so it is a very great disgrace to Christian religion when heathens, or such as are like heathens, void of the saving knowledge of God in Christ, may find Christians in those sins which their light leads them to punish, especially when Christians make their liberty by Christ a pretence and cloak to cover those sins: for it is here imported by the Apostle, that heathen masters did not only know somewhat of their servants' duty, but also would justly punish them for neglect of it; and that if Christian servants did by their miscarriage deserve sufferings from such masters (as they were in hazard to do by abusing their Christian liberty) this would prove a great disgrace to them, and to the profession of Christianity: *for what glory is it, if, when ye be buffeted for your faults, ye shall take it patiently?* [6.] Although patience under deserved strokes from men be in itself commendable, and will prove persons to be accepted with God, when they accept the punishment of their iniquity and fly to Christ for mercy, Luke 23:41, yet the patience of a professor of religion under those strokes which his own miscarriage has justly procured from wicked men will not remove his disgrace nor the disgrace of his profession, nor be any glory to him in comparison of what patience under sufferings for well doing would be: for this question, *What glory is it, if, when ye be buffeted for your faults, ye take it patiently?* imports that their sufferings for their faults, though never so patiently, would be no glory to them, to wit, in comparison of what it would be to suffer patiently for well doing. [7.] As none may expect that well doing will exempt them from trouble and suffering, but rather that it will occasion and increase the same, so the Lord's favour toward sufferers and His acceptation of them and of their sufferings as service to Him, should be thought a sufficient encouragement to patience under that lot, and should be often considered as a recompence of all the shame and pain of the cross: for with this encouragement, which the Apostle held forth for the substance of it in the beginning of the former verse, he closes this verse: *If when ye do well and suffer for it, ye take it patiently, this is acceptable with God.*

21. **For even hereunto were ye called: because Christ also suffered for us, leaving us an example, that ye should follow his steps:**

Here are some further arguments to press upon Christians'

patient suffering for the truth of Christ and duty to Him. The third in number is, that they were by the Gospel called to follow Christ with a cross upon their back. The fourth is, that Christ has in their room borne all the wrath that is due to them for their sins. And the fifth is, that He has cast a sweet copy and pattern of a right way of suffering for all His own to imitate: and therefore they should hold on in their duty notwithstanding of sufferings.

Hence learn, [1.] As Christ's followers are called by the Gospel to enjoy a sweet fellowship with Him here, 1 Cor. 1:9, and to the obtaining of glory with Him hereafter, 2 Thess. 2:14, so are they also called to endure a suffering lot in the world for following their duty to Him: for to those who were suffering wrongfully for well doing the Apostle thus speaks, *Even hereunto were ye called.* [2.] Christ does not hide this hard lot of suffering from His followers till they meet with it; but when first He invites them to engage with Him, He gives them forewarning of the worst that may befall them in His service, that so they may not be offended at it when it comes, John 16:1, that they may give proof of their esteem of Him by consenting to take up a cross for Him, Matt. 10:37,38, and by their former consent to follow Him upon these terms may be the more strongly engaged to adventure upon suffering for Him, John 11:16, 2 Pet. 1:14; for the Apostle brings this as an argument to patient and constant suffering, *that even hereunto were they called.* [3.] Jesus Christ has suffered in the room and place of the elect, so that none who are one with Him have any part of vindictive wrath to undergo, whatever fatherly displeasure they may be exercised with to humble them in the sense of sin and wrath due to them, that so they may flee to Him, Psa. 89:30, because *Christ also hath suffered for us.* [4.] Christ's suffering thus for believers strongly obliges and encourages them to suffer for Him, when they must either suffer or sin against Him, seeing His suffering for them has freed them from wrath, Gal. 3:13, and made everlasting blessedness sure for them, Rom. 8:34, &c, for this is the Apostle's fourth argument to suffer for well doing, because *Christ also hath suffered for us.* [5.] Although it be high presumption in any to aim at imitation of Christ in these acts of His which He did for the satisfying the Father's justice for sinners, for proving of His Deity, and the like, it being altogether impossible to imitate Him in these, John 15:24, yet Christians are bound to imitate Christ in these actions of His, which being in themselves moral, are purposely propounded in Scripture for Christians to imitate, such as meekness, Matt. 11:29, humility, John 13:12–15, self denial, Rom. 15:2,3 and here, patient and constant suffering for well doing: *Christ hath suffered for us, leaving us an example, that we should follow His steps.* [6.] Although the best will still be far short of conformity to their pattern Christ Jesus, even in these things wherein they are to imitate Him and in which some measure of conformity may be attained, yet ought we not to give over but still aim at the next time to come nearer our copy, which is perfect in itself and able to change those who by faith look on it, 2 Cor. 3:18, for there is a metaphor in the word here, taken from an exact copy which is cast to children, whereunto they are still to study more conformity, though after many essays they be very unlike it; *leaving us an example that we should follow.* [7.] Jesus Christ does not call His followers to step any hard step in His service, but such as He has trod before them Himself, whose paths drop fatness to them, Psa. 65:11, and who by His Spirit does yet go along with them through the hardest, Canticles 4:8, for His steps, here spoken of, are both the several kinds of His sufferings from wicked men which He went through, and the particulars of the right way of suffering wherein we are to imitate Him, *who hath left us an example that we should follow his steps.*

22. Who did no sin, neither was guile found in his mouth.
23. Who when he was reviled, reviled not again, when he suffered, he threatened not, but committed himself to him that judgeth righteously.

The Apostle insists in commending Christ as the believer's copy, from three particulars: which may be taken for so many further arguments to patient suffering for well doing. The sixth in order taken from Christ's innocency is, that seeing that He who did not in the least offend either God or man was handled as a sinner, His sinful followers should therefore take well with sufferings. The seventh, taken from His patience, is, that since the Son of God, when foul crimes were laid to His charge, did not at all requite His slanderers, nor give the least ill word for the worst usage, therefore patience under injuries, without studying revenge, becomes His followers. The eighth, taken from His faith and confidence, is, that seeing Christ did resign Himself to His righteous Father to deal with Him and His persecutors as He saw fitting, they that desire to be like Him should take the same course.

Hence learn, [1.] Christ Jesus our Mediator was altogether free of the least transgression of or defect in conformity to the Law of God, though the strongest of Satan's fiery darts were shot at Him, Matt. 4:1, &c, and 16:22,23. Yet His bow abode in its strength, Gen. 49:24, there being nothing in Him to befriend a temptation, John 14:30, He being by His miraculous conception exempted from the contagion of original sin, Luke 1:35, whence actual transgressions flow, Jas. 4:1. And it behoved Him to be so, that He might be completely lovely to God, as being the truth of all those spotless lambs that were offered under the Law, as types of Him, John 1:29, and that He might be a perfect pattern of holiness to His followers, *who did no sin*. [2.] There is nothing but truth and sincerity in all the words of Christ. He never expressed more willingness to receive and do good unto sinners than He does mind really to make out to all that come to Him. Nor has He expressed more wrath against slighters of Him than they shall find to be true: for this is another branch of the commendation of Christ from His innocency, *Neither was guile found in His mouth*. [3.] However innocent the children of the Lord may be of those crimes which are unjustly charged upon them by persecutors as the cause of their sufferings, yet the sense of their sinfulness in other things ought to make them submissive to and patient under hardest sufferings from men, considering that they suffer far less than they deserve, Ezra 9:13, and that it becomes them to bear indignation because they have sinned, Micah 7:9; for the Apostle proposes the innocency of Christ, who was a patient sufferer, as an argument from the more to the less, to move sinful things not to take ill with sufferings, since Christ was a patient sufferer, *who did no sin,* &c. [4.] As all that would glorify the Lord by their sufferings and have comfort under them, must study to imitate Jesus Christ in His innocency and sincerity, so they that have attained to the greatest measure of conformity to Him in these may not therefore expect exemption from sad sufferings, but rather, the more like to Him in these they are, to look for the worse usage from wicked men: for as Christ's innocency and sincerity are here held forth as steps of His which they that would honour Him by their sufferings and have comfort under them must follow, so He is here held forth as exposed to extreme grievous sufferings, notwithstanding He had these in their perfection: *He did no sin, neither was guile found in his mouth: yet He was reviled*, and put to hardest sufferings. [5.] It was the lot of our Lord Jesus, when He was in our place in the estate of His humiliation, not only to suffer hard things in His person, but likewise in His Name; to have that rent and torn with reproaches and to have foul crimes (as the word here rendered 'to revile' signifies) unjustly laid to His charge, such as compliance with Satan, John 10:20, blasphemy, John 10:33, sedition, Luke 23:2, and the like: and that because, though He never did anything worthy of blame, He stood in the room of many sinners really guilty of all these crimes, which were only upon Him by imputation so as He bear the curse of God and the shame of the world that was due to these sins: for this lot is here supposed to have been Christ's, that He not only suffered but was *reviled*. [6.] While our Lord Jesus was under this lot, He did not give a meeting of any kind to his enemies but was so far from charging them with foul crimes unjustly, which is reviling, that when they had done so to Him, calling Him a devil, John 8:48, He did not at that time so much as repeat the like challenge which He had before justly laid to their charge, John 8:44, and though He did sometimes threaten fearful judgments upon despisers of reconciliation with God through Him, Matt. 23:13, &c, yet upon His receiving of greatest personal wrongs He did not so much as renew any of these threatenings, but on the contrary prayed for His enemies, Luke 23:34, lest in the misapprehension of any onlookers, His sufferings might have been stained with imputation of passion or revenge and His followers might have abused His practice to vent their carnal passion against their persecutors; the hazard whereof is likewise imported in the Apostle's guarding thus against it: *Who when He was reviled, reviled not again; when He suffered, He threatened not.* [7.] As all Christ's followers should resolve to meet with grievous reproaches and slanders, joined with their other sufferings, as Christ did, so ought they to follow Christ's steps in not requiting their enemies or giving ill language for the worst usage, but must learn to die to their reputation as well as to other things for His sake, *who when He was reviled, reviled not again; when He suffered, he threatened not.* [8]. While Christ our Lord was suffering in our room He did with much confidence and willingness deliver Himself up to the will of His righteous Father to endure the utmost that was due to sinners, according to His undertaking in the covenant of redemption, Psa. 40:7,8, knowing that his Father's righteousness was engaged in the same covenant, to sustain his manhood under all His sufferings, Isa. 50:7, &c, to reward Him for them by giving Him all that He died for, as His seed to serve Him and praise Him for ever, Isa. 53:10,11, and to punish all the rest according to their deserving, Psa. 110:5,6, for this is here expressly asserted as the ground of the patience and submission of the man Christ to the Father's will, *He committed himself to Him that judgeth righteously.* [9.] Although these acts of faith which do necessarily presuppose guiltiness, or have with them any mixture of mis-belief or discouragement, could not be in Christ, who was holy, harmless, undefiled and separated from sinners, Heb. 7:26, yet His soul was eminently endued with the grace of faith as it is taken for resting upon the faithfulness of God and resignation of one's person and cause to Him under unjust sufferings from men: for thus is Christ here as a believer described, *He committed Himself to Him that judgeth righteously.* [10.] The oppressed and suffering people of God, who are not able to defend themselves from wrongs at men's hands, nor to redress the same, ought to commit themselves and their cause to God their Father as to a righteous Judge, not out of malice against or desire of judgment upon their persecutors, but as a means to prevent their own despondency of spirit and despair under their hard usage: for this practice of Christ's is one of His steps which suffering Christians ought to follow: *He committed himself to Him that judgeth righteously.* [11.] The best way for Christians to attain to true Christian patience under a cross for Christ, to keep down their carnal passions while they suffer wrongfully from men, and to guard their hearts against the study of revenge toward their persecutors, is to resign themselves and their cause into the hands of God the righteous Judge: for though there was no hazard of such sinful motions in Christ, yet He took that course which He knew would be most effectual to prevent them in His followers, whom He would have to follow His steps in this, as a means to keep them down: *When He was reviled, he reviled not again,* &c, *but committed Himself to Him that judgeth righteously.*

24. Who his own self bare our sins in his own body on the tree, that we, being dead to sins, should live unto righteousness: by whose stripes ye were healed.

The Apostle repeats and enlarges his fourth argument (it being the sweetest and strongest of all the rest) to press patient suffering for well doing, to wit, that since Christ has borne the weight of our sins by enduring the wrath due to us for them in His own Person upon the cross, how patiently should His redeemed ones bear light afflictions for His sake? And withal, he adds some further arguments to press the same point taken from the sweet ends of Christ's death and the advantages believers have thereby. The ninth in number is, that the very end of Christ's death being to purchase virtue for the slaying of sin in His own, and for quickening them to the duties of holiness, it becomes all His redeemed ones to follow their duty without desire of revenge upon those who put them to suffer wrongfully. The tenth is, that seeing the redeemed by Christ have spiritual and eternal health and welfare by virtue of those wounds which He received from God and men for them, therefore they ought not to take in evil part wounds and stripes from men for following their duty to Him.

Hence learn, [1.] Christ's suffering in the room of the redeemed is a subject that they should not soon weary to think and speak of, it being to them a ground of much patience and comfort under their sufferings, to consider that God cannot now be avenging Himself upon them for their sins, who are fled to Christ, nor taking satisfaction to His justice at their hands, He having received it already from Christ. Therefore the Apostle having held forth Christ's sufferings (v 21) as an argument to constancy in duty, notwithstanding of persecution from men, he loves to come over the same argument here again: *Who his own self bare our sins,* &c. [2.] The sufferings of Christ were not only exemplary that we might have a copy how to carry ourselves right under our sufferings, but they were expiatory of our sins and satisfactory for them to the Father's justice. For after the Apostle had set forth Christ in the former words as casting us a copy of the right way of suffering, lest any should think that to be his greatest design in suffering, he adds this, *Who His own self bare our sins in His own body.* [3.] Jesus Christ our Mediator who was altogether free of any guiltiness inherent in Himself (as was cleared from v 22) had all the sins of the elect upon Him by imputation and was handled by divine justice as if He had been guilty of them all, as is imported in this expression, *He bare our sins,* which frequently in Scripture signifies to bear the punishment of sin: see Lev. 20:17,20, Ezek. 23:49. [4.] As sin is to a waking conscience one of the heaviest burdens that ever was felt, Psa. 38:4, so Jesus Christ has by His satisfaction upon the cross lifted up (as the word here signifies) that weight from off the conscience of those who feel as much of it as chases them to Him for ease, so as it shall never press any such down to hell or to despair: for the Apostle speaks of his own sins and the sins of other penitent and believing sinners as a weight that none but Christ was able to lift, and which He has lifted up and borne: *Who His own self bare our sins*. [5.] That the second Person of the blessed Trinity might be fit to bear our sins, He behoved to be incarnate and to take on a true body, not borrowed or assumed for a time, but a body of His own which, with His soul being personally united to His Godhead, He will keep for ever and ever, that His conversing in heaven with His creatures that have bodies may be the more sweet: for, *He bare our sins in his own body*. [6.] Although the principal part of Christ's sufferings for us was in His soul, Isa. 53:10, Matt. 26:38, yet He is said to bear our sins in His body, not only because that is an ordinary designation of the whole person, consisting of soul and body, but because it is most wonderful that ever the Son of God should have assumed so frothy a being as a body of flesh; because His bodily sufferings did visibly represent His love to sinners and the desert of sin; and because His soul suffered only while it was in His body before His death: therefore the Apostle says, *He bare our sins in His body*. [7.] Our Mediator behoved to be put to a painful, lingering and shameful death because He was in the room of many who deserve such kind of deaths, even by human laws, that he might the better illustrate the terror of God against sin and might take the sting out of such kind of deaths to any of His own who should endure the like for His sake. For these causes *He bare our sins in His own body on the tree*, to wit, on the cross. [8.] That which most heightens our esteem of Christ's love in giving Himself to die for us, and most strongly obliges us not to spare our persons for Him, is the consideration of the excellency of His Person and of our unworthiness for whom He suffered; both which the Apostle leads believers unto here, while he does so often mention Him and us, *Who His own self bare our sins in His own body on the tree, that we* &c. [9.] Till the merit of Christ's death be applied by faith to the hearts of sinners they are alive to sin, being active, and delighting in the commission thereof; they are dead to righteousness, being no less impotent for any spiritual act or holy performance than dead men are for the actions of the living; as is supposed in this, that Christ's death was for these ends, *that we being dead to sin might live to righteousness*. [10.] Christ's intention in dying for sinners, which He does in some measure gain in all His redeemed ones in this life and will fully attain in the other, was that the love of sin in their hearts might, by the virtue purchased with His blood, be so weakened that they might have no more pleasure in the commission of it than dead men have in the delights of the living, and that their hearts might be quickened with spiritual life for holy performances, and they might live eternally praising their Redeemer for that righteousness of His bestowed upon them, whereby they are justified, sanctified and saved: for these two are here made the great ends of Christ's death, *that we being dead* (to wit, being made so in a spiritual sense by the virtue of Christ's death) *to sin, might live unto righteousness.* [11.] As every man in his natural state, before the application of the virtue of Christ's blood to His soul, is in no less dangerous and deadly a condition than a man that is wounded and bleeding to death, Luke 10:30 (which is not to be understood as if such had any spiritual life at all, but that while they live naturally, they are altogether dead spiritually, and posting toward eternal death as a man bleeding in his wounds is to his natural death), so it is only the virtue purchased by Christ's sufferings that brings true health to sinners, which consists in the pardoning of their sins, Isa. 33:24, the curing of their spiritual distempers, Psa. 103:3, and enabling them like healthy men to go about spiritual performances, Isa. 35:6, for it is here supposed that sinners are naturally in a deadly condition and that there is no health for them but from Christ's sufferings: *by whose stripes ye were healed.* [12.] Although we ought to conceive nothing of Christ's body now glorified, that may any way in our apprehension stain the incomprehensible glory and beauty thereof, Phil. 3:21, yet so deep were the wounds that Christ received from the Father's justice that we may safely conceive the impression of them to be no less biding in His heart for the entertaining of sympathy with His redeemed ones (who are wounded in their consciences with the sense of sin and fear of wrath, or in their bodies by stripes from men for their faithfulness to Him) than if He had yet in His body the print of those wounds to move His sympathy towards them: for the word here signifies the biding print or scar of a wound after it is healed: *by whose stripes ye were healed.* [13.] None can with patience and cheerfulness suffer wrongs for Christ but they that do by faith apply the virtue of His sufferings for them to their own souls for the pardoning and subduing of sin, quickening of their hearts in holiness, and healing of their spiritual distempers; which effects of His death are so sweet to them that partake of them, that they cannot but cheerfully endure the worst that men can do against them rather than do the least thing that may be offensive to Him: *Who His own self bare our sins in His own body on the tree, that we being dead to sins, might live unto righteousness; by whose stripes ye were healed.* All which the Apostle sets down as so many motives to constancy in well doing, notwithstanding of hardest sufferings.

25. For ye were as sheep going astray, but are now returned unto the Shepherd and Bishop of your souls.

The last argument to press upon believers, the patient sufferings of wrongs for Christ, and their duty to Him, is taken from that blessed change which by the virtue of His death is made upon them; and this the Apostle sets forth in two branches. The one contains the woeful case they were in before conversion, to wit, that they were then wandering in their ignorance and sinful ways to their own destruction like straying sheep. The other holds forth the blessed state they are now brought to, to wit, that by the powerful grace of Christ put forth in their conversion, they are brought back to Him, *the good Shepherd and Overseer of their souls*; and therefore they ought to follow Him and their duty notwithstanding of any hardship they can meet with in that way.

Hence learn, [1.] Before conversion, the elect as well as others are wandering toward their own destruction, unable to bring themselves into the right way and in hazard to be preyed upon by the roaring lion: which condition is fitly set out by this similitude, which the Apostle here makes use of from Isa. 53:6, *Ye were as sheep going astray.* [2.] True conversion is that change which Christ works upon sinners, whereby they are made not only to turn their back upon their former sinful courses, but also to betake themselves to Jesus Christ, seeking to enjoy His favour and fellowship, submitting to Him as their ruler and guide, and resigning themselves to be at His disposal: for so the Apostle here describes it: *Ye were as sheep going astray, but are now returned to the Shepherd.* [3.] This blessed change which is made upon sinners in conversion is that which evidences to them that they have received the healing virtue which flows from the wounds of Christ to His redeemed ones; none else can esteem themselves healed by His stripes, but those that find themselves brought back from their former sinful courses and made to follow Him as their leader: for after the Apostle had said, *by His stripes ye were healed*, he adds this as the evidence thereof, *for ye were as sheep going astray, but are now returned to* the *Shepherd*. [4.] Those whom Christ's powerful grace has thus turned toward Him shall find Him prove Himself to them a good and faithful Shepherd, and Ruler as the word also signifies, reclaiming them from their wandering not only before their conversion, Luke 15:4, but likewise after it, Psa. 119:176, providing plenty of wholesome food for them as His flock, Psa. 23:1, &c, tenderly leading and bearing them in His bosom, in their sick and weak conditions, Isa. 40:6, and so protecting and defending them that none can pluck them out of His hand, John 10:28, for He to whom they are returned is the *Shepherd of their souls*. [5.] It is not any one relationship among the creatures that can sufficiently set out what Jesus Christ will prove Himself to be to true converts, all the usefulness and sweetnesss which is but scattered among all the relations which one creature has to another, being but shadows of what He is to them that are truly turned to Him: for the Apostle says, *they are returned to Him who is not only their Shepherd, but their Bishop or Overseer* who foresees and guards them against hazards, so far as is fitting, and furnishes them with all necessary provision in His service and so proves himself the *Bishop or Overseer of their souls*. [6.] As the believers' outward man and the least thing that concerns the same is cared for and respected by Jesus Christ, Matt. 10:30, so He loves to commend his respect and oversight to them mainly in reference to their souls, which are their better part, the welfare whereof necessarily brings along with it the welfare of the body; and their souls being beyond peril, that may make them cheerfully adventure upon bodily hazards in following Him, *who is the Shepherd and Bishop of their souls*. [7.] That which engages the hearts of sinners to love Jesus Christ, and out of love to Him to follow their duty through hardest sufferings, is the frequently renewed sense of their woeful condition wherein sometimes they were, and of the blessedness and privileges of that state whereunto His grace has brought them: for after the Apostle had represented this change to them (vv 9,10) as a motive to holiness, he here holds it forth again as a motive to constancy in holiness, notwithstanding of sufferings: *For ye were as sheep going astray, but are now returned to the Shepherd and Bishop of your souls.*

CHAPTER THREE

This chapter has three parts. In the first, containing the duties of married persons, the Apostle presses upon Christian women, firstly, that they should make conscience of duty to their husbands, though they were pagans, that so they might be gained to fall in love with Christianity (v 1) by the sight of their chaste and religious carriage (v 2); secondly, that they should not be much taken up with trimming of their bodies (v 3). But thirdly, that their prime care should be to have their souls adorned with grace, especially meekness: because [1.] that is an ornament durable: and [2.] it is in high esteem with God (v 4). So should they resemble holy women recorded in Scripture (v 5), and prove themselves heirs of Sarah's blessedness (v 6). Next he exhorts husbands to a wise and tender walking toward them by some arguments (v 7).

In the second part, he exhorts all Christians, whatever their relations be, to the exercise of such graces and duties of holiness as serve for keeping up a comfortable communion among themselves and with the Lord (v 8), and dissuades them from some evils that might mar the same, because, firstly, they were all called to inherit the same blessedness (v 9), and secondly, because a holy walking with God and a peaceable carriage toward others is the only way to sweeten the lives of Christians under all their troubles (vv 10,11). Thirdly, that was the way to have God's favourable providence watching over them for good. Fourthly, to get acceptance to their prayers. And fifthly, to eschew his wrath (v 12).

The third part contains several motives to constancy in holiness and encouragements against suffering in that way. As first, that well doing was the way to ward off the evil of all their troubles (v 13). Secondly, that no trouble for well-doing should hinder but rather promote their blessedness: to which encouragements the Apostle subjoins six directions, for attaining a right carriage under suffering: (1) that they should labour to banish the fear of flesh (v 14). (2) that they should adore the holiness of God in carving out a suffering lot for them. (3) that they should betimes enrich themselves with the knowledge of the truth so that they might be able to give a reason of what they suffered for. (4) that they should manifest meekness toward their persecutors. (5) that they should entertain fear of their own miscarriage (v 15). (6) that they should labour still to keep a good conscience under their suffering so that their carriage might convince and make ashamed their very persecutors, which is their *third* encouragement (v 16). Fourthly, that their sufferings after this manner should prove much more comfortable to them than if they were procured by their own miscarriage. Fifthly, that the good will of God had the carving out of these sufferings (v 17). Sixthly, that innocent Jesus Christ had suffered to the death for reconciling them to God and, for the applying of His purchase, was raised by the power of His Spirit or Godhead (v 18). Seventhly, that there are many souls now imprisoned in hell for slighting such truths as Christ's Spirit, speaking through Noah and others of His servants, had pressed upon them (vv 19,20). Eighthly, that the spiritual safety of believers from the deluge of God's wrath was made no less sure to them by their baptism, and the work of Christ's Spirit with it, than the temporal safety of Noah and those few persons with him from the flood was made sure to them by the Ark (v 21). And ninthly, that their Surety is now in highest power and glory that He may bear them through all their troubles and possess them of that salvation which He has purchased for them (v 22). All which prove that believers ought to follow their duty to Him notwithstanding of all sufferings for Him.

1. **Likewise, ye wives, be in subjection to your own husbands; that, if any obey not the Word, they also may without the Word be won by the conversation of the wives;**
2. **While they behold your chaste conversation coupled with fear.**

The Apostle, in pointing out the duties of married persons, begins with and insists most upon the duties of the women, partly because they had most discouragements, and partly because their making conscience of their duty was the best means to provoke their husbands to their duty. Upon them he presses subjection or dutifulness to their husbands by two arguments. The first is, because their obligation to their duty was no less strait than the obligation of others who stood in any of those relations mentioned in the former chapter. The second is, because their unbelieving husbands might, through God's blessing, be moved to receive the Gospel which formerly they had rejected (v 1), providing they did mark nothing but chastity and holiness joined with the fear of God and reverence toward themselves, shining in the conversation of their wives (v 2). And therefore Christian women had reason to make conscience of duties even toward their pagan husbands.

Hence learn, [1.] They that would rightly divide the word of truth among the Lord's people must not content themselves to press the duties of holiness in general as they concern all Christians, but must learn in their doctrine to come down to the lowest relations that are among the Lord's people and to point out the particular duties of these, it being in the discharge of such duties mainly that religion is adorned, Tit. 2:10. Therefore the Apostle, after he has spoken at large of the duties of holiness belonging to all in general, he comes among other relations to point out the duties of wives to their husbands: *Likewise ye wives, be subject*, &c. [2.] The sum of a woman's duty to her husband is subjection, which consists in a reverent esteem of him, as of one placed by the Lord in a degree of superiority above her, which will produce reverent speaking of him, and to him (v 5), and in giving obedience to his commands in things lawful; both which are in the signification of this word whereby the Apostle expresses the whole duty of wives to their husbands, *Likewise, ye wives, be subject to your own husbands.* [3.] However, there be difference among those relations that are between the Lord's people, some of them having more of dominion and subjection in them, as those last mentioned in the former chapter between magistrates and subjects, masters and servants, others of them having more of equality and love in them, as this which is here between husband and wife, yet the obligation to the duties of the latter sort is no less strict than to the duties of the former, both being enjoined by the same authority and so to be made conscience of upon the same hazard. Therefore the Apostle presses the duty of women to their husbands by such an expression as imports a like strictness of tie upon them to their duty as was upon those mentioned in the last part of the former chapter, *Likewise, ye wives, be subject,* &c. [4.] The wickedness and disobedience to the Gospel of any married person, however it may draw themselves under the curse of God, yet it does neither loose the relation nor exempt the other party from their duty (excepting in the case of adultery and lawful divorce thereupon,

Matt. 5:32, or wilful desertion, 1 Cor. 7:15) but does rather tie
the better party the more strictly to a conscionable discharge of
that duty, for the conviction or gaining of the other party: for
though the Apostle here supposes husbands, some of them at
least, to be disobedient to the Word, yet he presses upon their
wives dutifulness to them, as to their own husbands: *Be in subjection to your own husbands, that if any obey not the Word* &c.
[5.] Although the public ministry of the Word be the ordinary
and principal means of sinners' conversion to the Lord,
Rom. 10:15,17, yet the Lord may and sometimes does make use
of the pains of private Christians for that effect: for it is
supposed that they who obey not the Word may be won to obey
it by the conversation[1] of their wives. [6.] Although the children
of the Lord be bound to deal with the unconverted or profane
among whom they live by discourse and conference, commending Christ to them, and pointing out the way of attaining
acquaintance and communion with Him, John 4:29,30,
Phil. 2:15,16, yet it is mainly a conversation[1] suitable to the
Word that God uses to bless, for gaining of such to fall in love
with religion, without which the best discourses will rather
harden folk in sin, than reclaim them from their sinful ways;
therefore the Apostle here presses practical duties upon Christian women as the best way to gain their unbelieving husbands,
*That if any obey not the Word, they may be won by the conversation of the
wives: while they behold your chaste conversation,* &c. [7.] The Lord's
people ought not to quit their hopes of the conversion of those
who have not hitherto been persuaded by the Word to follow the
directions thereof, neither yet do believe the truths revealed in it,
but they ought to continue their pains toward those with whom
the public ministry does not prevail: for even to these husbands
whom the Apostle supposes to be unbelievers, disobedient to
the Word, and such as will not be persuaded thereby (as the
word here signifies), he pleads for duty from their wives in hopes
of gaining them thereby, *That if any obey not the Word, they may
without the Word be won by the conversation of the wives.* [8.] The
winning of a sinner to Jesus Christ is an employment full of gain
and advantage (as the word here translated 'to be won' signifies)
both to the sinner itself, who is thereby made partaker of the
true riches, Jas. 2:5, and to those who are instrumental in that
work in regard of the comfort they may have from them,

[1] See page 40.

117

Phil. 4:1, and the reward they shall have from God, Dan. 12:3, and therefore it ought to be managed with a great deal of spiritual policy and skill, as the same word also signifies: *that if any obey not the Word*, &c, they may be won. [9.] There is no part of a Christian's conversation so prevalent to gain onlookers to fall in love with religion as that wherein the duties which we owe to others in the relation we have to them shines: for these two, chastity (which in the peculiar signification of it is one main duty of the wife in reference to her husband) and fear (signifying reverence to a superior, Rom. 13:7) are the qualities of a Christian conversation which the Spirit of God here condescends upon as most prevalent for gaining unbelievers to fall in love with religion: they may be won, *while they behold your chaste conversation, coupled with fear.* [10.] Carnal men do very accurately pry into all the secrets of the practice of those that are religious, which though it be done by them that they may find occasion against the godly, Psa. 56:6, who should therefore be the more circumspect, Psa. 39:1, and the more earnest for God's teaching, Psa. 27:11, yet the Lord may make use of it contrary to their intention to be a means of much good to their souls: for the word which the Apostle uses here, 'while they behold', signifies very accurately to pry into, and seriously to consider a thing: upon which the Apostle may be safely conceived to lay some weight for moving Christian women to the more holy circumspection in their carriage, which the Lord might bless for gaining of their husbands, *while they behold your chaste conversation.* [11.] There is no true purity or holiness of conversation which does not flow from fear of offending God in the heart, by which Christians depart from evil in their practice, Prov. 16:6. Nor is there any true fear of God in the heart where the conversation is not in some measure holy, Jer. 32:40, for though this chastity and fear of Christian women here spoken of may be taken with a special respect to their husbands, yet the words are of a larger signification and must necessarily include holiness of life and fear of offending God in the heart, whatever they might suffer from their husbands; the one whereof cannot be separated from the other, *A chaste conversation, coupled with fear.*

3. **Whose adorning, let it not be that outward adorning of plaiting the hair, and of wearing of gold, or of putting on of apparel;**
4. **But let it be the hidden man of the heart, in that which is not**

corruptible, even the ornament of a meek and quiet spirit, which is in the sight of God of great price.

The Apostle gives here two further directions to believing women for attaining to such a conversation as, through the Lord's blessing, might prove a means of gaining their unbelieving husbands. The one is negative, that they should not be too curious and superfluous in trimming their outward man. The other is positive, that their great pains should be to have their inward man adorned with the grace of God, especially meekness and peaceableness of spirit, in reference to their husbands, and the Lord's dispensation in tying them to such men, and to a cross with them: which last he presses by two arguments. The first is, that this was an ornament that would not wax old as others do. The second is, that it is in very high esteem with the Lord and therefore, as they desired to gain their husbands by their outward carriage, their great care should be to attain to a right frame of spirit within.

Hence learn, [1.] Even the children of the Lord are in hazard to offend Him and others in the matter of their apparel, while they labour not to have the same suitable to their several ranks and conditions, which God would have distinguished in some measure by apparel, Esther 5:1, Gen. 38:14, while they affect a newness and a strangeness whether in the kind of their apparel or in their way of using of it, Zeph. 1:8, and when much time and expenses are wasted about apparel, as is imported in the Apostle's words here. In all which, and the like cases, the Lord's people are ready to offend in the matter of their apparel; and that because there is in them much unsubdued pride and vanity ready to manifest itself that way, Isa. 3:16,18, &c, and because they forget that apparel is given to make them ashamed in remembrance of their sin, 1 Tim. 2:9,14, for the hazard of offending (by wasting both time and means) is imported in this dissuasive of the Apostle: *Whose adorning, let it not be that outward adorning of plaiting the hair, and wearing of gold, or of putting on of apparel.* [2.] Although the Lord allows persons who are in eminency above others to have ornaments beyond necessity, Isa. 22:20,21,22, and others to have more than ordinary at some special occasions, Gen. 24:30, and all of his people to provide for things honest in the sight of all men, Rom. 12:17, yet when any professor of religion becomes excessive in the use of his liberty in these things, he will be so far from commending religion to others thereby that his practice will rather be a hindrance to others to fall in love with it, who may or will readily take occasion thence to think that Christians have no better things to take them up than these whereupon they waste their time, pains and means; for, from this evil the Apostle here dissuades Christian women as they would gain their heathen husbands; importing that their vanity and excess in the matter of their apparel would rather hinder them than gain them to fall in love with Christianity: *whose adorning, let it not be that outward adorning, of plaiting the hair,* &c. [3.] They that would by their outward carriage commend religion and win others to fall in love therewith, must have their prime care exercised about their heart which if it be adorned with the graces of God's Spirit in life and practice, the conversation cannot but be lovely to all rightly discerning onlookers: for the Apostle having told those believing women before that it was their conversation mainly which would gain their husbands, he now condescends upon the way of attaining to such a conversation, *Whose adorning, let it not be that outward adorning,* &c, *but let it be the hidden man of the heart.* [4.] Those that waste much time, pains and means in decking and trimming of their bodies, do ordinarily neglect their souls, leaving these in a disorderly, sordid and filthy condition: for the Apostle dissuading from the one and (in opposition thereto) persuading to the other, imports the inconsistency of such an adorning of the outward man with the adorning of the inward; *Whose adorning, let it not be that outward adorning,* &c, *but let it be the hidden man of the heart.* [5.] The Lord has been pleased to hide the hearts of every one from the knowledge of another, who therefore ought not by their rash judging and censuring of the inward frame and state of others to invade the Lord's prerogative of searching the heart, Jer. 17:10, but ought to bestow much pains for keeping in a right frame their own hearts which are hid from all eyes but God's, as a prime evidence of their sincerity, Psa. 51:6,7. Therefore the inward frame of the spirit is here called *The hidden man of the heart.* [6.] That which mainly makes the carriage of a professor of religion a means to gain others to Jesus Christ is, the exercise of the graces of God's Spirit within, especially meekness and quietness of spirit; by the former whereof (to wit, meekness) they keep down their passions from rising against others that wrong them or against the Lord's dispensation in exercising them more hardly than others, Numb. 12:2,3 whereby also they essay all amicable and loving ways of reclaiming such as do wrong them, before they go to the rigour of justice, 1 Cor. 4:21, and by the latter (to wit, quietness of spirit) they do eschew all needless contradiction of others, Isa. 53:7, all rashness in their actions, Acts 19:36, all meddling with things not belonging to them, 1 Thess. 4:11, and all expressions of miscontent with that lot which the Lord has carved out to them, Psa. 131:2. All which are here required of Christian women tied to unbelieving and profane husbands as special means of gaining them to Christ: for in order to their gaining, the Apostle thus exhorts the wives to *put on the ornament of a meek and quiet spirit.* [7.] Where such a gracious frame of spirit is within, as the Apostle here exhorts Christian women to labour for, it will have visible effects that may be discerned without: for the Apostle exhorts Christian wives to the study of meekness and quietness of spirit as a means to gain their unbelieving husbands, which it could not prove, except the effects thereof were visible in their carriage. [8.] The grace of Christ is such an ornament, as being once put upon the soul does never altogether fade or wax old; the consideration whereof should make Christians more careful to have it in exercise in their hearts than to have on the best of their ornaments which will soon wear and wax old: for as an argument to move Christians to put on this adorning of God's grace, the Apostle affirms it to be that *which is incorruptible.* (9.) Although every grace be the Lord's own free gift, Jas. 1:17, and the most gracious cannot properly be profitable to Him, Job 22:2, yet He is pleased to esteem of His own grace, and graciously to reward the persons to whom He gives it, as if it were of much worth to Him. The consideration whereof should heighten the esteem of grace in our hearts and quicken us to pains for getting and increasing of it: for this end is the adorning of a meek and quiet spirit here commended from this, *that it is in the sight of God of great price.*

5. **For after this manner in the old time the holy women also, who trusted in God, adorned themselves, being in subjection unto their own husbands.**
6. **Even as Sarah obeyed Abraham, calling him lord: whose daughters ye are as long as ye do well, and are not afraid with any amazement.**

Here are two further arguments whereby the Apostle presses upon Christian women the study of such a carriage as might prove a means of gaining their wicked husbands. The one is taken from the example of holy believing women registered in Scripture, who counted it their best adornment to manifest their holiness and faith by their dutifulness to their husbands, and particularly of *Sarah* who testified her obedience to her husband by her respective and reverent language to him. The other argument is from the advantage of such a carriage, that if they did imitate these holy women, especially *Sarah*, in dutifulness to their husbands notwithstanding of any terror from them, they should prove themselves heirs of *Sarah's* blessedness.

Hence learn, [1.] The children of the Lord have not only need of precepts to press their duty upon them, but likewise of the examples of others held forth to them who have gone before them in the practice of these duties, that so they may apprehend them feasible, seeing others have attained to them; and sweet, seeing others have cheerfully practised them; and the neglect of them hazardous, since these who have made conscience of them may be brought as witnesses against the neglecters of them. Therefore after the Apostle has pressed by precepts and reasons the duty of believing women to their husbands, he here bears in the same further by the example of the saints: for after this manner also the holy women in the old time *who trusted in God, adorned themselves, being in subjection to their own husbands.* [2.] The approved examples of the most eminent of the saints making conscience of moral duties, which are registered in the Old Testament, are obligatory under the New to the meanest of believers in Christ who are not by their Christian liberty freed from imitating them in these: for here the Apostle presses upon Christian women dutifulness to their husbands, from the example of holy women under the Old Testament, and particularly *Sarah*, who was an eminent and in some respects an extraordinary person; *For after this manner in the old time the holy women also,* &c. *Even as Sarah,* &c. [3.] There is no true holiness which has not faith in God for the fountain and root of it whereby the heart relies on God for furniture for the duties of holiness, and encouragement against difficulties in the way thereof. Nor is there any real trusting in God which has not for the fruit thereof, holiness, consisting in the study of abstinence from every known sin, and endeavour after every known duty: for from these two jointly are those ancient believers described as examples to be imitated by others: *Holy women, who trusted in God.* [4.] True holiness and faith in God are mainly evidenced in the particular duties of these relations wherein the Lord's providence has placed His people; the consciable discharge whereof proves the principal ornament of professors: for, here the Apostle sets forth those ancient believing women as in their best ornaments while they are evidencing their holiness and trusting in God by their dutifulness to their husbands, to be imitated by Christian women under the Gospel, *The holy women who trusted in God, adorned themselves, being in subjection to their husbands.* [5.] The Lord takes notice of the least act of sincere obedience to His commands even when it is mixed with many sinful failings which He passes in penitents and would not have any of His people cast at any good in others nor be the less careful to imitate it, that they do discern much miscarriage joined with it: for in that passage of *Sarah's*, Gen. 18:12, which is here related to, there are many sinful failings and little thing commendable, beside that one word, evidencing her reverence to her husband, which the Lord here registers for her commendation and others' imitation, hiding the faults that were therewith: *Even as Sarah obeyed Abraham, calling him lord.* [6.] The want of these qualifications in parties to whom the Lord's people have relation, which have been eminent in others, does not exempt them from these duties which by virtue of that relation have been performed to others, endued with these qualifications: for here the Apostle from *Sarah's* reverencing of *Abraham*, an extraordinarily and eminently gracious man, infers upon Christian women reverence to their wicked infidel husbands: *Even as Sarah obeyed Abraham, calling him lord.* [7.] When we obtain grace from the Lord to follow the footsteps of the saints registered in Scripture, especially in the faithful discharge of the duties of our particular stations and relations, then do we prove ourselves to be partakers of the same spiritual privileges with them and heirs of the same eternal blessedness which they now possess: for as those who imitate the faith and obedience of *Abraham* are for that called his children, Rom. 4:11,12; Gal. 3:7,9,29, so these women here who imitate *Sarah* in well-doing, particularly in obedience to their husbands, are called her daughters, *Whose daughters are ye, as long as ye do well*; which is not to be understood as if they were cast out of the number of her daughters for every shortcoming in their duty, but that it is in the way of their duty that they will clear to themselves their right to her blessedness and enjoy the sense of their interest in the spiritual privileges which she had. [8.] They that resolve to hold on in the way of well doing may resolve to meet with as much of terror and fright therein as wicked men can make them; yea, even from those of their nearest relations, whose enmity against godliness before the Lord change them is greater than any natural affection they have to those they are most strictly tied to: for it is mainly against the terror and amazement of wicked husbands that the Apostle here guards Christian women, encouraging them by this that they should prove themselves daughters of *Sarah* if they held on in their duty, and *were not afraid with any amazement*. [9.] It is perseverance in the way of duty when there is not only small appearance of success but much terrible opposition from wicked men in following of it, which mainly clears to believers their right to the heavenly inheritance: for this the Apostle presses upon Christian women as that which would prove them daughters of Sarah, that is, co-heirs with her of the heavenly inheritance, *if they did well and were not afraid with any amazement*.

7. **Likewise, ye husbands, dwell with them according to knowledge, giving honour unto the wife, as unto the weaker vessel, and as being heirs together of the grace of life; that your prayers be not hindered.**

In the next place, the Apostle presses the duties of husbands to their wives, which he comprehends in two branches. Firstly, that they should manifest a special measure of prudence and heavenly wisdom in conversing with them. And secondly, that they should season their authority over them with tenderness and respect to them; both which he presses by several arguments. [1.] From the strictness of their obligation to these duties, which was the same with that of the wives to theirs. [2.] From the weakness and infirmity of the women, which calls for the more wise and tender dealing. [3.] From the equality of both in partaking of spiritual and eternal privileges. And [4.] From the hazard of the neglect of those duties, to wit, the interrupting of their service to God, particularly the marring of their access to him in prayer.

Hence learn, [1.] Husbands are no less strictly tied to duty toward their wives than the wives are to duty toward them, or any inferior toward their superior; and therefore they ought not to make their superiority a pretence to the neglect of their duty, as if their wives were tied and themselves left at liberty: for the

Apostle uses the same word in pressing the duty of husbands to their wives which he did before in pressing the duty of wives to their husbands and of servants to their masters: *Likewise, ye husbands*. [2.] It is the duty of husbands to cohabit with their wives and to labour for much prudence and wisdom in conversing with them, that they may not only know their own duty toward them but may be able to instruct them in theirs, 1 Cor. 14:35, that they may discern how far to entrust them with their affairs and counsels, Prov. 31:11, and how far they ought to keep up the same from them, Micah 7:5, and that they do not rule them according to their passion and will but according to that wise rule set down in the Word: for the Apostle here presses upon husbands both cohabitation and wise walking with their wives; *Ye husbands, dwell with them according to knowledge.* [3.] There is not only love required of the husband toward his wife, but likewise some respect and honour, such as makes them signify their sympathy with them under their crosses, 1 Sam. 1:8, their high esteem of the virtues they discern in them, Prov. 31:28 and such as may conciliate respect to them from the rest of the family, Gen. 16:6, for this is the other branch of the duty of husbands, *giving honour unto the wife.* [4.] It has pleased the Lord to exercise the woman with a special measure of weakness and infirmity, both natural, by imposing upon her much pain and labour in bringing forth and educating of children, and moral by giving her fewer opportunities than the man has of means for perfecting of her natural parts which likewise are not ordinarily so strong in her as in the man: in which respects she is here called *the weaker vessel*. [5.] The consideration of this weakness of the woman should be so far from making husbands to despise and slight them, that by the contrary it should increase their respect to them, considering that by reason thereof they are the more easily crushed and broken in their spirits, especially by the austere and undutiful carriage of their husbands, and the more apt to apprehend themselves slighted: for so it is here made an argument to procure respect to them from their husbands, *giving honour unto the wife as unto the weaker vessel.* [6.] Both the work of God's saving grace in His own, which is here called the grace of life, because it quickens the soul, where it is, for spiritual performances and clears its right to eternal life; and likewise eternal life itself, which may be safely conceived to be comprehended in the same expression, are the free gift of God's grace, proceeding merely from His favour and love, bestowing the same upon sinners, as their inheritance never to be taken from them: for of both these the Apostle may be understood while he calls Christian women and their husbands to whom he speaks as being believers, *Heirs together of the grace of life*. [7.] The difference of sex or outward condition among the Lord's people does not hinder their equality in the participation of spiritual and eternal privileges which free grace bestows without respect to these differences, Gal. 3:28, for here husbands and wives are called *heirs together of the grace of life*. [8.] The consideration of this equality should strongly move superiors to make conscience of duty toward their inferiors, considering that because of this equality their inferiors are no less dear to God than themselves, and that they are fellow-heirs with them of that which is much better than anything of a temporary concernment wherein they do excel them: for this is here brought as an argument of husbands' dutifulness to their wives, *That they are heirs together of the grace of life*. [9.] Although none can be so infallibly persuaded of another's being in the state of grace and salvation, as they may be of their own, Rev. 2:17, yet ought every professor to entertain so much charity of another concerning that as may make them no less conscionable in every duty toward them, than if they were such, and not upon slender grounds to question the same or admit of thoughts to the contrary, lest thereupon Satan make them apprehend exemption from duty toward them: for, so much is imported here, while husbands are exhorted to duty toward their wives and that because they ought to judge them in charity, *heirs with them of the grace of life*. [10.] When Christians are not making conscience of the faithful discharge of the duties of their particular relations, especially of this between husband and wife, then the duties of God's service chiefly in their families, and in secret, will either be broken off or the success of them marred; for however the one party may be more innocent than the other, yet the guilt of the injuring party and the grief and passion of the injured will not only indispose the hearts of both for duties and mar their hearty joining in them, but will also readily cut off (as the word here rendered *to hinder* signifies) the very external performance of the duty of prayer (under which all other religious performances may be comprehended) and mar their access to God and the success of their duties: for so much is imported in this last reason, *That your prayers be not hindered*. [11.] The more conscionable Christians are by the grace of God enabled to be in the discharge of the particular duties of their several relations, the more access to God and success of all their religious performances they may expect: for this motive, as it imports the hazard to follow upon the neglect of duties of that sort, so it imports also the advantage to follow upon the conscionable discharge thereof, to wit, *that their prayers should not be hindered.*

8. **Finally, be all of one mind, having compassion one of another, love as brethren, be pitiful, be courteous:**
9. **Not rendering evil for evil, or railing for railing: but contrariwise blessing; knowing that ye are thereunto called, that ye should inherit a blessing.**

Here is the second part of the chapter wherein the Apostle exhorts to the exercise of such graces and duties of holiness as do concern every Christian; and do serve in a special way for keeping up a profitable and comfortable communion with God and with His people: of which sort the Apostle condescends upon seven. Firstly, that they should labour for unity of judgment among themselves. Secondly, that they should be affected with one another's condition, as if it were their own. Thirdly, that their love one to another should resemble that which is among brethren. Fourthly, that they should pity the infirmities one of another. Fifthly, that they should show themselves courteous in their carriage and easy to be conversed with, v 8. Sixthly, that they should not study to requite mutual injuries but, seventhly, rather seek the happiness of them that wrong them. All of which, especially the last two, the Apostle presses by this reason, that they were all called to inherit one common blessedness.

From v 8 learn, [1.] Although complete oneness of judgment cannot be expected among the Lord's people, while knowledge is imperfect in all, 1 Cor. 13:9, and dispensed in different measures, Rom. 12:6, yet it ought to be the sincere endeavour of every one so to drink in the knowledge of all saving and necessary truths themselves and to employ their power, according to their calling, to make all others do the same, that they may be, so far as is possible, as if one and the same mind were in them all (as the word here signifies), which is in some good measure attained when Christians do agree in all saving and fundamental truths, and when their prime projects and designs (as the word also signifies) do meet in one, to wit, the advancement of the glory of Jesus Christ; without which unity of judgment, there does ordinarily follow among the Lord's people alienation of affection, Gal. 4:15,16, and a loss of the consolations of Christ's Spirit, which uses to be given through their communion among themselves, Phil. 2:1,2, for this is it which the Apostle here expressly presses, *Finally, be all of one mind.* [2.] Every one of the children of the Lord ought to be so affected with the condition of another as if it were their own, mourning with and for one another in affliction, as if they were afflicted with them, Heb. 13:3, rejoicing in and praising for their welfare as if they were in their case, Rom. 12:15, considering that they are all members of one body, 1 Cor. 12:26, and that this sympathizing frame of spirit is a special part of our conformity to Jesus Christ, Heb. 4:15, for this is the second duty here pressed, *having compassion one of another.* [3.] Whatever differences for worldly respects or measures of spiritual gifts there may be among the children of the Lord, there should be, notwithstanding, such affection and love in the most eminent and strongest toward the meanest and weakest, as is among brethren, they being all children of one Father, John 1:12, and the weakest owned by Christ as his brethren, Heb. 2:11, and co-heirs, not only with the strongest, but with Jesus Christ Himself of everlasting blessedness, Rom. 8:17. And therefore that measure of affection which may be found among men without the church, who have not put off humanity, is not sufficient for one of the Lord's people toward another: for this is the third duty here pressed, *Love as brethren.* [4.] There can neither be unity, sympathy nor brotherly love among the Lord's people unless they have hearts to pity the infirmities one of another, and some proneness of spirit to do good to others, even when they deserve the contrary at their hands: for this word, whereby the Apostle presses the fourth duty, is often used to signify Christ's compassion to His own which is manifested in bestowing favours notwithstanding of provocations, and signifies such a tenderheartedness as is evidenced by forgiving of wrongs, Eph. 4:32; *Be pitiful.* [5.] They that would keep up a sweet and profitable society with others of the Lord's people must show themselves affable and pleasant in their carriage towards them, studying to speak and do so far as they may with a good conscience what may be acceptable, and engaging of their affections to them: for this duty, which is the last in the eighth verse, as also all the former, may be taken in reference to the keeping up of society with others; *Be courteous.*

From v 9 learn, [1.] Even those who have attained to such a carriage as ought in all reason to be lovely and honoured by all with whom they converse, may notwithstanding resolve to meet with much hard usage and many slanders: for the Apostle presses here patience, in the sixth place, importing that they who had attained to all the former five would, notwithstanding, have ado with their patience: *Not rendering evil for evil, or railing for railing.* [2.] The children of the Lord may resolve not only to meet with hard usage and bitter language from the profane or those that are without, but even from their fellow professors, whether hypocrites who will still be maligning the sincere, Gal. 4:29, or even truly gracious whose corruptions oppose grace in others, Job 16:20, for this last grace of patience, pressed in the beginning of the eighth verse, cannot well be taken in reference to other persons than these, in reference to whom the exercise of the former graces or duties were pressed which do clearly relate to other professors; and therefore this imports that they might be tried both with evil deeds and words from such, while the Apostle thus dissuades, *Not rendering evil for evil or railing for railing.* [3.] However, the best of the children of the Lord are prone to study revenge and requital of private injuries, as is supposed in this dissuasive, yet must they not allow themselves in so doing as they love their own and others' peace, and desire to eschew the displeasure of God for usurping His place, Rom. 12:19, Prov. 23:2: *Not rendering evil for evil, or railing for railing.* [4.] So far should the Lord's people be from the study of private revenge and retaliation of wrongs done by one of them against another, that by the contrary the greatest personal wrong by word or deed should not hinder one of them to procure the bestowing of blessings if they be able upon another, to commend in them what they can discern to be praiseworthy, or to pray for their true blessedness, which is a special draught of the image of the Lord, Matt. 5:44,45. All which is in the signification of this word whereby the Apostle expresses the duty opposite to rendering evil for evil, or railing for railing: *but contrariwise, blessing.* [5.] The consideration of that everlasting blessedness which consists in the clear vision and full fruition of God in Christ through the Spirit, and which sinners who are naturally under the curse are called to possess as their free-gifted inheritance (as the word here translated, *to inherit,* signifies), should comfort the hearts of believers against the worst usage and vilest reproaches of men, which will be sufficiently made up when they come to possess that blessedness: the thoughts whereof should take them off from all study of revenge toward those who may be heirs with them of the same inheritance; and who could never wrong them so far as they have wronged the Lord, who has graciously called them to possess that free-gifted inheritance; for this is here proposed by the Apostle as an argument to patience under wrongs and a dissuasive from revenge among the Lord's people: for even *hereunto were ye called, that ye should inherit a blessing.*

10. **For he that will love life, and see good days, let him refrain his tongue from evil, and his lips that they speak no guile:**
11. **Let him eschew evil, and do good; let him seek peace, and ensue it.**

Here is a second motive to the study of the duties formerly pressed, to wit, that that study was the way to have a sweet life and many good days in communion with the Lord, notwithstanding of all their troubles. This argument is taken out of Psa. 34:12,13 and contains four several directions for clearing the way of attaining to that sweet fellowship with God, and among themselves. The first is, that they should watch against the evils of the tongue. The second is, that they should set against every known sin. The third is, that they should set about the practice of every known duty. And fourthly, that they should earnestly pursue peace with others of the Lord's people; so might they expect sweet communion with Himself.

Hence learn, [1.] Although the most part of men esteem their life happy and their days good enough, if they enjoy abundance of earthly comforts, Psa. 4:6,7 and 49:16,18, yet there is no life that deserves the name of a life except it be sweetened sometimes with tastes of the Lord's special love; nor are there any days that are worthy to be called good days which are not spent in fellowship with God: for this life and those good days here spoken of are the same with tasting how gracious the Lord is, as appears by comparing these words with the ninth verse of the psalm whence they are cited. [2.] There is no way to live that sweet life and to see those good days that sinners may attain to, even here away in communion with the Lord, but by the study of holiness, eschewing everything that grieves the Spirit of God and aiming sincerely at the practice of everything that is well pleasing in His sight: for both these are here pressed *as the way to have that life, and to see those good days.* [3.] Although men are prone to count very little of the sins of their tongue, Psa. 12:2,4, yet much of that guilt which mars sweet fellowship with God will be found in sins of that kind; partly in idle and unprofitable discourses, whereof men must give an account, Matt. 12:36, foolish talking and jesting which is not convenient, Eph. 5:4, rigid censuring of and bitter inveighing against others which makes all that Christians do in religion useless, Jas. 1:26, and grieves the Spirit of God, Eph. 4:29,30,31, meddling with those things in discourse wherein folks are not concerned, 1 Tim. 5:13, and the like, which may be comprehended under that which is here called *Evil*; and partly in equivocation, Gen. 20:2,12, venting of error under fair speeches and pretences, Rom. 16:17, and hypocritical or feigned discourses whereby Christians do give out themselves to be what they are not, which resembles that whereunto David relates in that passage of the psalm which is here cited, as appears by comparing the words with the title of that psalm. All which and the like may be comprehended under *guile*; and both sorts of sins of the tongue are to be abstained from by those that would enjoy communion with the Lord: for in order to that, this is the first direction: *He that will love life, and see good days, let him refrain his tongue from evil and his lips that they speak no guile.* [4.] Were Christians never so innocent in their discourses and watchful over their tongue, except also they make it their serious study to keep a distance in heart and practice from every known sin, and that as it is evil and contrary to the holy nature and will of God, they cannot expect to keep up that sweet communion with God which He allows upon His own: for this is the second direction necessary for attaining to that end, *Let him eschew evil.* [5.] It is not simple abstinence from sin (suppose that could be attained to without further) that fits souls for entertaining fellowship with God, unless there be also joined therewith a sincere and universal aim at everything that is well pleasing in the sight of God, both in duties relating more immediately to God, and His public matters in the world, 2 Chron. 24:16, and in duties toward others of His people, whether those of our particular relations, 1 Tim. 5:4, or others, Gal. 6:10, to which these Scriptures give the name of doing good: for this is the third direction for attaining and enjoying communion with God, *Let him do good.* [6.] They that desire to have much peace in fellowship with God must be very serious in studying peace with others, both by living peaceably with them themselves, so far as is possible, Rom. 12:18, without prejudice to truth, Zech. 8:19, or holiness, Heb. 12:14, and procuring and cherishing peace among others of the Lord's people, Matt. 5:9, both which are comprehended in this fourth direction for attaining to and enjoying of communion with God: *Let him seek peace, and ensue it.* [7.] As there will be no small difficulty from Satan, our own and others' corruptions, in the way of attaining and entertaining peace among the Lord's people, so none of them must stand upon their pains in the pursuit thereof, nor quit the same though upon many former essays they have not had success and though peace seem to be flying from them. All which is imported in the signification and doubling of the word here, *Seek peace and ensue it.*

12. For the eyes of the Lord are over the righteous, and his ears are open unto their prayers: but the face of the Lord is against them that do evil.

Here are three further arguments to press the forementioned duties. The first is that the watchful providence of God is exercised about them for their good, who, having fled to the righteousness of Christ, do also walk in the way of righteousness or holiness formerly described. The second is that He does favourably accept of their prayers. And the third is that the terror and wrath of God is employed against those that walk in the contrary way.

Hence learn, [1.] It is the privilege of justified persons walking in the way of holiness to have the favourable providence of God watching over them for good; which comprehends His furnishing of them with everything necessary for their welfare, Deut. 11:12, warding hazards off them as far as shall be for their good, 2 Chron. 16:9, rendering ineffectual all opposition made to them while He has service for them, Ezra 5:5, supporting them under and delivering them from all their troubles in due time, Psa. 33:18, and making out his covenant to them, Jer. 24:6,7. All which the Scriptures cited make clear to be comprehended in this expression which holds forth their privileges: *The eyes of the Lord are over the righteous.* [2.] Although for wise reasons the prayers of the Lord's people may have no answer for a time, even after frequency and importunity in that duty, 2 Cor. 12:8, yea, and to their sense may seem to be misregarded by the Lord, Psa. 22:2, yet their requests have always a favourable acceptance with Him, insofar as He delights to hear them, Prov. 15:8, Canticles 2:14, and during the delay is preparing them for a good answer, Psa. 10:17; Isa. 30:18,19. Providing they be praying for things agreeable to His will, 1 John 5:14, not to gratify their lusts, Jas. 4:3, but for His glory, and building their confidence of acceptance upon Christ's merits and intercession, John 14:13, for this must be some special notice He takes of their prayers, since He hears also the prayers of the wicked though with detestation, Prov. 28:9, *His ears are open to their prayers.* [3.] Only those who in the sense of their own unrighteousness are fled to the righteousness of Christ that so their persons may be accepted with God, and have obtained grace to be sincere students of true holiness, may lay claim to these privileges, the Lord's favourable providence exercised about them for good and His acceptance of their prayers: *for the eyes of the Lord are over the righteous, and His ears are open to their prayers.* [4.] That which makes the life of believers a life indeed and their days good days to them in the midst of many troubles is this favourable providence of God watching over them for their good and His gracious acceptance of their prayers through his Son: for these privileges are brought in to clear wherein that life and those good days spoken of in the former words do stand, even in this that *the eyes of the Lord are over the righteous, and His ears are open to their prayers.* [5.] However the Lord may long spare wicked men in their sinful courses, from which indulgency of his they take occasion to do more and more wickedly, Eccles. 8:11, yet His constant purpose is to destroy all of them who make a constant trade of provoking Him, Psa. 68:21, and that without any battle or reluctancy in their heart, Ezek. 11:21, and at last He will employ his power and terror for their ruin; as is imported in this, *The face of the Lord is against them that do evil.* [6.] It is both lawful and necessary for the Lord's people to encourage their own hearts in the duties of holiness by the consideration of that sweetness which the Lord uses to let out to them, while they hold that way; and to deter their hearts from those sins whereunto they do strongly incline, by the consideration of the hazard abiding them that continue in sin; for both the gain of godliness and the hazard of sinful courses, is here proposed to be considered by them for these ends; *for the eyes of the Lord are over the righteous,* &c. *But the face of the Lord is against them that do evil.*

13. And who is he that will harm you, if ye be followers of that which is good?

Follows the last part of the chapter which is full of encouragement against sufferings and of motives to the duties of holiness notwithstanding thereof, together with several directions for attaining to a right carriage under the same. The first encouragement is that the following of duty, notwithstanding of suffering, would prove the best way of any to eschew the hurt of all trouble from wicked men, with whom the Lord would assuredly reckon for molesting of His people, while they were following their duty to him.

Hence learn, [1.] Although the godly, in following their duty, may expect the hardest usage that wicked men can devise or inflict upon them, Heb. 11:34, yet properly there can be no harm or evil done to them in regard the nature of all afflictions, especially for well doing, is charged to them, Rom. 8:28, their persecutors cannot at all reach their better part, Luke 12:4, and all their losses by suffering for truth are more than sufficiently made up to them, Matt. 19:29; for this question may be safely conceived to have the force of a denial, *None shall be able to harm you, if ye be followers of that which is good.* [2.] The best way to eschew, at least to mitigate trouble, even from wicked men, is close adherence to that which is right in the sight of God: not because wicked men favour the way of well doing; but because the Lord sometimes allays their fury against those that follow it by putting convictions upon their conscience of the equity of the cause which they persecute, 1 Sam. 24:17, &c., and sometimes works in their heart some reverence toward it and them that follow it, Mark 6:20, for here the Apostle mentions the following of that which is good, as the best way of eschewing trouble from wicked men, who would be glad to see the miscarriage of the godly that they might thence have occasion to trouble them: *And who is he that will harm you if ye be followers of that which is good?* [3.] Whoever shall enterprise to harm or evil intreat (as the word here signifies) the children of the Lord for their dutifulness to him, the Lord shall enquire after them: He shall find them out, and reckon with them, be they who they will: for this question may be taken for the Lord's challenge of them and His enquiry for them to judge them; *Who is he that will harm you?* [4.] The children of the Lord are not only to go about their duty in obedience to His commands, but likewise in imitation both of Christ Himself as their prime pattern, Eph. 5:1, and of the rest of His saints who have walked in that way before them, Heb. 6:11, for this is the description of those to whom this encouragement is given, that they are *followers* (or as the word is, *imitators*) *of that which is good.*

14. But and if ye suffer for righteousness' sake, happy are ye: and be not afraid of their terror, neither be troubled.

The second encouragement to constancy in duty notwithstanding of sufferings is that if Christians be put to suffer for adhering to the way of free justification by Christ's imputed righteousness (which legalists did then persecute) or for any duty of holiness (which libertines opposed), those sufferings should evidence and promote their true blessedness: from which encouragements the Apostle infers, in the following words, several directions for attaining to a right carriage under suffering; whereof the first is in this verse, to wit, that they should labour to banish the fear of what flesh could do to them, and not suffer their hearts to be terrified or perturbed by the terror or hard usage of wicked men, while they suffered for so honourable a cause.

Hence learn, [1.] Were the cause which the Lord's people maintain never so good, and their carriage in following of it never so innocent, it is in vain for them to dream of exemption from trouble at the hands of wicked men who are oftentimes the more incensed against them that their cause be good, John 7:7, and their carriage a shame and reproof to others, 1 John 3:12, for lest from the former encouragement any might expect exemption from trouble by following that which is good, Peter does in this suppose that they might expect to be put to *suffer for righteousness' sake.* [2.] The sufferings of the godly for righteousness' sake are so far from making them miserable, as themselves are apt to apprehend, Psa. 73:13, and the wicked world do ordinarily judge, 2 Cor. 4:13, that by the contrary they serve both to promote their spiritual happiness, the times of suffering being the times wherein every grace thrives most, Rom. 5:3, and divine consolation abounds most in their hearts,

2 Cor. 1:5, and likewise to evidence and prove to them their right to everlasting blessedness, Phil. 1:28, a special measure whereof is reserved for the greatest sufferers, Rev. 7:13, &c. For this second encouragement contradicts the Lord's people's ordinary apprehension of themselves and the profane world's opinion of them under suffering: *If ye suffer for righteousness' sake, happy are ye.* [3.] The best of the children of the Lord are in hazard to have their spirits troubled and perplexed with the fear of hazard from flesh which is then exceeding sinful when it makes them deny the truth, Matt. 26:70, or take any sinful course for their temporal safety, 1 Sam. 21:10,13, or when their spirits are thereby defiled and mudded (as the word in the original here signifies) with passion against the instruments of their trouble, Matt. 26:51, which hazard is imported in this dissuasive given to those that suffer for righteousness: *Fear not their fear, neither be troubled.* [4.] They who are fled to the righteousness of Jesus Christ and desire to adhere to that which is right in His sight notwithstanding of suffering, have no cause to fear what flesh can do unto them, or to have their spirits perturbed under the hardest of their sufferings, considering that whatever they suffer is according to the Lord's fore-appointment, 1 Thess. 3:3, and carved out by His all-ruling providence, Matt. 10:30, that they have the promise of His presence with them under their sufferings, Heb. 13:5,6, and are sure of a glorious issue out of them, 2 Cor. 4:17. Upon which grounds they ought to banish fleshly fear and perturbation out of their hearts as the Apostle here exhorts, *Fear not their fear, neither be troubled.*

15. But sanctify the Lord God in your hearts: and be ready always to give an answer to every man that asketh you a reason of the hope that is in you with meekness and fear.

This verse contains some further directions to persecuted Christians for attaining to a right frame of spirit and carriage under their sufferings. The second in order is, that they should reverence and adore in their hearts the sovereignty and holiness of God, especially in that dispensation of His toward them in putting them to suffer while their wicked persecutors prospered; which direction, as also the former, is taken out of Isa. 8:12,13. The third is, that they should betimes furnish themselves with such clear knowledge of the truth, that they may be able to hold forth from the Word of God reasons of what they believe and

suffer for. The fourth is, that their testimony for the truth should
be seasoned with meekness even toward their persecutors. And
the fifth is, that they should entertain in their hearts some holy
fear of miscarrying in the way of giving that testimony.

Hence learn, [1.] It is a principal part of a right disposition for
sufferers to entertain in their hearts the sense and acknowledgment of the holiness of God who, though He be matchless in
holiness, 1 Sam. 2:2, and can have nothing added to that or any
other of His infinite perfections by any creature, Rom. 11:35,36,
yet esteems Himself sanctified in the hearts of His own, while
they are by the consideration of His holiness made submissive to
the hardest of His dispensations toward them, Psa. 22:3, afraid
to offend so holy a majesty, Isa. 29:23, and thereby also are
confirmed in the faith of His performing all His promises, Psa.
111:9, and executing of His threatenings upon His enemies and
theirs, Hab. 1:12, for this is the Apostle's second direction for
attaining to a right frame of spirit under sufferings: *Sanctify the
Lord God in your hearts.* [2.] The children of the Lord, while they
are under hard usage from wicked men, are in great hazard not
only to forget the sovereignty of God over them, to use them as
He pleases for His own glory, which occasions much perturbation of spirit in them, Isa. 51:12,13, but likewise to entertain in
their hearts thoughts unsuitable to the holiness and purity of
His nature, as if their sufferings and the wicked's prosperity were
not consistent therewith; both which are imported in this exhortation to acknowledge the holiness of God, whom the Apostle
represents under such names as hold forth also His sovereignty:
Sanctify the Lord God in your hearts. [3.] Although the godly ought
not to be anxious concerning their furniture[1] in a time of trial,
Matt. 10:19, yet ought they not to neglect ordinary means of
preparation for trials, such as the drinking in of the solid and
clear knowledge of the truth, 1 Tim. 6:19, entertaining the
presence of that Spirit who reveals truths not yet known and
brings known truths to remembrance when it is necessary, John
14:26, that so they may be able to defend the truth by holy
reason drawn from the Scripture, or make apology for it, as the
word here signifies, and answer objections that may be made
against the same, Prov. 15:28 as is imported in this third direction: *Be ready always to answer every man that asketh you a reason of the
hope that is in you.* [4.] Although in some cases the children of the

[1] See page 62 (used here to signify spiritual gifts and graces).

Lord may safely answer their adversaries with silence, to wit, when they have sufficiently and frequently born testimony to such truths before, Matt. 27:12,14 or when questions are propounded to them by wicked men out of scorn, Prov. 26:5 or curiosity, Luke 23:8,9,11, or to be a snare to the godly, Isa. 36:21, yet ought they still to keep themselves in a readiness of mind and fitness of disposition for defending the truth and giving a reason of what they hold, when the glory of God and edification of others call for it, the season and manner whereof every humble waiter on God shall know from Him, Luke 12:11,12 and 21:14,15, Hab. 2:1, for the Apostle does not direct them here to answer always every man that asks them, but *to be ready always to answer every one that asketh a reason.* [5.] The children of the Lord ought not to satisfy themselves with any confidence or persuasion concerning the truths of the Gospel, whereof they have not such clear and rational grounds from the Word as may not only convince themselves, but such as they are able to hold forth to others, when they are called: *Be ready to give a reason to every man that asketh you.* [6.] Every testimony that God's people give to His truth before the enemies of it ought to be seasoned with meekness of spirit, evidenced in their carriage toward their persecutors by their eschewing all signs of carnal passion and revenge against them, 1 Thess. 5:15, by their respective and sober language to them, Acts 26:25, which may be blessed of God to procure a mitigation of their trouble, Prov. 15:1, at least to put convictions upon the wicked of the equity of the cause which they persecute, as the following verse clears: for this is the fourth direction for a right carriage under sufferings, that they *be ready to give a testimony to the truth with meekness.* [7.] Although the fear of flesh, which mars confidence and peace in the heart, be most unsuitable for sufferers, as was cleared from the Apostle's first direction, yet a holy fear of miscarriage under trials by denying or concealing any necessary truth, by bringing forth the same untimeously,[1] or mixing our own passions with our testimony to the truth, is a prime qualification of a right sufferer for Christ and His truth, for this is the Apostle's fifth direction, that they should be *ready to bear testimony to the truth with fear.*

16. Having a good conscience; that, whereas they speak evil of

---

[1] 'untimeously': unseasonably, unopportunely.

you, as of evildoers, they may be ashamed that falsely accuse your good conversation in Christ.

Here is a sixth direction for attaining to a right carriage under suffering. That they should labour to have their conscience purged from guiltiness and so made good in God's sight, the study whereof, as also of all the former, the Apostle presses by a third motive, which is also an encouragement against suffering; that if they made conscience of following those directions their slandering persecutors would be convinced and ashamed by reason of their Christian behaviour.

Hence learn, [1.] None can rightly undergo a suffering lot for Christ and His truth who do not labour to get and keep a good conscience within, by the application of Christ's blood for purging of it from guilt, and of the virtue of His Spirit for subduing the power of corruption, Heb. 10:22, which proves a continual feast to them that have it, Prov. 15:15, and so makes them cheerful under their hardest sufferings, 2 Cor. 1:12; for this is the Apostle's sixth direction, for attaining to a right frame of spirit and carriage under suffering: *having a good conscience*. [2.] Even those who have attained to a good conscience within and an honest conversation without may resolve not only to meet with hard sufferings, but as a principal ingredient embittering the same, to have many false and grievous crimes laid to their charge, and those not only forged and spread in a private way for their disgrace, but (as the word here translated *to speak evil* signifies) given-in judicially against them, that so they may be the more like to their Lord, Mark 15:3, and may learn to die to their credit before men, while they are honoured to suffer for Him, 1 Cor. 15:31; for this the Apostle supposes to be the lot of those who have both a good conscience and a good conversation, *that they shall be evil spoken of, as evil doers, and have their good conversation falsely accused.* [3.] It is the Lord's wise way to bring the shame and confusion of wicked men out of the integrity and uprightness of His suffering people and the endeavours of their enemies to disgrace them, by drawing a testimony of His people's innocency from some of their adversaries, to the shame of the rest, Acts 23:29 and 26:31, by enabling His suffering servants to maintain His truth and their own innocency with such clearness and power as sometimes confounds their opposers, Titus 2:8, by making use of the enemies' fury, and His people's constancy, to disappoint wicked designs and directly to promote the cause which enemies intend to crush, Phil. 1:12, that so they may either be reclaimed from their opposition to His truth and people or have everlasting shame poured upon them, Psa. 83:16,17, for this is the result which God brings out of all the wicked's slander and persecution of the godly, that they *may be ashamed who falsely accuse their good conversation in Christ.* [4.] The consideration of the disappointment and shame which the Lord sometimes makes wicked men to meet with here for their persecuting and slandering of His people should be a strong motive to the godly to constancy in following their duty, whatever they may suffer: for this is given to them here for their encouragement, *that whereas they speak evil of the godly, as evildoers, they may be ashamed who falsely accuse their good conversation in Christ.* [5.] To the end that the conversation of a Christian may be good in God's sight, and so may serve to make slanderers and persecutors ashamed, it must flow from a good conscience within and must be a conversation in Christ, the person being by faith united to Him, and enabled to draw virtue from Him for walking unto well-pleasing, John 15:5, and to aim at conformity in the conversation to His carriage, 1 John 2:6; for both these are necessary for that conversation of a Christian which may make persecutors ashamed and which deserves to be called a good conversation: *Having a good conscience, that whereas they speak evil,* &c, *they may be ashamed who falsely accuse your good conversation in Christ.*

17. For it is better, if the will of God be so, that ye suffer for well doing, than for evil doing.

The fourth motive to press the former directions and to encourage against suffering is, that in their suffering for Christ and their duty to Him they should find much more comfort and spiritual advantage than if they did procure sufferings to themselves by their miscarriage. And this fourth motive, or encouragement, has a fifth in the bosom of it, that they should not be put to a necessity of suffering except it were the good will of the Lord so to dispose.

Hence learn, [1.] Christians have much more spiritual advantage, honour and sweetness in suffering for Christ and in duty to Him than they could have in suffering for their faults, though they had obtained mercy for them from the Lord, and had peace in their spirits while they did stoop to the stroke of human justice inflicted for these faults; the former sort of sufferings being more conformed to Christ's, and having ordinarily a larger allowance of peace and cheerfulness than uses to be let forth to them who suffer for their faults, though they were never so sure of God's mercy: for in this sense must the Apostle be understood here to compare suffering for well doing and for evil doing, and to prefer the one to the other; because suffering from men for evil doing, without obtaining mercy from God, has no goodness in it at all; and so cannot be compared in that with suffering for well doing, as here it is by the Apostle: *For it is better to suffer for well doing, than for evil doing.* [2.] The consideration of this difference in regard of comfort and spiritual advantage, which is between suffering for well doing and for evil doing, should move the Lord's people to watchfulness and tender walking, lest by their miscarriage, they deserve suffering at men's hands; and to constancy in suffering for well doing, considering that they have within them strong inclinations to such evils as, being acted, might justly put them to suffer before men; and that if they shift duty to Him, for fear of suffering from men, He may justly leave them to fall into those sins which may procure harder sufferings, with less comfort, than what they should have met with in suffering for well doing: for this is here brought in as a motive to constancy in duty and suffering in the way of duty, *that it is better to suffer for well doing, than for evil doing.* [3.] Suffering for well doing is a duty that does not bind, as negative precepts do, at all times and in all cases; nor are the children of the Lord tied to it as they are to some other positive duties, for the opportunity whereof they are to watch, 1 Pet. 4:7, but is only binding when the Lord by His providence has brought His people under the power of persecutors, and they do put them to a necessity either of suffering or sinning: in which case only, the Lord manifests His will to His people that they should suffer: for the Apostle here commends suffering not absolutely as other duties, but only upon this supposition, that it be manifested to be the will of God; *For it is better, if the will of God be so, that ye suffer for well doing, than for evil doing.* [4.] When God's will that His people should suffer is manifested to them by leaving them no midst[1] between sin and suffering, then they ought with courage and cheerfulness to choose suffering as the only best course for them, considering that His will is a good will

[1] 'midst': middle way.

to them and so would have prevented their suffering if it had been good for them; that without His will no creature could bring them to that necessity: and that, as it is His will that they should suffer for Him, so it is His will they should reign with Him: for this is here cast in as a special encouragement to constancy in suffering for well doing, that they should not be put to undergo that lot, except *the will of God be so.*

18. For Christ also hath once suffered for sins, the just for the unjust, that he might bring us to God, being put to death in the flesh, but quickened by the Spirit:

The sixth motive or encouragement to constancy in duty, notwithstanding of hardest sufferings, is taken from Christ's sufferings for us, whence many encouraging arguments to suffer for Him may be drawn. The sum of all which is, that since the innocent Son of God has completely satisfied God's justice for unworthy sinners that He might reconcile them to God, having for that end suffered to the very death in His humanity; and that He might apply His purchase, is raised up again by the power of His Spirit or Godhead; it does therefore well become His sinful followers, for whom He died and rose again, to undergo cheerfully a suffering lot in following their duty to Him.

Hence learn, [1.] Of all motives that may prevail with Christians to suffer for Christ when they are called, His suffering in their room is one of the strongest and should be most frequently made use of by them for that end, considering that He by His sufferings has taken the sting out of all theirs, Isa. 53:4, has defeated all their enemies, John 16:33, Col. 2:15, has cast them a sweet copy to follow concerning the right way of suffering, Heb. 12:2, has engaged them not to desire a better lot than He had, John 15:20, and has made sure their perseverance and eternal happiness, which none of their troubles can mar, Rom. 8:38, for the Apostle, having made use of this same argument to this same purpose in the close of the former chapter, does here again insist upon it as the strongest, and that which should have most weight with all His redeemed ones, to move them to suffer for Him: *For Christ also hath suffered for sins.* [2.] As the whole time of Christ's humiliation was one uninterrupted course of suffering, so by that whole course, and especially by His offering Himself a sacrifice for us upon the cross, He has so completed the work of satisfaction to God's justice for the sins of the elect, and of purchasing grace and glory to them, that nothing thereof remains to be done, nor need that sacrifice be again repeated: for though His sufferings were finite in regard of duration, yet in regard of the worth which the excellency of His person who was God did add to them, they were infinite: for both in respect of the continuation of His sufferings throughout His state of humiliation, and in regard of the completeness of them for satisfaction to God's justice, as also in opposition to all the legal sacrifices which for their imperfection behoved to be often repeated, Heb. 7:27, the Apostle says here *He hath once suffered for sins*. [3.] Although our blessed Mediator had all the sins of all the elect upon Him by imputation, 2 Cor. 5:21, and the punishment laid upon Him of all the heinous crimes that ever were, or ever shall be committed by the elect, Isa. 53:6, yet was He in Himself completely just and righteous, not only as He is God, Isa. 45:21, but even as Man, He being wholly freed of that original contagion, Luke 1:35, wherewith all others that are come of *Adam* are defiled, Job 14:4, and completely conformed to the Law of God in heart and practice, Matt. 3:15, that so, as our Mediator, He might be lovely to God, Psa. 45:7, and to all the saints, Canticles 5:16, for so the Apostle sets Him forth who suffered for sins, *the Just for the unjust*. [4.] There was nothing in those for whom Christ suffered to have moved Him to lay down His life for them, many of them who were then living being His actual persecutors and murderers, and all of them being still at enmity with Him, till He by the virtue of His death changed them; and yet His free love made Him suffer for their sins: *The Just for the unjust*. [5.] As all are naturally far from God, Eph. 2:13, and the godly at their best at a distance and unable to come nearer, Canticles 1:4, so this is the comfortable end of Christ's death and His intention in dying, that sinners might be brought to a state of nearness, to wit, of favour and reconciliation with God, Col. 1:21, and that being done, to a growing nearness, to wit, of communion and fellowship till they be completely one with Him, John 17:11,20,21, &c, for thus does the Apostle express the end of Christ's death and His intention in dying that He might lead us by the hand (as the word here signifies) and give us ready access to a reconciled God; He has suffered for sins, the Just for the unjust, *that He might bring us unto God.* [6.] No lesser degree of suffering could be accepted from our Cautioner[1] than the suffering of death, there being no other way, except all had eternally died, to illustrate the exact justice and righteousness of God in punishing sin, Rom. 3:24,25, and his faithfulness in executing that just threatening, Gen. 2:17, to take away the sting out of the first death to His own, 1 Cor. 15:55, and keep them from tasting of the second, John 8:51, for which cause the Apostle here affirms of our Mediator, that *He suffered, being put to death.* [7.] Although Christ did truly humble Himself, even in respect of his Deity, by assuming frail flesh, in a personal union therewith, John 1:14, and obscuring the glory thereof for a time with the veil of flesh, Phil. 2:6,7, yet (the Godhead being altogether impassible), His sufferings were properly in His humanity, to wit, both in His soul which suffered the unspeakable wrath of God, John 12:27, Matt. 26:38, and in His body which suffered all sorts of torments whereof it was capable, Luke 22:44, both which parts of human nature are here comprehended in one, because His soul suffered only while it was dwelling in flesh, before His death: *being put to death in the flesh.* [8.] Our Cautioner[1] having paid our debt could not be held in the prison of death, but, by the power of His own Spirit, or Godhead, which are essentially one, was quickened in His humanity by the union of His soul to His body, and raised up as an evidence that He was discharged of our debt and we in Him, Rom. 4:25, as a pledge that we shall be quickened by the virtue of His resurrection to newness of life, Rom. 6:4, &c, and after death raised to possess glory with Him, 1 Cor. 15:20, for He was *put to death in the flesh, but quickened by the Spirit.* [9.] All the considerations of our suffering Mediator whereof the Apostle here mentions several, are strong inducements to His redeemed people to suffer for Him when He calls them to that honour: for so may every particular here mentioned be applied; that since the Son of God, being so innocent and just, did suffer, and by suffering did so completely satisfy justice for such mis-deserving wretches, and did suffer to the very death for so sweet an end to bring sinners to God, and had so glorious an outgate,[2] it becomes all His redeemed ones to adventure cheerfully upon suffering for Him: to which every expression here may be

---

[1] See page 13.
[2] 'outgate': a passing from one state to a better.

applied as a motive: *For, even Christ hath suffered for sin, the just for the unjust, that he might bring us to God: being put to death in the flesh, but quickened by the Spirit.*

19. **By which also He went and preached unto the spirits in prison.**
20. **Which sometime were disobedient, when once the long-suffering of God waited in the days of Noah, while the Ark was a preparing, wherein few, that is, eight souls, were saved by water.**

Here is the seventh argument, pressing upon Christians constant obedience to the Gospel, notwithstanding of hardest sufferings. The sum whereof is that since there are many souls of men and women to whom Christ did once by his Spirit, in the ministry of *Noah* and others of his servants, make plain the way to life and salvation, who are now imprisoned in Hell for ever-more, because of their slighting so much patience and pains as the Lord did exercise toward them, especially during the time of Noah's preparing the Ark, wherein a few only escaped destruction by the flood; therefore it concerns those who have the Gospel more clearly preached to them to give obedience thereunto, whatever they may suffer for it within time.

Hence learn, [1.] The second Person of the blessed Trinity has been exercising His mediatory office long before His incarnation; and by His Spirit, the third Person, speaking through His servants, has been publicly inviting sinners to repentance, and faith in himself: for this preaching to the old world here spoken of must be the same in substance with that which is more clearly held forth now under the Gospel, it being Jesus Christ, the same yesterday, and today and for ever, Heb. 13:8, who did then preach by His Spirit, who speaks His mind only, John 16:13,14. *By which he went and preached.* [2.] When the mind of Christ is plainly held forth by the ministry of His servants, then Christ Himself comes to them, to bestow Himself and fellowship with Him by His Spirit, upon them that receive His Word; and to deal with others in wrath as if they had rejected Him, immediately and in His own Person dealing with them: for though Christ did not preach in Person to the old world, but only in the ministry of Noah and others of His servants, yet of Him it is here said that *by His Spirit He went and preached.* [3.] It pleases the Lord to invite to repentance and make offers of His grace unto many

145

who will never obey His counsel nor embrace His offers, that He may make His grace more manifest while He does more effectively prevail with His own that are among them, Acts 18:10, and may take away all excuse from them that wilfully disobey His counsels and reject His offers, John 15:22, for there are spirits or souls who once had Christ preached to them that are *now in prison*. [4.] The souls of men and women do not go to nothing, nor die as do their bodies; but so soon as they are separated from the body must either go immediately to the place of blessedness, Luke 23:43, or else to this place of their everlasting imprisonment: for though it could not be told where their bodies were that drowned in the flood, yet their souls are to the fore and existing as *spirits in prison*. [5.] Hell is a place of safe custody, as the name of it here imports, where there is no liberty but for devils and damned souls to torment one another, out of which there is no possibility of escaping, for by this prison can be meant nothing else but Hell (which elsewhere in Scripture has this same name, Rev. 20:7) it being the place where only the spirits of them who were disobedient to the Lord are *now in prison*. [6.] Of all the sins that men and women commit who have the way of salvation truly preached to them, this is of the highest nature and the chief cause of their damnation, that they will not be persuaded to accept the offers of God's grace and mercy in Christ, will not obey the sweet directions of His Word, will not follow the motions and strivings of His Spirit with them thereby; in which course whosoever do continue, they look like those that are appointed for the prison of Hell: for it is clear by comparing this text with Gen. 6:3, that these here spoken of had offers of forgiveness of sin, and eternal life through the Messiah, invitations to repentance and holy walking, and some motions of His Spirit working with His Word; and yet though they were guilty of many gross and filthy sins, as appears by the sixth and seventh chapters of Genesis, their disobedience to the Gospel, or unwillingness to be persuaded thereby (as the word signifies) is here set down as the chief cause of their perpetual imprisonment in Hell; those *spirits are in prison, who sometime were disobedient*. [7.] The Lord does not at the first give over dealing with despisers of His saving counsels, and rejecters of His blessed offers, but does defer their deserved punishment, and draw out His patience in length toward them, as the word here signifies, that they may be the more inexcusable and He may have the glory of long-suffering and patience after it is expired: for upon those *who are now in prison, the long-suffering of God once waited in the days of Noah.* [8.] No length of time can make the Lord forget His mercies, which impenitent sinners have abused. Even when they are in Hell He will remember them, and make them to remember them, for the increase of their unspeakable torment and vexation, Luke 16:25, for here the Spirit of the Lord, speaking by this Apostle, declares to the world that He is mindful of the despising of His patience and pains, manifested many thousand years ago, toward them that are now in Hell: *Once the long-suffering of God waited in the days of Noah,* &c. [9.] Even those who may have good hope through grace that they are delivered from the pit of destruction ought to consider the woeful case of them that are there as a means to keep them from provoking the Lord by those sins which bring souls to that prison; and as a motive unto thankfulness to Jesus Christ and constancy in duty to Him, notwithstanding of temporary sufferings, who has delivered them from the same: for here the case of the damned for disobedience to the Gospel is presented by the Apostle to the consideration of those who (as he supposes in the former words) might comfort themselves in their exemption from wrath by Christ's sufferings, as an argument to constancy in holiness, notwithstanding of hardest usage from men: which is the Apostle's scope to press. [10.] When the Lord vouchsafes to send His Word unto a people, He uses also with it to frame His workings and dispensations so as may be most fitting for bearing-in His Word upon them, that if they reject and slight both, their stripes may be double: for beside that Christ went and preached to the old world, He made a work to be wrought before their eyes which was a visible preaching of wrath to come upon them except they did repent, and a real invitation of them to repentance, that they, seeing such a small vessel in comparison of the great multitude that were upon the face of the earth, every one might have studied to be one of those who might have had entry into it; *He went and preached, and his longsuffering waited while the ark was a preparing.* [11.] Whensoever the Lord has judgments to bring upon the generality of a people, it is His way to provide sufficient means of safety for His own that are among them; sometimes, from the outward judgment, as here, and always from the evil of it, Psa. 91:10; for while judgment was approaching upon the old world, *the Ark was a preparing, wherein few, that is, eight souls, were saved.* [12.] Though there never were wanting, nor will be at any time, some true

147

believers in Jesus Christ, in regard of His standing relation of a husband and head to the church, yet so far may profanity or error overspread the face of the church that the number of visible professors may be very few; and therefore the multitude of such can be no real mark of the true church: for here in all the world there are but a few (and of those, a great part wicked, for what may be gathered from the Scripture history) *that is, eight souls, saved by water.* [13.] It may fare the better with the wicked in this life (though nothing in that which is to come) that they have been in society with the godly, and have outward relations to them, partly for the more satisfaction and encouragement of the godly who are tied to them by natural bonds or affection, and partly that they may be some way serviceable to the godly in the work of the Lord; for which causes, among others, there are here *eight souls* (whereof some were of a wicked disposition, and cursed, Gen. 9:22,25) *saved by water.* [14.] The Lord can make that which is the means of destruction to the wicked a means of safety to His own; for the water which drowned the rest of the world bears up the Ark; and so proves a means of the safety of these eight, *who were saved by water.*

21. **The like figure whereunto, even baptism, does also now save us (not the putting away of the filth of the flesh, but the answer of a good conscience towards God) by the resurrection of Jesus Christ:**

The eighth encouragement to constancy in suffering for Christ and His truth is that since believers have a spiritual privilege answerable to the Ark, sealing their safety from the deluge of God's wrath, to wit, their baptism; not the external part of it alone, which can only remove the filth of the body, but the internal, to wit, the application of Christ's blood to the conscience of believers which the Apostle expresses here by the effect thereof, that thereby believers may challenge all Christ's purchase as theirs, and answer all challenges to the contrary; and that upon this ground, that their Cautioner[1] is absolved from their debt, whereof His resurrection is the evidence. Therefore they have no reason to faint in following their duty or fear to be lost in the midst of their sufferings.

[1] See page 13.

Hence learn, [1.] Whatever outward privilege any of the Lord's people had of old when he was working in a more extraordinary way than now, every ordinary believer may find in Jesus Christ a spiritual privilege answerable to it: faith can feed upon Christ the bread from heaven, John 6:32,35, as the *Israelites* did upon the manna; it can draw spiritual life and health from Him as the stung *Israelites* had health to their bodies by looking to the brazen serpent, John 3:15,16, and can find spiritual and eternal safety in Him through His own means as in an Ark, when others are perishing in the deluge of His wrath: for though believers in the Apostle's time had not such an extraordinary way of preservation from persecution as *Noah* and the few with him had from the flood, yet they have a spiritual privilege answerable to it and of a far better nature: *the like figure whereunto even baptism doth also now save us.* [2.] Baptism does in a spiritual sense resemble the Ark in so far as few in comparison of the rest of the world do partake even of that outward ordinance, as few were in the Ark, in that it is equally dispensed to good and bad who are within the visible Church; as but such were admitted into the Ark; in that it exempts all that partake of it according to Christ's appointment from the common case of the rest of the world and does seal to the elect safety from that wrath which destroys the greatest part of the world: in which and the like respects it is here compared with the Ark; *The like figure whereunto even baptism doth also now save us.* [3.] Although the spiritual and eternal salvation of believers be only the effect of the merit of Christ's blood applied to the conscience, yet does the Spirit of Christ in Scripture oftentimes ascribe the same to the instrument or means by which He conveys that salvation to them (compare with this place, Luke 7:50, 1 Tim. 4:16) that so he may keep up due respect to His own means, which if they be neglected or despised by them that have the opportunity of them, salvation cannot be expected. Therefore says the Apostle, *Baptism doth now save us.* [4.] There is no small hazard of people's placing too much in the external and outward part of the ordinances, as if that of itself were of some efficacy for salvation; against which the ministers of Christ have no less need to guard in their doctrine, than against people's undervaluing of the ordinances: for after that the Apostle has asserted baptism to be the means of our salvation answerable to the Ark, lest any might persuade themselves of salvation because they had received the external baptism, he adds as a guard, *not the putting away of the filth of the flesh*. [5.] The internal baptism, to wit, the application of Christ's merits, is known to be bestowed upon sinners by the effects thereof upon their conscience: which do appear, first, when they answer to the Lord's offers and commands in the gospel, by their hearty acceptation of the one and engagement in His strength to obey the other. Secondly, when they become humbly familiar with God, in laying claim to the purchase of Christ's death as theirs. And thirdly, when they are taught of Him to answer the accusations and challenges that may be brought against them in doing of the former two: for all these three which make a good conscience, to wit, *stipulation* or engagement, *claim* or challenge, and *apology* or answer, are in the signification of this word which the Apostle makes use of here to express the internal part of baptism, to wit, the application of Christ's merits by the effect thereof, which effect manifests the cause, *even the answer of a good conscience*. [6.] Christ's resurrection, is to the believer one chief ground of this answer of a good conscience formerly described, from whence he may justly claim to absolution from guiltiness, since His Cautioner's[1] discharge is evidenced by His resurrection, Rom. 4:25, and to virtue for subduing of his corruptions, since He who purchased it is risen to apply it, Rom. 6:9,11,12, and to through-bearing strength under all trials, since, the Head being risen, the members must needs be where it is, John 14:3, and from thence also may answer all objections drawn from his guiltiness and from the strength of his corruption and from his weakness to go through trials, which might discourage his heart or dispute his faith, Rom. 8:33, for here the Apostle shows how the believer has this answer of a good conscience, to wit, *by the resurrection of Jesus Christ*.

22. **Who is gone into heaven, and is on the right hand of God; angels and authorities and powers being made subject unto him.**

The last encouragement to Christians under all their sufferings has three branches. Firstly, that since their Head and Mediator is gone in their nature and name to possess heaven. Secondly,

---

[1] See page 13.

CHAPTER 3 : VERSE 22

since He is in highest dignity and power with God. And thirdly, since He has all the heavenly hosts of angels at His command, therefore none of His followers need to fear suffering in following their duty to Him.

Hence learn, [1.] Christ's withdrawing of His bodily presence from His people at His ascension is so far from being matter of discouragement to them as the disciples did mistake it, John 16:5,6, that by the contrary it is to them a well-spring of much consolation whence they may with joy draw answers to every discouragement. He being gone to heaven that He may pour out of His Spirit more plentifully than He did before His ascension, John 7:39, Eph. 4:10, and having in that very act of His ascension triumphed over all our spiritual enemies, Psa. 68:18, and made a patent access to us to enter heaven by our faith and prayers since He is gone there in our nature and name, Heb. 6:19,20, and 10:19, &c, for, as a consolation against sufferings and ground of the answer of a good conscience, is this brought in, that *Christ is gone into heaven*. [2.] The high esteem and power which Christ as our Mediator has with the Father, signified by His sitting at His right hand, Eph. 1:20, &c, having the fulness of grace and glory given Him to dispense to His redeemed ones, Acts 5:31, is another strong ground of believers' consolation, whence also they have the answer of a good conscience to all challenges given-in against them, His sitting there, being a clear evidence to them that the work of their redemption is completely done, Heb. 10:11,12, that the Father is abundantly satisfied therefore, Psa. 110:1, Rom. 8:33,34, for this is another branch of their encouragement, that *Christ is on the right hand of God*. [3.] Whatever be the order or several degrees that are among the angels in heaven, into which we are not curiously to enquire, seeing it is not made known in Scripture, yet this is sure, that Jesus Christ, not only as He is God but as He is our Mediator, has all of them subject to Him, as His messengers and mighty hosts, having authority from Him for the defence and comfort of the godly, Psa. 34:7, Heb. 1:14, and for the terror and punishment of His and their enemies, Psa. 68:16,17, for of Him as our Mediator is this spoken, that *He has angels and authorities and powers subject unto Him*. [4.] The consideration of this subjection of all the angels and heavenly host to Jesus Christ the Mediator may be very comfortable to the few oppressed godly, especially when the

151

powers and authorities on earth and their messengers and hosts are employed against them, as in this Apostle's time they were: for this is here given to believers as the last branch of their encouragement in this chapter, that they serve and suffer for such a Master as has *angels and authorities and powers subject unto Him.*

CHAPTER FOUR

In this chapter (which contains an enlargement of the former purpose) the Apostle does, by several arguments, press upon the redeemed the study of holiness; and gives them many encouragements against suffering in that way, which are the two principal parts of the chapter. The sum of the first is that believers should renounce the slavery of their sins. Firstly, because they were esteemed judicially to have suffered for sin in their Cautioner,[1] Christ (vv 1,2). Secondly, because they had already followed too long the filthy fashions of the profane (v 3). Thirdly, because those who did wonder at and slander them for changing their course and company, behoved to give a sad account thereof to their Judge (vv 4,5). Fourthly, because censure and opposition from the profane had been the lot of the saints departed (v 6). And fifthly, because time was now near an end, therefore they should keep themselves in a praying disposition (v 7), make conscience of love (v 8), and of hospitality toward the saints (v 9), and employ their talents and gifts in their several places for the glory of Christ (vv 10,11).

The sum of the second part is that hardest sufferings should not seem strange to believers: considering, firstly, that they were sent to try their graces (v 12); secondly, that by them they were made conformed to their Master; and thirdly, should share of His glory (v 13); fourthly, that even reproach for faithfulness to Christ should prove them happy; fifthly, that they should be sure of the presence of His Spirit with them; sixthly, that He did resent their wrongs as done against Himself; seventhly, that He did esteem Himself glorified by their sufferings (v 14), providing they did not procure these sufferings by their miscarriage (v 15) but endured them with courage and cheerfulness for the truth of Christ (v 16); eighthly, that God's appointed time was now come for purging of His Church by such hot persecution that even the godly could not come to heaven but with great difficulty; and lastly, that the end of their ungodly persecutors behoved to be unspeakably terrible (vv 17,18). It was therefore

---

[1] See page 13.

153

their best to commit themselves to Him whose power and faithfulness is engaged to bear them through all their trials (v 19).

1. Forasmuch then as Christ hath suffered for us in the flesh, arm yourselves likewise with the same mind: for he that hath suffered in the flesh, hath ceased from sin;

The Apostle's scope in the first part of this chapter being to stir up the redeemed of the Lord to fight against sin and to give themselves wholly away to the obedience of their Redeemer, as appears from vv 2 and 7, &c, he brings his first and principal argument for that purpose from Christ's sufferings for them and their interest in these sufferings: the sum whereof is, that seeing Jesus Christ had in their name and nature suffered the wrath due to them for their sins, they ought to put on this very same consideration as a complete armour against all temptations, and that because believers being esteemed judicially to have suffered in the Cautioner,[1] they are thereby strongly obliged to desist from those sins for which Christ has suffered and for which they are reckoned to have suffered in Him. So that the last clause of this verse cannot be understood of Christ who never sinned; but of the believer who is reckoned a sufferer in Christ and to have ceased from sin in regard of Christ's undertaking to make him cease from it, and of the obligation that Christ's suffering in his room puts upon him to mortify it, which makes the matter as certain as if it were done: and therefore the Apostle speaks of it in the past time as if it were already done.

Doctrine: [1.] They that would make use of Christ's sufferings for them as a motive to suffer for Him must learn to make use of them for mortifying of their lusts, by faith drawing virtue out of His death, for weakening the love of sin in their hearts: the strength and vigour whereof is the main thing that makes Christians shift[2] a cross for Christ and indisposes them for carrying it aright, Matt. 16:24, for the Apostle, having taught believers in the last part of the former chapter to make use of Christ's sufferings for them as a motive and encouragement to suffer for Him, he here teaches them to make a further use of His sufferings as necessary to be joined with the former, if so be they

[1] See page 13.
[2] 'shift': to decline, escape from.

would attain unto it, to wit, that by faith they should draw virtue from His sufferings for mortification of their corruptions; *Forasmuch then as Christ hath suffered, arm yourselves,* &c. [2.] Christ our Mediator has taken true flesh upon Him and in it has suffered all that wrath which was due to the elect for their sins, so that His sufferings were not to be a pattern only to Christians of a right way of suffering, but they were in the room and place of the elect as is clearly imported in this ground which the Apostle lays down in the beginning of this chapter, from whence he is to infer and press upon believers the study of mortification: *Christ hath suffered for us in the flesh.* [3.] As those for whom Christ has suffered in the flesh and who cannot therefore be overcome by their spiritual enemies, Col. 2:15, must, notwithstanding, make them for a battle and a fighting-life with those enemies; so they are of themselves naked and without armour for this spiritual warfare till they receive the same from Jesus Christ; and not only so but they are often found secure and forgetful of their warfare and therefore have need to be roused up to lay hold upon their spiritual armour and to accept of the same from Jesus Christ, as is imported in this military exhortation, *Arm yourselves.* [4.] The believer's best armour against his spiritual enemies, especially temptations to sin, is the believing consideration of Christ's suffering in His name and nature, which cannot but give him courage and strength in the battle, seeing by these sufferings of Christ for him his spiritual enemies are spoiled of all power of overcoming though not of molesting; and so he may be sure of victory, 1 Cor. 15:55,56,57 for with this very same consideration or notion (as the word signifies) that Christ has suffered in our room and nature, the Apostle exhorts believers to arm themselves against all temptations; *Forasmuch then as Christ hath suffered, arm yourselves,* &c. [5.] Whatever sufferings were inflicted upon Christ, the same are judicially reckoned to be inflicted upon believers in Him, He being their surety, Heb. 7:22, and a common person representing them all, Rom. 5:18,19, for the Apostle having in the first part of the verse asserted Christ's sufferings for believers, in the close of it he designs[1] the believer as if he had suffered in his own person; *he that hath suffered in the flesh.* [6.] None that do truly believe their union with and interest in suffering Christ Jesus can continue in the slavery and servitude of sin, they being, by their believing of their union with

---

[1] See page 37.

Him who suffered for them, certified of the mortification of sin, Rom. 6:6, and so encouraged in the battle against it; and by His love manifested in His suffering, powerfully constrained never to take pleasure in that which put Him to so much pain and does so much grieve His Holy Spirit, 2 Cor. 5:14,15. Therefore the Apostle speaks of their ceasing from sin, as a thing already done in regard of the certainty of it and their obligation to it, it being ordinary in Scripture to affirm the duty of believers as already done by them, thereby to assure them that it shall be done, and to oblige them the more strongly to the study of it, Col. 3:9,10. *He that hath suffered in the flesh, hath ceased from sin.*

2. That he no longer should live the rest of his time in the flesh to the lusts of men, but to the will of God.

In this verse, the Apostle expresses the end of Christ's sufferings and of believers' interest therein: the attaining whereof should be their constant aim, to wit, that no more of their time in this mortal state should be spent in the service of those lusts, whereunto corrupt nature leads unregenerate men; but that their life and time should be wholly spent in conforming themselves to the will of God, who gave Christ to suffer for them: whereby it appears that the *ceasing from sin,* spoken of in the former verse, must be understood of the believer's obligation to the study of mortification of it, and of Christ's undertaking to make him cease from it, as the original word there used, signifies.

Hence learn, [1.] Whoever believes that Christ has suffered for them should think themselves thereby obliged not to give the least part of their life or time in the flesh to the service of their lusts, or to take the least part thereof from obedience to the will of God, but to employ the same entirely and wholly in the mortifying of sin, wherein they should have no more pleasure than if they were dead men; and in conforming themselves to the will of God, in doing and suffering which should be the great business of their life, considering that their time is short and their strength while they are in frail flesh but small, which is here insinuated as a reason of this truth: for this the Apostle makes the end of the believer's union with suffering Christ and the use that he should make of this privilege, that Christ has suffered for him and that he is esteemed to have suffered in Christ, to wit, *that he no longer should live the rest of his time in the flesh to the lusts of men, but to the will of God.* [2.] Christians cannot but be slaves to their own unmortified corruptions, and servants to the lusts one of another, making it their very trade of life so to do, until they do by faith *arm themselves* with the consideration of Christ's undertaking to deliver them from that servitude and of His purchasing virtue by His death for that effect: for while the Apostle exhorts them thus to *arm themselves*, that they might no longer live to the lusts of men, he does clearly import that before their so doing they had been slaves; and until they did so they could not but live the rest of their time *in the flesh, to the lusts of men.* [3.] Then it is made clear to the believer that Christ has suffered for him, and that he is reckoned to have satisfied God's justice in Christ his Cautioner[1] when by faith he draws virtue from Christ to make him aim at the mortifying of his corruptions, and at conformity to the revealed will of God in heart and practice: for this may be looked upon as the clear mark of those who may conclude that Christ has suffered for them in the flesh and who are esteemed to have suffered in Him, that they have now ceased from sin and *live no longer to the lusts of men, but to the will of God.*

3. **For the time past of our life may suffice us to have wrought the will of the Gentiles, when we walked in lasciviousness, lusts, excess of wine, revellings, banquetings, and abominable idolatries:**

The second argument whereby the Apostle presses upon believers the study of holiness, especially that part of it which consists in the mortifying of sin, is that they had given too much of their time already to the service of their lusts, wallowing themselves in all sorts of vileness against both Tables of the Law, after the manner of the heathen, among whom they were scattered: whereof the Apostle gives here some instances. The first is *lasciviousness*, whereby is meant such open vileness and wantonness in sin as is contrary to common honesty. The second he calls *lusts* which signifies those strong and burning desires which are in unrenewed hearts after more and more wickedness, especially their sinful pleasures. The third, fourth, and fifth point out their excess in drinking and belly-cheer, with their shameless and unseemly carriage while they kept up a sinful society together. And the last is, their idolatry or false worship in

---

[1] See page 13.

a special way detestable to God. In all which steps, and others of that kind, they having too long walked already, ought therefore now to think it more than time to break off that course and to consecrate the remnant of their time to the study of holiness, for His honour whom they had formerly so much dishonoured.

Hence learn, [1.] Whenever the Lord makes a gracious change upon the hearts of sinners they will be so far from putting off and delaying the forsaking of their sins till afterward that they will with grief look back upon the time they have already given way to them, as very long and too long to have been employed that way: so that they who mind to live any longer in the course of their sins have no ground to think that they have yet met with the power of converting grace, seeing they say in substance that they have not yet taken time enough to dishonour God, and destroy their own soul: for this is the sad language of every real convert: *the time past of our life may suffice us to have wrought the will of the Gentiles.* [2.] The longer sinners have continued in the course of their sins, and the greater height of wickedness they have been at before their conversion, the more eagerly should they set about the mortifying of sin and the more assiduous and serious should they be in the study of holiness after their conversion, that so they may, so far as they can, restore the Lord to His honour, 1 Cor. 15:9,10, reclaim, if it be possible, some of those whom formerly they have hardened in their sin, Gal. 1:13, and get their own hearts loosed from the love of those sins which long continuance and custom have deeply rooted in them, Jer. 13:23; for the Apostle makes this a reason why believers should give no part of their life or time to the service of their lusts, but employ the same wholly in obedience to the Lord that they had spent so much thereof in the slavery of sin already and had been at so great a height in wickedness: *For the time past of our life may suffice us to have wrought the will of the Gentiles, when we walked in lasciviousness, lusts,* &c. [3.] Jesus Christ has suffered for and conferred His saving grace upon some of the vilest of the children of men, that He may proclaim His grace and love to be most free by bestowing it upon those who have nothing in them but what is loathsome in His sight, and most powerful in coming over and doing away so much vileness, and adorning the soul where it was with his beautiful grace: for the Apostle clearly supposes here himself and other converts for whom Christ had suffered in the flesh to have been really such as are here described, *working the will of the Gentiles, walking in lasciviousness, lusts, excess of wine,* &c.

[4.] It does much concern all true converts to entertain in their hearts the lively apprehension of the several steps of their former vileness, wherein they have wallowed themselves before their conversion, that they may be still vile in their own eyes, considering how dishonourable to God they have sometimes been, and may have their hearts frequently raised in the praises of Him who has graciously pardoned and powerfully changed them, 1 Tim. 1:13, &c., and may manifest much compassion and meekness in their carriage toward those who yet remain in that condition wherein themselves once were, Tit. 3:3,3, for here the Apostle represents to his own heart and the hearts of other converts the several branches of that profane disposition and course wherein they had lived before their conversion, to wit, *that they had wrought the will of the Gentiles, walked in lasciviousness, lusts, excess of wine,* &c. [5.] True penitents will not stand to[1] proclaim and aggreage[2] their own vileness, when it may serve for the glory of Christ's free grace in pardoning and changing of them, and may provoke others to mortification and holiness: for here the Apostle puts himself in the catalogue of these who had *walked in lasciviousness, lusts, excess of wine,* &c. [6.] They who would reflect aright upon their disposition and carriage before their conversion, should not only make their more gross practices, but the very inward motions and lusts of their hearts toward those sins which possibly they have never committed, and consider with what strong bensell[3] of spirit they have been inclined to, or did commit those iniquities, and call to mind the several sorts of their sins against both Tables of the Law, such as their abusing of God's good creatures to be fuel to their lusts, their following the example of others, their serving of others, or hardening of them in their sins by evil example, their forsaking or corrupting of the right worship of God and the like: that by the distinct and clear up-taking of all, they may be the more humble and the more provoked to praise God and to be diligent in their duty: for such a representation is here given to converts of their former disposition and carriage that they had in time past *wrought* (with great intention and bensell[3] of spirit, as the word signifies) *the will of the Gentiles* (by following their examples, serving and encouraging them in their sins), *walking* in outward *vileness,* and inward *lusts,* in *excess of wine,* and such other gross

---

[1] 'stand to': to refrain from.
[2] 'aggreage' (aggrege): to make to appear more grave.
[3] 'bensell': determination.

sins against the second Table: and in abominable idolatries against the first Table. [7.] Where the love of sin is entertained in the heart and profanity given way to in the practice, contrary to the second Table, there is ordinarily joined therewith a forsaking or corrupting of the right worship of God, contrary to the first Table; a spirit of strong delusion in the matters of religion and God's worship being the ordinary and just plague of God upon those who frame not their heart and manners according to the rule of the Word, 2 Thess. 2:10,11,12, for this is the last instance of their profane course and may be taken for the consequent of the rest, that *having walked in lusts, excess of wine*, &c., they did also *walk in abominable idolatries*. [8.) As every sin is hateful to the Lord, Psa. 45:7, and should for that cause be so to all His people, Zech. 8:17, so He has a special detestation of the sin of idolatry, whether that more gross kind of it whereby that external worship which is due to God is any way given to a creature, Exod. 32:5, Psa. 106:19,20, or that which is more spiritual, whereby the affections of the heart are poured out excessively upon anything beside God, were it never so lawful in itself, Col. 3:5. Therefore is this epithet expressly added to the last step of their wicked course here mentioned: *abominable idolatries*.

4. **Wherein they think it strange that you run not with them to the same excess of riot, speaking evil of you:**
5. **Who shall give account to him that is ready to judge the quick and the dead.**

Follows a third argument whereby the Apostle presses the study of holiness upon believers and removes a great discouragement out of their way. The sum whereof is, that however they who had now changed their course and company might expect to be made a wonder to the profane, and disgraced by them so far as they could, for not joining with them in their profane courses formerly described, yet this ought to be no discouragement to the godly in the way of holiness in regard that these their mockers and persecutors behoved shortly to give a strict and sad account of their way to the Judge of all.

Hence learn, [1.] Men that are left of God to live in any sinful course are very unwilling that any should part company with them in their way, and are strongly desirous to have others infected with their sins, that so there might be none to make them ashamed and many to encourage them in their evil way, Psa. 64:5, for so much is imported in this, that *they think it strange that others run not with them to the same excess of riot*. [2.] Were the course of profane men never so vile, and even such as nature's light cannot but condemn, yet it is to them matter of great admiration[1] that any should abandon the course which they follow, because they apprehend a paradise in the satisfaction of their lusts, 2 Pet. 2:13, and the true sweetness which is in Christ's service is wholly hid from them, Prov. 14:19. Therefore *they think it strange that others run not with them to the same excess of riot*. [3.] It does not satisfy graceless persons to go at leisure in the way to their own destruction, but being acted upon by that violent spirit of Satan they make all the haste they can toward their own ruin, as men in a race do for a great prize, as the word here signifies, and will not spare to spend their bodies and spirits and waste their means in the service of their lusts, and cannot be satisfied with any that will not do the like, as is imported in the signification of these words: *They think it strange that ye run not with them to the same excess of riot*. [4.] Profane men cannot abide that the godly should be in credit and reputation beside them, partly because of their natural enmity against them, Gal. 4:29, and partly because their way is a shame and reproof to theirs, as Christ's was to his enemies, John 7:7; therefore they devise and spread false calumnies to hurt the credit (as the word here signifies) of the godly, *speaking evil of you*. [5.] Even the godly are so little mortified to their credit before the world, and do so little prize esteem with God and his people, that the mockery and slanders even of profane men are ready to prove a great discouragement to them in the ways of the Lord: for the Spirit of God finds it necessary here to guard against this discouragement by discovering of it and threatening the slanderers; *they think it strange that ye run not with them*, &c, *speaking evil of you; who shall give account*, &c. [6.] Although the saving grace of Christ does not loose those upon whom it is vouchsafed from the relations they may have to graceless persons, nor from the duties of those relations, neither yet from fellowship with them in necessary commanded duties, 1 Cor. 5:9,10 and 7:12,13, 1 Sam. 11:6,7, 2 Cor. 11:20, &c, yet it will make them separate from their sinful fashions and loathe their company in their sinful courses, even though they should be wondered at and evil spoken of for

---

[1] 'admiration': wonder, perplexity.

so doing: for the Apostle imports clearly that those converts to whom he speaks would not now keep fellowship with their former companions in their sinful courses whatever they might suffer at their hands, while he says, *They think it strange that ye run not with them to the same excess of riot.* [7.] Although a long-suffering God may let wicked men have a long time of prospering in their sinful ways and persecuting of His beloved people, yea, and may defer His reckoning with them the whole length of their time, yet, of necessity, they must all of them at last appear before Him as their Judge at the great day, when both those of them that have died before that time and such as shall then be found living be present to give account to Him *that judgeth quick and dead.* [8.] The delay of the last reckoning with wicked men is not because the Lord is not ready for that work, but because there is yet a number of the elect to be gathered, Rev. 6:11, their faith and patience are to be tried, Rev. 14:12, and the wicked to be more ripened for judgment, Rev. 14:15. So that there is nothing upon the Lord's part that hinders the day of account; for He is *ready to judge the quick and the dead.* [9.] So dear are the Lord's people to Him, and so exact is He in his justice, that there is not a thought in wicked men's hearts, nor a word in their mouths contrary to Him or His people, but He takes notice of it and will exact a strict account thereof from them: for here the Spirit of God signifies His notice-taking of their admiring[1] thoughts of the godly and their ill speeches of them, and assures His own that for these they shall give account to Him who is ready to *judge the quick and the dead.* [10.] Although the children of the Lord should not desire a woeful day upon the most wicked for any personal injury they have received from them, Jer. 17:16, nor rejoice when it comes upon them, because they are their enemies, Prov. 24:17, but rather should pray for their conversion and salvation, Matt. 5:44, yet it is both lawful and necessary for the Lord's suffering people to consider how glorious the Lord will be in His justice upon so many of them as are irrecoverable and without the compass of his electing love; and thereby they ought to comfort their hearts against their bitter slanders and other injuries of that kind: for this is here given as an encouraging motive to the study of holiness, notwithstanding of any discouragement from such, that they shall *give account to Him, that is ready to judge the quick and the dead.*

[1] See page 161.

6. For, for this cause was the gospel preached also to them that are dead, that they might be judged according to men in the flesh, but live according to God in the spirit.

The fourth argument to constancy in holiness notwithstanding of any discouragement from the profane world is, that seeing the Gospel had been preached to the saints who are now at their rest for this very end, that they being exercised in their external condition with the hard censures and persecution of the profane, might have the life of grace promoted in their hearts, and so be fitted for life eternal, there was therefore no reason why the Lord's people should be discouraged in that way because of such a lot as all the saints departed had met with.

Doctrine, [1.] All that believe the Gospel and give themselves up to the obedience of it may resolve to have many hard censures passed upon them by those that do not profit by it, to be judged of them, a deceived and accursed people, John 7:47,49, a proud and precise company, who will not do as neighbour and others do, Mark 7:2,5, to have many false calumnies raised and spread of them, Rom. 3:8, and to be condemned to the worst usage that wicked men can bring upon them, Jas. 5:6, for this is here set down as the lot of the saints departed and the consequent of their embracing the Gospel: For, *for this cause the gospel was preached to them that are dead, that they might be judged according to men in the flesh*. [2.] Although the Gospel of itself tends to the making of peace both with God and amongst those that hear it, Rom. 10:14, Luke 19:42, and the Lord does no way approve profane men's censuring, or condemning them that embrace it, Luke 10:6, yet does the Lord send the Gospel among men for this very end, that upon occasion of His people's embracing of it, wicked men may vent their natural enmity against Him by their persecuting of His people, that so they may be justly punished for that and other of their sins, and His own people may be exercised by their opposition for their good; which are just and holy ends upon God's part: For, *for this cause was the gospel preached to them that are dead, that they might be judged according to men*, &c. [3] It gives much encouragement to the Lord's people in the way of their duty against all discouragements from the profane, to consider, firstly, that they are not singular in a suffering lot, seeing the same has fallen to the saints before, in whose person God has given a proof of His power and goodwill to bear His own through all their trials;

secondly, that the troubles from wicked men can reach no further than their flesh or outward man and the concernments thereof; thirdly, that those troubles can continue no longer than their dwelling in the flesh; and fourthly, that all their hard exercises are carved out not by the lusts of men but by the holy and wise providence of God: for these considerations are here presented to the godly for their encouragement against the mockery and persecution of the profane, that the same had been the lot of the saints now departed, that it was measured out by the Lord, that it could only reach their flesh, and them only while they were in frail flesh, as is imported in these words; For, *for this cause was the gospel preached to them that are dead, that they might be judged according to men in the flesh.* [4.] God's great end in sending and keeping up the Gospel among His own is that they, being quickened by His Spirit, which He communicates to them through the preaching of the Gospel, Gal. 3:2, may be enabled to live the life of faith, John 20:31. and holiness, 2 Cor. 3:18, and may have also a life of consolation here, 1 John 1:4, and a life of glory hereafter, 1 John 5:13. All which is imported in this great end of preaching of the Gospel to the Lord's people. *that they might live according to God in the spirit.* [5.] The life of grace and of consolation could not thrive so well in the hearts of the godly, nor could they be fitted for the life of glory, except they met with trials and opposition from the wicked world, to stir them up to the exercise of their grace, Rom. 5:3, and to cry for a further measure of it, Psa. 119:25, to loose their hearts from this life, and make them long for a better, 2 Cor. 5:2. *For, for this cause the gospel was preached to the saints departed, that they might be judged according to men in the flesh, but* (by the blessing of God upon the Gospel and upon their hard exercise from the wicked) *might live according to God in the spirit.*

7. **But the end of all things is at hand: be ye therefore sober, and watch unto prayer.**

The fifth argument to the study of holiness, notwithstanding of discouragements in the way thereof, is, that wicked men's opposition and the godly's sufferings, and all things of that nature, would shortly be at an end: from which , together with the former arguments, the Apostle infers seven directions for attaining to a right carriage in duty, under so much opposition from wicked men, whereof three are comprehended in this verse. The first is, that they should manifest moderation and prudence in their disposition and carriage. The second is, that they should be much with God in prayer. The third is, that they should carefully watch against every thing that might mar their intercourse with God in that duty.

Hence learn, [1.] It cannot now be long to the end of time and all things in it, whether we compare the remainder of time with that which is already past, or the whole of it with eternity; or whether we consider how near the end of time and all things in it is to every particular person: in all which respects the Apostle expressly asserts here that *the end of all things is at hand.* [2.] The Lord's people could not faint in their duty, nor be discouraged because of opposition in the way of it, if they entertained the believing consideration of the nearness of the end of wicked men's persecution and of their pains in duty and sufferings for it: for this is here given as an encouraging argument to constancy in duty, notwithstanding of opposition in the way thereof; *That the end of all things is at hand.* [3.] They that would carry themselves aright under much discouraging opposition in the ways of the Lord, and would keep themselves in a fit disposition for meeting with Him at the end of all things, must study sobriety, which consists in a mean esteem of ourselves for our gifts or graces, Rom. 12:3, in the exercise of right reason and Christian prudence in compassing our affairs, Mark 5:15, and in a spare meddling with such earthly delights as may indispose us for our Christian warfare, 1 Thess. 5:8; for this is the first particular direction which the Apostle gives for a right carriage in duty under opposition, and which he infers upon the nearness of the end of all things as the way to be prepared for the same: *Be ye therefore sober.* [4.] None can hold out in their duty when they meet with discouragement in the way of it, nor can keep themselves in a right disposition for the end of all things, but those only who keep much correspondency with God by prayer; in which exercise His people receive from Him light and strength to carry themselves aright, and encouragement against all that might discourage them in His way: for this is the second thing recommended to them that would persevere in their duty, even under opposition, and be fit for the end of all things, that they should *watch unto prayer.* [5.] None can expect acceptance or success of their prayers except they join therewith watchfulness, that so they may furnish themselves beforehand with matter for prayer, Psa. 5:1, that they may discern and make use of the fittest opportunities for the discharge of that duty, Psa. 55:17, that they may eschew in their ordinary carriage what may mar their access to God in prayer, and the return of the same, 1 Pet. 3:7, and may carefully observe what answers of their former prayers they have from God, Hab. 2:1, for in order to this duty and as a necessary prerequisite of it, watchfulness is here pressed: *Watch unto prayer*.

8. And above all things have fervent charity among yourselves: for charity shall cover the multitude of sins.

The fourth direction to the Lord's people for attaining to a right carriage under so much opposition from the profane, which the Apostle infers from the former arguments to the study of holiness, especially that taken from Christ's love to His own manifested in His sufferings, is that they should labour for fervency of affection one towards another; and this the Apostle presses with great earnestness as the sum and chief of all the duties we owe to our neighbour; and bears it in by this argument, that love will prevent and pass many mutual wrongs which cannot but mar comfortable society among the Lord's people.

Hence learn, [1.] Next unto our love to the Lord Jesus which is the first and great command in the law, Matt. 22:38, love to His people ought to be studied above all other things, it being the main evidence of our love to Him, 1 John 5:1, and His love to us, 1 John 3:14, and that which makes way for every other duty to our neighbour, 1 Cor. 13:4; for the Apostle, supposing love to Christ to be in the hearts of those to whom he writes (chap. 1:8), presses this love to others of His people in the next room as that which should have the precedency of any other duty: *Above all things have fervent charity among yourselves*. [2.] They that love Christ should not only entertain love in their own hearts to others of His people, whatever their estate or condition be, but should likewise labour to procure and cherish hearty love in and among all the rest of God's people: for this direction, as it presses upon every one of the Lord's people love toward one another, so it presses upon every one of them the entertaining and promoting of mutual love among others: *Have fervent charity among yourselves*. [3.] The more hatred and opposition the children of the Lord meet with from the profane world, the more warmness of affection should they entertain and express towards one another, that so the comfort they have in one another's affection may make up to them the discouragement they have from their wicked enemies; for while this people were exposed to many discouragements from the profane, as is clear from the former words, the Apostle with great earnestness presses them to this as that which would sweeten their sad lot: *Above all things have fervent charity among yourselves.* [4.] It is not enough that the Lord's people keep themselves free of malice and hatred one of another; neither yet that they have such a measure of affection toward one another as they ought to have toward all men, Tit. 3:2, yea, even their very enemies, Matt. 5:44. but they must beware of all cold-riseness of affection one toward another, and labour for such a height of love as may keep them always in a bensell[1] to do one another good, and such as may not be interrupted by the failings one of another: for such a measure of affection is here pressed by the Apostle in these words, wherein there is a metaphor from a bow that is bent: *have fervent charity among yourselves.* [5.] None of the children of the Lord have ground to expect such a society of His people to converse with in this life, in whom they may not discern many failings and wrongs, and those often reiterated both against God and against one another, which cannot but mar the benefit and comfort of their society, unless one of them can pardon and pass by a multitude of such in others: for this argument imports that there will be among the saints, *a multitude of sins to be covered.* [6.] Although the Lord's people ought not to justify or connive at the faults one of another, Lev. 19:17, but with zeal and meekness point them out to them and reprove them, Gal. 2:11, which should be much desired and well taken by one of them from another, Psa. 141:5, yet where true love is it will not be interrupted by the discerning of these, but will cover them by pardoning the wrong done to the person that has love, Eph. 4:32, interceding with God for pardon of the wrong done against Him, Jas. 5:16, hiding our knowledge of such wrongs from the party injuring, as we may in charity think they will challenge themselves for, Prov. 12:23, and all of them, so far as may be, from the profane, Prov. 11:13, who can make no better use of their knowledge of them than to take occasion from them to loathe and disgrace religion, 2 Sam. 12:14, Rom. 2:24, and especially by furthering the repentance of the guilty

[1] See page 159.

person and their use-making of the blood of Christ, Jas. 5:20, whereby alone sin is covered from God's justice, Psa. 31:1,2; for the covering of sin here spoken of is not attributed to love, as if it could either justify ourselves or others, but because it is a grace that pardons and hides wrongs done against them that have it and furthers others, what it can, to seek the Lord's forgiving of these wrongs also; *Love covereth a multitude of sins.* [7.] The consideration of the many wrongs and sinful infirmities that one of the Lord's people may discern in another should be so far from weakening the affections of one of them toward another and so marring their comfortable society, that by the contrary it should move them to study the greater fervency of affection, that thereby they may cover these infirmities and by their so doing be the more like their Lord whose love kythes[1] in covering a multitude of sins in every one of His own, Eph. 4:32, for it is here brought in as a reason encouraging to the study of fervent charity, that thereby they should *cover a multitude of sins.*

9. Use hospitality one to another without grudging.

The fifth direction is that they should prove the fervency of their love one to another by their kindly entertainment of such Christians as wanted those outward accommodations which others had; and this duty the Apostle qualifies, that it ought to be made conscience of without any fretting or mal-content-ment.

Hence learn, [1.] It may be the lot of the Lord's dear people to be without house or harbour,[2] or any such worldly accommodations of their own, and to be put to live upon the charity of others: for in such a case are several of the Lord's people here supposed to be, while the Apostle commands them to *use hospitality one towards another.* [2.] The Lord does not ordinarily bring all of His people in a like hard condition at once, but in hardest times uses to keep some of them in a capacity to be helpful and comfortable to others: for while there are some that want lodging and accommodation of their own, there are others of His people that have these things to give to such as want them, as is supposed in this exhortation, *Use hospitality one to another.* [3.] Although human laws do not bind Christians to the duties of

---

[1] 'kythes': becomes known or manifest.
[2] 'harbour': shelter.

charity, nor punish them for the neglect thereof, yet the supreme Law-giver has enjoined these duties as strictly as any other, and therefore, no question, will be as terrible to the neglecters of these duties as of any other duties, Matt. 25:44, for this text is the poor's right to a share of the accommodations and society of the rich, and the Lord's order to the rich for giving the same to the poor: *use hospitality one to another.* [4.] Duties of charity to the Lord's people in necessity ought to be done without fretting or mal-contentment, either at the poor as being burdensome, or at God's providence for casting so many objects of charity in our way; and consequently they ought to be gone about willingly and pleasantly, considering that the Lord esteems of them as done to Himself, Prov. 19:17, and that He delights exceedingly in our cheerful performance of such duties as are expensive to us, 2 Cor. 9:7, for thus does the Apostle qualify the right manner of performing this duty of hospitality, that it be *used without grudging.*

10. **As every man hath received the gift, even so minister the same one to another, as good stewards of the manifold grace of God.**

The sixth direction which the Apostle infers upon the former arguments is that they would mutually communicate all their receipts for the glory of Christ and the good of others: and this he presses by two arguments. The one is that whatever they had was a free gift flowing from the grace of God. The other is that they were not absolute owners but dispensers or stewards of those various gifts and graces of God.

Hence learn, [1.] There are none of the Lord's people who have not received some gifts from Him, which being rightly employed may be made forthcoming for His glory and the good of others of His people. This is supposed while the Apostle thus exhorts, *As every man hath received the gift so let him minister the same*, &c, *that God in all things may be glorified.* [2.] It has pleased the Lord to dispense His gifts variously among His people, giving to some more talents and to some fewer, Matt. 25:15, and different measures of the same gifts to several persons, Rom. 12:3, that all may know that all fulness is only in Himself, Col. 1:19, and that every one may make use of that gift or degree of gift in another which themselves lack, 1 Cor. 12:21. For this variety of the Lord's dispensing of His gifts is imported in this direction of the

Apostle's, while he thus exhorts in the beginning of the verse, *As every man hath received the gift*, &c, and while he calls those gifts in the latter part of the verse *the manifold grace of God*. [3.] Whatever gift or talent any of the Lord's people have that may be any way useful for His glory and the good of others, that is a free gift to them, flowing from the undeserved grace of God, there being nothing foreseen or found in any that can merit the least good at God's hand, Rom. 11:35, as is clearly held forth in the signification of this word, *As every man hath received the gift*. [4.] None of the Lord's people have received any gift from Him for themselves alone, but that they may lay forth the same for His glory and the good of others, as is imported in this direction, *As every man hath received the gift so let him minister the same*. [5.] The children of the Lord have much need of His Spirit, that they may discern the gifts they have received and so may know what is freely bestowed upon them, 1 Cor. 2:12, that they may neither undervalue their receipts as useless and so hide their talents in a napkin, nor yet take upon them what they are not able for, but may put forth their gifts in their stations for the glory of God and others' good, suitably to the measure they have received; *As every man hath received the gift, so let him minister the same*. [6.] All our receipts ought to be communicated with much diligence and activity, as also with humble condescendency, to profit those that are inferior to us, as being in that, servants to others: for both diligence and condescendency are imported in the signification of this word, *Let him minister the same*. [7.] The consideration of the freedom of God's grace in bestowing any of His gifts should strongly move all His people heartily to lay out the same for His glory and the good of others. So that we may never think upon any of our receipts but as free gifts, and thereby may be moved to communicate the same, the Spirit of the Lord has put such a name upon them here as in the original signifies a gift of grace, and a gift whereby others may be gratified: *As every man hath received the gift*. [8.] The Lord's people are not to look upon themselves as owners of any gifts they have, so as they may use the same at their pleasure, but as dispensators and stewards, as the word here signifies, who ought to dispose of their receipts according to the mind and direction of the Giver of them, communicating the same seasonably and with discretion, considering the several tempers of the rest of the family, to whom they are to give out these gifts, and faithfully as those that must give account how they have employed all that they have received, as good stewards use to do. All which is imported in the manner of Christians dispensing of their gifts, here held forth in a metaphor, *As good stewards of the manifold grace of God.*

11. If any man speak, let him speak as the oracles of God; if any man minister, let him do it as of the ability which God giveth: that God in all things may be glorified through Jesus Christ, to whom be praise and dominion for ever and ever. Amen.

The last direction is concerning the right manner of communicating what they have received; of which the Apostle gives two instances. The first is concerning the communication of things spiritual, which are to be communicated by word: and for that he exhorts that it be done (whether by public ministers or private Christians in their stations) with that reverence and confidence which is suitable to the majesty and certainty of divine truths. The second is concerning the right way of communicating things temporal; and for this he exhorts that those be given forth (whether by all Christians, whom charity obliges to supply one another's necessities, or by those who have an office in the House of God, to gather and distribute the charity of the rest) in a way suitable to every one's ability, and with such a willing and cheerful frame of spirit as the Lord vouchsafes upon them; and withal he proposes the right end that Christians should have before them in all their duties, and especially in this, the communication of their receipts, to wit, the glorifying of God through Jesus Christ: upon the mentioning whereof the Apostle's heart rises to ascribe eternal praise to Him, wherewith the first part of the chapter is closed.

Hence learn, [1.] All that speak anything to others of the matters of God (as private Christians in a private way may do, for their mutual edification, Judg. 5:10,11, Mal. 3:16, especially to those under their charge, 1 Tim. 5:4), and more especially those who have an office in the House of God for that end, ought to study the right manner of delivering the mind of God, that they speak nothing but what they understand and are clearly persuaded to be His truth, as the word here signifies; that they speak the same with plainness, that there may be no ground for people to doubt the meaning, as ordinarily there is of Satan's oracles, which use to be doubtful and ambiguous; that they speak seasonably, with reverence and humility, as becomes the mind of God: all which is imported in this direction, prescribing the right manner of communicating spiritual receipts, which is to be done by speech, *If any man speak, let him speak as the oracles of God.* [2.] As every Christian ought willingly to give out of his worldly substance for the supply of the necessities of others of the Lord's people, and that with due consideration how far his ability may reach, so as his charity may neither be unsuitable to the Lord's liberality towards him, 1 Cor. 16:2, nor prejudicial to duties of equity, Rom. 13:8, especially to those of his near relations, 1 Tim. 5:8; so those who have an office in the House of God for gathering and distributing the charity of others ought to discharge the same with faithfulness and diligence, cheerfully going about the meanest duty of their office; for this last part of the Apostle's direction may be understood both of the deacons and of every private Christian, and likewise of the proportion which should be between their charity and their ability; as also of their stretching themselves to the utmost of the grace given unto them, to do those duties of charity in a right manner; *If any man minister, let him do it as of the ability which God giveth.* [3.] As there is a great proneness in all men naturally, whereof the regenerate are not free, to seek their own glory, especially in the giving out of their receipts, as is imported in the Apostle's proposing this end to believers in the communication of their gifts that God may be glorified, so none can acceptably employ their best gifts unless their main end be that God the Giver may be praised, both by the dispenser of these gifts, and by those that are profited by them, for the giving of such gifts to men, and the heart to let them forth for so holy an end as this, *that God in all things may be glorified.* [4.] As every gift we have comes to us through Jesus Christ, John 1:16, so all the glory that redounds to God by the right use of these gifts must be given to Him (whether by the dispenser of them or those who are profited by them) through Jesus Christ, in whose strength they are rightly employed, John 15:5, who makes His people intend the glory of God in all things, Isa. 61:3, John 17:10, and makes their intention to glorify Him accepted by his merits, Heb. 13:16; for this glorifying of God, which is here proposed as the end to be intended both by them that let out their gifts to others and by those to whom they are dispensed, must be through Jesus Christ: *That God in all things may be glorified through Jesus Christ.* [5.] Although the essential glory of God be so infinitely great that it can receive no addition, Neh. 9:5, and His dominion in itself so absolute and large that it cannot be more, Psa. 115:3, yet it is the duty of all His people, especially His ministers, to declare that glory of His, to wish that it may be ascribed to Him by all, and that His dominion may be voluntarily acknowledged and submitted to by all: for, so does the Apostle here: *To Him be glory and dominion for ever.* [6.] So full of desires to have Christ glorified and submitted to by others, should the hearts of all be that love Him, especially His ministers, that they should be ready to intermit other purposes and burst forth in His praise, thereby to provoke others to that duty: for so does the Apostle here: *To Him be glory and dominion for ever.* [7.] Our desires to have the glory of the Lord manifested, and His dominion over all acknowledged, and willingly submitted to, should reach the length of eternity in regard we are obliged to Him by favours of infinite worth, for which we will never be able to give Him the glory due to Him: *To whom be glory and dominion for ever.* [8.] We ought to raise our hearts in praise by the consideration of the Lord's faithfulness in performing of His promises, and to close that exercise for the time with the hearty acknowledgment thereof and with our faithful engaging of ourselves to glorify Him, by believing of His faithfulness; for this Hebrew word *Amen* signifying faithfulness, is used in all languages, importing that all tongues should, and must, at last give to God the glory of faithfulness; and is made the ordinary close of our prayers and praises to signify our acknowledgment of His faithfulness and engaging of ourselves faithfully to every duty that may honour Him. *Amen.*

12. Beloved, think it not strange concerning the fiery trial which is to try you, as though some strange thing happened unto you:

The second part of the chapter contains several directions for attaining to a right disposition and carriage under a cross for Christ, and several encouragements against the same. The first direction propounded negatively is, that they should not be amazed or perplexed at their hottest sufferings, as men used to be when they meet with some new and strange thing. The first reason pressing this direction is that their hardest sufferings were but to try their graces and purge away their corruptions, and therefore ought to be well taken.

Doctrine, [1.] Christians under a cross, especially for Christ and truth, stand in need of frequent directions and encouragements, and those borne-in with much affection, they being then in hazard to take some sinful course for their ease, or else to suffer heartlessly and in a way unbeseeming their Master; and ready also to think themselves forgotten or slighted by others: for which and the like causes it is that the Apostle, having been upon this subject of directing and encouraging sufferers frequently before in this Epistle, does here return to it again and make way for it by this loving compellation, *Beloved, think it not strange*, &c. [2.] The children of the Lord have not only trials, but fiery trials to prepare for, which are such as do deprive them of the sweetest of earthly comforts and reaches to that which is dearest to them as men, their credit, liberty and life, Matt. 16:24, and such as few professors will abide, Zech. 13:9, for such trials are the godly here forewarned of, and supposed to be in, while the Apostle thus directs, *Think it not strange concerning the fiery trial.* [3.] So unwilling are the children of the Lord to forecast sore trials and so make them familiar to themselves before they come, Heb. 12:5, so subject to security even when trials are nearest, Matt. 26:40, so ready to dream of much worldly ease, Act 1:6, and when they get but a little breathing-time from trouble, to promise themselves perpetual exemption therefrom, Psa. 30:6, that they are in great hazard to be surprised and perplexed at the sight of approaching trials, as men used to be at the sight of anything strange and terrible, which they did not forecast and prepare for; as is imported in this direction, *Think it not strange concerning the fiery trial, &c, as though some strange thing had happened unto you.* [4.] However fiery the trials of the Lord's people be, there is no reason why they should seem strange to them, seeing they are so frequently forewarned of them in Scripture, considering that the best of the saints, and the Captain of our salvation, have gone through trials as hot, Heb. 12:1,2,3 and especially that they are assured of One with them in the hottest furnace of affliction they can be put in, who will quench the violence of the fire that it shall not consume them, Isa. 43:2,5. Therefore they should not think it *strange concerning the fiery trial, as though some strange thing had happened unto them.* [5.] One main end for which the Lord exercises His people with fiery trials is that they may have proof of the strength of His grace in them for their comfort, Rom. 5:3, and a discovery of their weakness thereof also, and of the much dross of corruption which is with it, for their humiliation and purging, Isa. 27:9, for this the Apostle affirms of the hottest sufferings of the godly, *that they are only to try them.* [6.] The consideration of these excellent advantages which the Lord's people have by trials should guard their hearts against offence thereat: for this, that afflictions are but to try them, is here held forth as a special reason why they should not take uncouth[1] with them: *Think it not strange concerning the fiery trial which is to try you, as though some strange thing happened unto you.*

13. **But rejoice, inasmuch as ye are partakers of Christ's sufferings; that when his glory shall be revealed, ye may be glad also with exceeding joy.**

The second direction for a right disposition and carriage under the cross for Christ which the Apostle propounds positively is, that they should count it great matter of joy to be honoured to suffer for Christ. And this, together with the former direction, the Apostle bears in by two further arguments. The one is that by their sufferings for Christ they were made conformed to Him in His suffering, and did partake of the fruits of His sufferings for them. The other is, that their sufferings for Christ were to them sure pledges and forerunners of their sharing with Him of His glory at His second appearance.

Hence learn, [1.] It is not enough for the Lord's people to have their hearts kept free of discouragement under the cross, or amazement at it, as a strange lot; but they ought also to rejoice in their sufferings for Christ as the matter of their great honour and happiness: which frame of spirit may be attained to under the hottest trials wherewith the Lord's people can be exercised: for after the Apostle has exhorted them not to think it strange concerning the fiery trial, he adds this second direction, *But rejoice,* &c. [2.] Those who are honoured to suffer for Christ do in a special manner partake of His sufferings, in regard they have a special measure of that wisdom and strength which He purchased by His death, communicated to them under their trials, Rev. 12:11, are then brought to a nearer conformity with Him in his estate of humiliation, Rom. 8:29, do undergo what He esteems done to Himself, Acts 9:4, and do fill up their share of these sufferings which divine providence has carved out for Christ mystical, Col. 1:24. In all which respects, sufferers may be said to partake of the sufferings of Christ; every one whereof

---

[1] 'take uncouth': that is, view (the afflictions) ignorantly.

ought to be a strong motive to cheerfulness and constancy under sufferings for Him: for to this end does the Apostle give this reason, comprehending all these privileges: *Inasmuch as ye are partakers of the sufferings of Christ.* [3.] Although Christ's essential glory be always one and the same, Heb. 13:8, yet His declarative or manifested glory is sometimes much hid and veiled, as it was in a special way during the time of His personal humiliation, John 17:5, and will be so in a great measure till all His suffering members share in His glory at the last day, at which time He shall be clearly manifested to be fully glorious; as is imported in this other reason of joy in suffering for Christ: *That when His glory shall be revealed, ye may be glad also,* &c. [4.] The Lord has reserved the fulness of the joy of His people till the time of the full manifestation of His own glory at His last appearing, that His own may long much for that day and may not take it ill to suspend their joy while His glory is under a veil: for *when His glory shall be revealed, they shall glad with exceeding joy.* [5.] As Christ's second coming will be a glad day to all that believe in Him, 2 Thess. 1:10, so there is a special measure of joy and gladness reserved for them who get grace to go cheerfully through a sad suffering lot in the world for His sake; in the consideration whereof He does allow them to comfort themselves against their sufferings, and does not esteem it a mercenary disposition in them so to do: for to sufferers is this consolation given, as especially verified in them, *That when his glory shall be revealed, they shall be glad with exceeding joy.*

14. If ye be reproached for the Name of Christ, happy are ye; for the Spirit of glory and of God resteth upon you: on their part he is evil spoken of, but on your part he is glorified.

The Apostle adds to the former three arguments several others, to encourage them against sufferings. The fourth is, that even their enduring disgraceful speeches for Christ should prove a means and evidence of their happiness; and therefore much more their greater sufferings. The fifth, which explains their happiness, is, that the glorious Spirit of the Lord delights to reside in the hearts of sufferers; which must be understood of some special operations of Him, seeing He dwells or rests in the hearts of all His own whether they be put to suffering or not. The sixth is, that the reproaching of the godly is taken as done against that glorious Spirit of God residing in them. And the seventh is, that the constant enduring of that and other degrees of their sufferings is esteemed much glory to that glorious Spirit.

Hence learn, [1.] Although even those of the Lord's people who do not decline suffering for Him are very strongly desirous to suffer with credit before men, Psa. 119:22, yet they ought to expect reproach as a main ingredient in their trials, whereby their reputation will be stained in the minds of many, and foul crimes to make them detestable laid to their charge, as the word here signifies: for this is supposed to be a part of their trial against which the Apostle here guards and comforts them: *If ye be reproached*, &c, *happy are ye.* [2.] As there are several kinds of trials wherewith the Lord's people are exercised, and every one is not tried with the same kind; so the Lord takes notice of all the degrees and kinds of their trials, were it but an envious look, 1 Sam. 18:9, or the least disdainful gesture, Psa. 22:7, Isa. 58:9, and will not suffer the lesser sort of their sufferings to lack their own consolation and reward; and particularly He takes notice of all disgraceful expressions against His people, which is the particular trial here spoken of: for having comforted them against fiery trials in the former verse he here comforts them against reproach, *If ye be reproached for the Name of Christ, happy are ye.* [3.] Even those who are not put to the hottest kind of sufferings are ready to miscarry and be discouraged under the lesser, because the best are not easily brought to deny their own strength, till they be under some extremity, 2 Cor. 1:9, for this is imported in the Apostle's guarding and comforting against reproach, *If ye be reproached for the Name of Christ, happy are ye.* [4.] The consideration of the greatness of the reward which the Lord graciously bestows upon the least degree of suffering for Him should make His people joyfully undergo the greatest and most fiery of their trials. If it be a happiness to be reproached for His sake, it must be a great happiness to be killed for His sake: for the Apostle makes this a reason why they should rejoice under fiery trials, that to be reproached for Him was a happy thing: *If ye be reproached for the Name of Christ, happy are ye.* [5.] It is not the sufferings of Christians, but the cause for which they do suffer, which makes them happy, to wit, their suffering for the profession of the Name of Christ, for adhering to His truth and their duty to Him and out of respect to His glory: for this is the qualification of a right sufferer, who may count himself happy in his sufferings: *If ye be reproached for the Name of Christ, happy are ye.* [6.] The third Person of the blessed Trinity is glorious in

177

Himself, being God equal with the Father and the Son, 1 John 5:7, and works glorious effects in the hearts where He dwells, such as the bestowing and increasing of grace which is begun glory, 2 Cor. 3:18, giving clear foresights of glory, Eph. 1:17, and sometimes sweet foretastes thereof, Rom. 8:23; in which respects He is here called *The Spirit of glory and of God*. [7.] As the Spirit of the Lord constantly abides in the hearts of all believers, in regard of some of His operations, John 14:16, especially in regard of His preserving the seeds and habits of grace, and keeping the saints from final apostasy, 1 John 3:9, so He has ordinarily a more glorious and more constant residence in regard of His comfortable and supporting operations, in the hearts of sufferers than of others; and though He has not tied Himself to fill the hearts of His suffering people always with sense and comfort, but may withhold the same from the dearest of them under their sharpest sufferings, and put them to live by faith as it was with David and Christ Himself, Psa. 22:1,2, &c., yet oftentimes their allowance of comfort is larger and their enjoyment of His sensible presence longer than what others have who are not put to suffer, and sweeter than what themselves have had before suffering: for this is here held forth as an encouragement made out in a special way to sufferers: *The Spirit of glory and of God resteth upon you*. [8.] The true happiness of believers stands in their enjoyment of the presence of Christ's Spirit, residing in their hearts, and proving Himself to be there by His gracious operations, which may be had in the midst of sharpest sufferings: the consideration whereof ought to make great joy in the hearts of sufferers: for the Apostle having pronounced such happy, he explains their happiness, which is the reason of their joy under their sufferings, *That the Spirit of glory and of God resteth upon them*. [9.] The more glorious and constant the residence of Christ's Spirit in the hearts of His suffering people appears to be, the more enraged will their profane persecutors be to speak evil of that Spirit that dwells in them, which they will be esteemed to do (though they do not expressly blaspheme the Spirit) when they father the operations of the Spirit upon Satan, Matt. 12:24,28 or when they wilfully resist and oppose His known mind delivered to them by His suffering people, Acts 7:51, for though the Spirit of glory and of God rests upon these persecuted saints, yet upon the part of their persecutors *He is evil spoken of*. [10] It may allay to the godly the bitterness of reproaches and disgraceful expressions against them, to consider that by these the Spirit of the Lord counts Himself evil spoken of, and takes as done directly against Himself those wrongs which are done to His people, who are His temple, and His workmanship and He will punish wicked men accordingly: for this may be taken as a particular encouragement against reproach that even the Spirit of God was, upon the part of them that did reproach His followers, *evil spoken of.* [11.] The Lord esteems Himself much glorified by His people's constancy in suffering for Him, while His terror, sweetness, power and other properties are proclaimed and commended by that practice of His people in choosing of affliction rather than sin against Him; and His esteeming so of it should be a strong motive to cheerfulness and constancy in suffering for Him: for this the Apostle expressly asserts as an argument to constancy and cheerfulness under suffering, *On your part He is glorified.*

15. But let none of you suffer as a murderer, or as a thief, or as an evildoer, or as a busybody in other men's matters.

Here is a third direction for attaining to a right carriage in a time of persecution; the sum whereof is that as they desire to find the sweetness of the former consolations which the Apostle had held forth to sufferers, they would keep themselves free of those evils, which even heathen magistrates under whose power they lived, would readily punish; such as wronging the persons or estates of their neighbours, meddling with things without the bounds of their calling, and other wickednesses of that sort, so should they be the less moved with their sufferings.

Hence learn, [1.] It is the duty of those who have power and authority over others to prove themselves keepers of both the Tables of the Law of God, by punishing without respect of persons, not only the grosser sorts of transgressions, such as murder and theft, whereby men injure the persons or estates of their neighbours, but also those more subtle and specious sins such as invading the rights of others, going beyond the bounds of folks' calling, which often are veiled with the pretences of zeal for God, and the public good, Numb. 16.3, which kind of sins the Apostle understands here by being busy in other men's matters; yea, all other known iniquities, whether against the first Table, such as idolatry, Job 31:26,27,28, blasphemy, Lev. 24:11, Sabbath-breaking, Numb. 15:32, or against the second Table, such as disobedience to parents, Deut. 21:18, &c, adultery, Job

31:11. All which, and the like, are iniquities to be punished by the Judge, and are comprehended here under this general clause, *evildoers*: for the Apostle supposes here that even Christians, being found guilty of any of those iniquities, ought to be put to suffer for them, while he gives them this caution, *But let none of you suffer as a murderer, or as a thief, or as an evildoer, or as a busybody in other men's matters.* [2.] Even nature's light will speak against the toleration of several sorts of evils, and will not suffer men that have power and have not put out that light, by frequent sinning against it, to pass them without punishment. What a shame then is it for these within the church to commit such things or tolerate them in others? For the Apostle supposes here that Christians who lived under heathen magistrates would certainly be put to suffer by them if they were found *murderers, thieves, evildoers, or busybodies in other men's matters.* [3.] As it is the duty of all who, by their miscarriage, have deserved the stroke of human justice, willingly to submit to the same, Luke 23:41, so it should be the great care of the Lord's people to eschew those sins which may draw them under that stroke, it being a great reproach to Christianity when the professors of it are found guilty of those things which even heathen, or such as are no better, cannot but punish, and a great hardening of wicked men in their evil ways: for which and the like causes, the Apostle gives this third direction, *But let none of you suffer as a murderer*, &c. [4.] Except Christians employ Christ's Spirit to apply that virtue which He has purchased by His death, for the changing of their nature, and mortifying of the love of sin in their hearts, and study watchfulness in their carriage, they will readily break out in those abominations for which even the heathen would justly put them to suffer: for this direction of the Apostle's does import that except Christians did watch and pray, and make use of Christ's death for mortification of sin within, to which duties He had stirred them up before, they were in hazard to break out in the sins here mentioned, and so be put to suffer as *murderers, thieves, evildoers, and busybodies in other men's matters.*

16. Yet if any man suffer as a Christian, let him not be ashamed; but let him glorify God on this behalf.

The Apostle gives some further directions for attaining the forementioned end. The fourth in number is implied in the beginning of this verse, that they should cleave to the profession of the name and truth of Christ, carrying themselves under their sufferings as His anointed ones; upon which he infers the fifth, that if they did so suffer they ought not to be ashamed of their sufferings. But on the contrary (which is a sixth direction) they should take occasion from such sufferings of giving much glory to God for honouring and enabling them so to suffer.

Hence learn, [1.] They that would have true comfort under their sufferings for Christ must first study to be real Christians, taught of Christ to know Him and His will, Acts 11:26; to have from Him the anointing of His Spirit, 1 John 2:20, whereby they are made in some measure to resemble Him in His nature and disposition, 2 Cor. 3:18, 2 Pet. 1:4, and in His offices to which He is anointed, by having power over their lusts; and in His strength, overcoming all opposition in the way of their duty, 1 John 5:4, as anointed kings to God, by offering up themselves as a sacrifice to God, Rom. 12:1, and their service through Jesus Christ, 1 Pet. 2:5, as a spiritual priesthood; by communicating the knowledge of Christ to others, especially those under their charge, Gen. 18:19, whereby they do resemble Him in the exercise of His prophetical office; and especially to be conformed to Him in suffering for Him and showing forth that meekness and constancy and other of His communicable perfections which shined in Him under His sufferings, avowing His Name and offices to which He is anointed upon all hazards: for this is to suffer as a Christian (whose name signifies an anointed one) which the Apostle here implies as necessary for all that would taste the sweetness of the former consolations; *But if any man suffer as a Christian, let him not be ashamed.* [2.] Profane Christians who may be justly put to suffer for their faults are very ready to entitle themselves to the honour of suffering for Christ; and therefore it concerns Christ's ministers to clear the cause of suffering in which Christians may comfort themselves and the right manner of suffering for a right cause: for the Apostle in this and the preceding verse sets a guard about the former consolations given to sufferers for Christ, lest they might be usurped by profane professors, justly put to suffer for their miscarriage: *Let none of you suffer as a murderer,* &c., *but if any man suffer as a Christian, let him not be ashamed.* [3.] There is no shame or contempt that the world can pour upon sufferers for Christ whereof they ought to be ashamed, but rather to despise shame for Him, as He did for us, Heb. 12:2, as they would not have Him dealing with them as if He were ashamed of them another day, Mark

8:38, for this is the fifth direction; *If any man suffer as a Christian, let him not be ashamed.* [4.] When the Lord by His providence brings a necessity upon Christians of suffering for Him and His truth, and by His grace enables them to carry themselves Christianly under the same, they owe much praise and glory to Him for putting that honour upon them; especially considering that His grace alone has prevented their falling into those sins which might justly have brought them to no less suffering and with far less credit and comfort than now, while they are put to suffer for Christ and their duty to Him: for this is the sixth direction, *Let him glorify God on this behalf, to wit, that he is put to suffer not as a thief, nor a murderer, but as a Christian.*

17. For the time is come that judgment must begin at the house of God: and if it first begin at us, what shall the end be of them that obey not the gospel of God?

Here are two further arguments to move the godly to courage and constancy under their sufferings; the one is that now God's appointed and fit opportunity was come wherein He would have His just displeasure against the sins of men, beginning first to kith[1] in his own family, the church under the New Testament, by trouble and persecution for the correction and trial of His own; and therefore they had no reason to faint under these trials, seeing the time of them was of God's appointment, and that the godly were only to endure the beginning of that which would make an end of their persecutors. The other argument is, that seeing God's just displeasure against sin was first manifested toward His own people, the end of their wicked enemies behoved to be unspeakably terrible, and therefore they had no reason to fear sufferings from them, nor to join with them in their evil ways to eschew the same.

Hence learn, [1.] Trouble and persecution cannot arise in the church when wicked men please to plot it, or set a time to the beginning of it, were their power, policy and malice never so great, but only when that fit and prefixed opportunity (as the word here signifies) is come, which has been condescended upon in the eternal counsel of God, who has also determined how long the troubles of the church shall continue, Hab. 2:3, and at what period of time they shall end, Psa. 102:13. The con-

[1] 'Kith' (Keth): See page 168.

sideration whereof should quiet and comfort the hearts of the godly under their sufferings; for it is here held forth as a ground of cheerful submission to a suffering lot that the time prefixed and fittest for that business (as the word signifies) is come. [2.] The church is the house of God whereof Himself is both the Builder, Psa. 147:2 and the foundation and chief corner stone, Isa. 28:16, wherein He delights to dwell, Psa. 132:14, and which He will therefore protect and defend, Zech. 2:5, wherein there should be everything belonging to a well-ordered family, 1 Tim. 3:15, especially holiness in the members thereof, Psa. 93:5, for so the church is here called the *house of God.* [3.] As the Lord is pleased sometimes to begin His judgments at the sins of men without the church, that thereby His own may take warning, Zeph. 3:6,7, so He sees it fitting at some other times to take another method, and to begin at his own church with sore corrections, while His enemies (who must drink the dregs of that cup, whereof His own taste but a little, Psa. 75:8, Jer. 25:29 and 17:18) are spared, that He may make use of them as a rod wherewith to scourge His children, Isa. 10:5,12, that He may prove Himself impartially just in correcting the sins of His own which are oftentimes more dishonourable to Him than the sins of others, Amos 3:2, for which and the like causes it is that *judgment must begin at the house of God.* [4.] Although there be no vindictive wrath in any of the troubles and sufferings of the godly, since Christ has borne that to the full, Rom. 5:9, and so all His paths toward His own, and consequently even persecution itself, must be mercy and truth, Psa. 25:10, yet those calamities wherewith the Lord exercises His visible church may be called judgments, not only because they are properly such, to many wicked and profane, with whom God deals by these calamities, as a just Judge punishing unpardoned iniquities, and because that same calamity, which is a merciful trial to the godly, will be turned into a judgment to their persecutors, as the Apostle imports in the latter part of this verse, but also because even persecution itself and suffering for Christ and His truth in reference to the godly, as they are always acts of the Lord's love to them, Heb. 12:6, so they may be also acts of His holy justice, correcting and humbling them for those iniquities which He has pardoned, Psa. 99:8, so that those same sufferings which the godly endure for Christ and His truth may be to them also fatherly chastisements for their faults, which in Scripture are called judgments even upon the godly, Psa. 119:75, for here the

Apostle, speaking of the trials and sufferings of the godly, says, *Judgment must begin at the house of God.* [5.] The trials and hard exercises of the church are certain forerunners of a woeful end abiding the instruments thereof, when the Lord has done His work by them; the consideration whereof should keep the Lord's people from fainting under their sufferings from wicked men, and from inclining to join with them in their evil ways, for present ease; for *if judgment first begin at us what shall the end be of them that obey not the Gospel?* [6.] As the end of all wicked men, even of these who have not heard the Gospel, shall be everlasting destruction, because they have not made use of those natural impressions of God and His will that are left in them, Psa. 9:17, so the judgment abiding those who have heard the Gospel and would not suffer themselves to be persuaded to embrace the blessed offers made therein, nor give up themselves to Christ's obedience (which is the description the Apostle gives of those whom he here threatens, supposing them to have been hearers of the Gospel) shall be so terrible as no words can express; therefore the Apostle uses this question which none can answer, *What shall the end be of them that obey not the Gospel?*

18. And if the righteous scarcely be saved, where shall the ungodly and the sinner appear?

Here the Apostle clears his former argument, to this purpose, that if even justified persons and holy walkers had such a hard lot in the world that they could not but with great difficulty, and through many fiery trials, win to the Kingdom of Heaven, those who did cast off all religion and gave themselves up to all wickedness might expect in the day of God's reckoning with them to find no place to shelter themselves from His everlasting wrath; and therefore there was no reason why the godly should fear them or join with them in their evil ways, to shun sufferings from them, seeing their end should be so terrible.

Hence learn, [1.] Although the salvation of all that fly to Christ and take themselves to the study of holiness be most sure in regard of Christ's undertaking to cause them persevere till they come to it, John 10:28, and the way to that salvation be in itself sweet, Prov. 3:17, and in regard of Christ's large allowance of strength and comfort, easy to the renewed man, Matt. 11:30, yet considering the many fiery trials that are in the way, and the believer's own weakness, it is no easy matter for them to win through to the possession thereof. The consideration of which difficulty should be so far from discouraging them in the way, that it should provoke them to put on much resolution to hold on that way in Christ's strength, notwithstanding all difficulties: for not the possibility of the elect's losing salvation but the difficulty of attaining it, by reason of many trials and their own weakness, is imported in this expression, as a motive to constancy, *If the righteous scarcely be saved*, &c. [2.] While the Lord's people are suffering and wicked persons prospering, they should put their hearts frequently to consider how woeful and unspeakably terrible the end of these wicked enemies must be when they shall be forced to appear before their Judge and shall find no place to shelter them from His fierce wrath which shall pursue them to Hell and torment them there for ever; that by such thoughts the suffering children of God may be moved neither to envy them for their present prosperity, nor incline to join with them in their sinful courses for eschewing trouble from them, Psa. 37:1,2, &c, and 73:2,17, but rather to endure sufferings from them that they may not share with them in their woeful end: for that the godly might not run with their prospering persecutors to the same excess of riot, nor faint under sufferings from them, the Apostle does again represent to their hearts the consideration of their unspeakably terrible end by this other question, *Where shall the ungodly and the sinner appear?* [3.] The consideration of this difficulty in the way of the godly's salvation is sufficient to convince us that their end must be unspeakably terrible, who are so far from taking pains to be saved that they shake off all duties of religion, as the word *ungodly* signifies; and give themselves up to all wickedness as the word *sinners* imports, and so haste their own destruction: for so much is imported in the connection of the first part of this verse with the latter: *If the righteous scarcely be saved, where shall the ungodly and the sinner appear?*

19. **Wherefore let them that suffer according to the will of God commit the keeping of their souls to him in well doing, as unto a faithful Creator.**

Lest the sharpness of the trials whereof the Apostle gave forewarning in the former words, and the difficulty of attaining salvation by reason thereof might discourage the hearts of the godly, the Apostle gives here the seventh and last direction, which is that they should give up their souls to the keeping of the Lord for whom they suffered, and so hold on in their duty notwithstanding of sufferings. And this direction the Apostle bears in by two arguments: the one is that whatever they did suffer was carved out to them, not by the lust of men, but by the goodwill of their God. The other is that under their sufferings for well doing they might be at quietness concerning the eternal salvation of their souls, and their through-bearing till they come to the possession thereof having put them in His hand who is both able to save them, having made them, and all things, of nothing; and in testimony of His good will to save them, has engaged His faithfulness in His promises to that end: and therefore believers had no reason but to go on cheerfully and constantly in their duty, notwithstanding of all their sufferings.

Hence learn, [1.] The consideration of the difficulty that is in the way of the salvation of the Lord's people, by reason of the many fiery trials they have to go through, should stir them up to make sure work about their souls by putting them in Christ's hand, so shall they have courage and strength under their sufferings: for this last direction is inferred upon the former purpose, as the first word makes clear, *Wherefore, let them that suffer*, &c, *commit the keeping of their souls to Him*. [2.] The Lord's people should more highly esteem of and be more solicitous about the preservation of their souls, especially in a troublesome time, than of all things else in the world, it being a special part of heavenly wisdom and prudence to ensure that by faith putting it in Christ's hand, so will they be sure of quietness of spirit under all their sufferings, Psa. 31:5, and will value the less other losses, their best jewel being in safety, 2 Tim. 1:12, for the Spirit of God does not mind them of taking course to preserve other things, knowing they were ready to spend too much of their care that way in an evil time, but gives them this direction for quieting their hearts, however other things went: *Commit the keeping of your souls to Him*. [3.] They that have committed the keeping of their souls to Jesus Christ, as they would have comfort under their sufferings, must hold on in the way of well doing; considering that however their souls that are committed to Him cannot be lost, yet their assurance and comfort cannot be kept but in that way: therefore the Apostle qualifies this direction, *Commit the keeping of your souls to Him in well doing*. [4.] They who, from the sense of their souls' hazard to perish for any ability themselves have to preserve them, and from their desire to have their souls in safety above all other things, do by faith, put them in the hand of a Saviour for mercy and salvation, and having so done, do betake themselves in His strength to the way of their duty, whatever they may suffer in it, they need not doubt of Christ's taking the charge and custody of the souls thus committed to him. For that they may be confident He will take the charge of them, and safely keep what is committed to Him, He thus by his Spirit, speaking through the Apostle, commands, *Commit the keeping of your souls to Him.* [5.] The sufferings of the Lord's people come not according to the lust and will of their adversaries, but are measured out and ordered by the will of the Lord, which is always a good will towards his own, making all things work for their good, Rom. 8:28. The consideration whereof should hearten them under all their sufferings: for this is here asserted as an argument to constancy and cheerfulness under their sufferings, that *they did suffer according to the will of God.* [6.] They that would have courage under their sufferings from powerful adversaries must by faith lay hold upon God's omnipotency, manifested in the words of creation. The consideration whereof cannot but give strength and courage to believers under their sufferings, they having the Lord and all His properties engaged to be forthcoming for them in the Covenant of Grace; and especially considering that their through-bearing and deliverance cannot but be easy to Him who made all of nothing: so for that the Apostle may encourage sufferers, he represents the Lord to their faith under the consideration of *a Creator.* [7.] The consideration of the Lord's faithfulness in keeping of his promises is a strong pillar of the saints' confidence, that they shall be well borne through all their trials, seeing His good will has moved him expressly to pawn His faithfulness for everything they need; particularly for pardoning their sin upon their confession, 1 John 1:9, for enabling them to the duties of holiness, 1 Thess. 5:24, and for bearing them through all their sufferings, 1 Cor. 10:13, 1 Thess. 3:2,3. For this consideration of the Lord, joined with that of His omnipotency, is here held forth to the faith of sufferers as a strong ground of their confidence, concerning the safety of their souls and their being well borne through all their trials: *He is a faithful Creator.*

CHAPTER FIVE

This chapter has three parts. In the first, the Apostle, having in-sinuate himself upon the officers of the Church, (v 1) persuades them to the prime duties of their calling, and dissuades them from the main evils incident to them, (vv 2,3) by the considera-tion of the glorious reward abiding Christ's faithful servants (v 4).

In the second part he pressed the duties of the flock, that they should be subject to their officers and one of them to another; that they should study humility, which he urges by several arguments (vv 5,6), that they should trust God with their through-bearing in these duties (v 7), and prepare themselves for the battle against Satan, their cruel and restless adversary (v 8), by faith opposing all his temptations, notwithstanding of afflictions in that way, considering that all the rest of the saints were their fellow-soldiers in this warfare (v 9).

The third part contains the close of the whole Epistle, wherein the Apostle prays for their perseverance and perfection (v 10), praises in confidence of hearing (v 11), commends the bearer of the Epistle and the Epistle itself (v 12), delivers commendations to them from other saints (v 13), exhorts them to mutual expressions of love and wishes to them all true happiness (v 14).

1. **The elders which are among you I exhort, who am also an elder, and a witness of the sufferings of Christ, and also a partaker of the glory that shall be revealed:**

The Apostle, being to press the duty of the church officers, he does in the first place insinuate himself upon them, by drawing several reasons from his own person to make his following exhortations have the more weight with them. The first is, that he who was so earnest with them had the same office with them, to the duties whereof he did excite them. The second is, that he had been an eye-witness of Christ's sufferings for the church; which did oblige him and all Christ's servants to faithfulness. The third is, that he did by faith share with them and other believers of the right to and first fruits of that blessedness which

Christ had purchased, and will in due time manifest to His redeemed ones. All which considerations might move them to take an up-stirring message well off his hand.

Hence learn, [1.] Even in the midst of persecution, and while the Lord's people are in exile and under the power of enemies to the truth, the Lord can keep up a standing ministry and his ordinances among them, in despite of Satan and all his instruments: for the Apostle, writing to the dispersed and persecuted Christian Jews supposes them to have officers, and those officers to have opportunity of going about their duty, while he thus exhorts them to it: *The elders which are among you I exhort*, &c. [2.] Even those whose calling it is to stir up others to their duty, and in whom there is no such remarkable defect in the discharge of their duty as deserves any public notice to be taken of it, have notwithstanding great need to be very earnestly stirred up to greater diligence and progress in their duty than what they have already attained, there being in the best even of Christ's ministers a strong party drawing them back from their duty, Matt. 26:41, and at their best much shortcoming in what they might attain to, Phil. 3:12,13, for here the Spirit of the Lord whose love makes Him publish the faults of His dearest servants when it is necessary, Rev. 2:4, although He see it not meet before the church in this Epistle to reprove the officers for any failing, yet does He by His Apostle very earnestly stir them up to their duty: *The elders which are among you I exhort*, &c. [3.] The duties of ministers and other office-bearers of the church ought to be pressed upon them in the hearing of the people, that so those officers may be the more engaged to their duty, and the people the more able to discern between those of them that are conscionable in the discharge of their duty and others that are not. Therefore the Apostle does not satisfy himself to write to the church officers concerning their duty in any private letter, directed to themselves alone, but insists upon their duty in this public letter directed to the whole church; and while he begins to deal with the officers he directs his speech to the people: *The elders which are among you I exhort*, &c. [4.] Those that bear office in the house of God ought to be such as are come to some maturity of age and such as are of some considerable standing in the profession of Christianity (see 1 Tim. 3:6), and especially such as for their wisdom, experience and gravity may deserve that reverence and respect which is suitable for the aged: for this title of presbyters or elders here given to the officers of the church may be safely conceived both to point at their age and their qualifications suitable to the aged: *The elders that are among you.* [5.] Christ's ministers have not only the charge of His flock, but also of their fellow-labourers, with whom they have society or correspondence in the work of the Lord and so are bound to stir up and encourage one another in their duty: for this Apostle does not only press the duty of the people but also of their church officers; and while he does it he represents himself as a fellow-presbyter or colleague with other ordinary ministers: *The elders which are among you I exhort, who am also an elder.* [6.] No minister of Jesus Christ ought to affect or usurp any superiority over other ministers, considering how much Christ was displeased with it in His own disciples, Matt. 20:25,26; and that this great Apostle, from whom the anti-christian church pretends her warrant for prelacy among ministers, while he speaks to other church officers holds forth himself only as their equal: *Who am also an elder.* [7.] As the ministers of Christ ought to take well with exhortation to their duty even from the people under their charge, who though they have no jurisdiction over their officers to call them to a judicial account, or inflict censures upon them for their faults, which does belong to their fellow-presbyters, 1 Cor. 14:32, yet they have good warrant to warn them of their duty and incite them to it with due reverence and modesty suitable to their station, Col. 4:17. So should they receive counsel and warning, especially from their fellow-labourers who ought to have more courage and skill than ordinarily the people have, to point out the duty of church officers, and ought to be looked upon by other officers who hear them point out their duty as having a calling from God through virtue of their office so to do: for the Apostle, speaking to the officers of the church, makes this an argument to prevail with them, that he who brought this message was *also an elder.* [8.] It is no easy thing for one of Christ's ministers to prevail with others of that same sacred calling by counsel and exhortation, every one of them being apt to lift up themselves above another, Luke 22:24, and at the apprehension of that frame of spirit in their fellow-labourers to have their passions stirred against them, Matt. 20:24. The consideration whereof should move all ministers to much humility and loving earnestness in dealing with their fellow labourers: for the Apostle here uses many insinuations upon the church guides, as arguments to bear in his following exhortations upon them, thereby importing some difficulty of prevailing with them, and is very humbly earnest with them, thereby casting a copy to one minister how to deal with another, as is imported in the signification of these words, *The elders which are among you I exhort, who am also an elder.* [9.] It pleased our Redeemer to suffer before witnesses, both in his agony in the Garden, Matt. 26:37, and upon the Cross, Matt. 27:39, and likewise to employ some of these witnesses to preach Him crucified to the church, thereby condescending to beget the greater certainty in the hearts of believers that God's justice is satisfied for them, Acts 5:30,31, to give us the more lively description of his sufferings, Acts 3:15, and to let us know that he has borne shame for us, as a part of the punishment due to our sins, Heb. 12:2, for which and the like causes the Apostle calls himself here, *A witness of the sufferings of Christ.* [10.] However these whom the Lord makes most instrumental to gain others to himself may expect a special reward from him, Dan. 12:3, yet everlasting blessedness, or glory, is not a thing proper to them alone, but is the common portion of all faithful ministers and believers in Jesus Christ: for the Apostle only calls himself *a partaker* (or as the word signifies, a sharer together with others, to wit, the flock of Christ, to whom his speech is directed, and their officers, whose duty he presses) *of the glory that shall be revealed.* [11.] Although the saints in this mortal state could not well endure the least glimpse of glory, much less partake of it as they shall do afterward, Mark 9:6, yet even while they are in the midst of much outward misery, and in the expectation of more, they have a right and may attain to some real participation of glory, while they are by faith united with Christ the Lord of glory, Col. 1:27, and do sometimes taste of the first fruits of that whereupon glorified spirits do live, Rev. 2:17; for the Apostle, a persecuted man and looking for martyrdom, 2 Pet. 1:14, calls himself *a partaker* (or sharer with other believers) *of the glory that shall be revealed.* [12.] Although Christ's ministers should detest the seeking of their own glory before the world, as they desire to resemble their Master, John 8:50, and the best of his servants, 1 Thess. 2:6, yet may they humbly assert any special honour that Christ has put upon them when it is manifest that their so doing may tend to His glory and the advantage of the message they carry: for that the Apostle may make way for the receiving of the message which he has to the church guides, he commends himself from the honour Christ had put upon him, to be a personal witness of His sufferings, *and a partaker of the glory to be revealed.* [13.] The greater certainty of the truth and comfort by it appear to be in them that deliver it, and the more charity they may express concerning the good estate of those to whom they do deliver it, the better acceptance and success of their message may they expect: for the Apostle, that his message might be the better taken, represents himself as one to whom the truth of the Gospel was most certain, he being *a witness of the sufferings of Christ*, as one that had much courage and comfort in adhering to it, and much charity toward those with whom he deals as being a co-partner with them of *the glory to be revealed.*

2. **Feed the flock of God which is among you, taking the oversight thereof, not by constraint, but willingly; not for filthy lucre, but of a ready mind.**
3. **Neither as being lords over God's heritage, but being ensamples to the flock.**

The Apostle having insinuated himself in the former verse upon the officers of the church, that so his counsel here might have the better acceptance with them, he does in the next place branch out particularly their duty, exhorting them to feed the Lord's people with His truth and rule them by His discipline; both which are in the signification of the first word. And that these might be the better done he presses them to take diligent inspection of the manners and several conditions of the people: which duties he bears in by an argument taken from the relation that the people of their charge had to the Lord as being His flock; and withal, points out the right manner of going about these duties, in six several directions; one whereof is still negative, dissuading them from evil, incident to men of that calling; and another positive, persuading to the study of some necessary qualification requisite in such, to wit, firstly, that they should not go about their duty as if they were forced to it; but secondly, from an inward inclination to serve their Master and profit His people. Thirdly, not from so base an end as their outward gain, but fourthly, from a heart fitted by Jesus Christ for their duty. Fifthly, that they should not affect any dominion over the Lord's people; but sixthly, in their whole carriage cast them a copy of holy and humble walking.

Hence learn, [1.] Every minister of Christ ought both to be able to feed His people with His saving truth, Jer. 3:15, rightly divided and applied, 2 Tim. 2:15, to every one of them, according to their several conditions, Matt. 24:45, which is no less necessary for cherishing and increasing their spiritual life, than their ordinary food in season is for their bodies, Job 23:12, and likewise they ought to have wisdom, authority and equity for ruling of the Lord's people by the right exercise of discipline and application of censures: for both feeding and ruling is expressed by one word in both the original languages, to signify that they are jointly requisite in every minister, whose duty here is mainly held forth: *Feed the flock*, &c. [2.] It is not enough for the ministers of Christ to hold forth sound and saving truths to His people in their doctrine and to rule them by the application of censures and discipline, unless they also take diligent inspection of their manners, and of their several conditions and necessities, by frequent conversing with and visiting of them, as this other word, holding forth their duty, signifies, without which they can neither apply the truth nor censures to the people as they ought: for this is the second principal part of church officers' duty, especially ministers, toward the flock of God, *taking the oversight thereof.* [3.] It should provoke ministers to fidelity and diligence in their calling, to consider that the people of their charge are the flock of God who therefore will provide for them, Isa. 40:11, and will be very terrible to them that have the charge of them in case they slight or wrong them, Ezek. 34:2,10, &c. For to move the church officers to faithfulness and painfulness in their duty, the Apostle thus designs[1] the people of their charge, *the flock of God.* [4.] Although none that are sensible of their own weakness and the weight of the charge of souls will be very forward to thrust themselves into that employment, Exod. 3:11, Jer. 1:6, yet being once called to it and engaged therein, they should not go about the duties thereof as being constrained thereunto by their fears, lest they discover their own weakness, or lest they fall under the censure of others, or lest their own conscience may vex them for neglect of their duty: for this is the first evil from which the Apostle dissuades Christ's ministers, as that which would mar the right manner of going about their duty, *Not by constraint.* [5.] There should be in the heart of every faithful minister so much love to Jesus Christ, arising from the sense of his personal obligation to Him, 2 Cor. 5:14, and so great a desire of the salvation of souls, 1 Cor. 10:33, as may beget in him such a strong inclination and inward bensell[2] of

[1] See page 37.
[2] See page 159.

spirit to his duty that though there were no external consideration of gain, glory or the like, to hold him on, yet may he not be
suffered to neglect it: for this is the first positive qualification of
a minister going rightly about his duty: *but willingly*.
[6.] Although Christ's ministers may with His allowance
challenge from the people under their charge a competent
means of outward subsistence, according to their ability,
1 Cor. 9:14, yet for any of the ministers of Christ to make their
worldly gain their great inducement to undertake that calling, or
their prime encouragement in going about the duties of it, is a
filthy frame of spirit which appears to be in them when they
stretch themselves to the utmost to please them most from
whom they expect most gain, Numb. 23:1, and to oppose and
discourage others from whom they expect least, Mic. 3:5, for
from this evil as abominable to God, detestable to faithful
ministers, and a thing that indisposes them for the right discharge of their duty, the Apostle here dissuades in the third
direction: *not for filthy lucre*. [7.] A minister of Christ that would
go rightly about his duty must lie in wait for every opportunity
thereof, keeping himself in some fitness of disposition for every
part of his calling, whether the opportunity of discharging the
particular duties thereof do presently offer or not, as is imported
in the fourth direction, which is positive: *but of a ready mind*.
[8.] It is an evil to be abhorred by all that would expect the
reward of faithful ministers, to affect or usurp any lordship or
dominion, whether over their fellow-labourers, which appears
in their seeking preference over them, 3 John 9, or over the
people of their charge; which appears by their taking a way with
people rather to compel them to subjection to the Gospel, than
to persuade them to it, contrary to the apostles' practice,
1 Cor. 4:21, 2 Cor. 12:20, by their making use of the Word, or
discipline, to vent their own private revenge or to carry their
point by mere violence and outwearying of those that oppose
them, Ezek. 34:4, contrary to the Apostle's precept,
2 Tim. 2:24,25, for this is the third evil the Apostle dissuades
from, in his fifth direction: *neither as being lords over God's
heritage*. [9.] The church and people of God are His inheritance
which He has purchased to Himself with His blood, Acts 20:28,
in which He is the only Lawgiver, Isa. 33:22, and therefore will
never cast off or alienate the same, Psa. 94:14. The consideration whereof should make all afraid to lord it over His people, or
to appropriate this style to themselves which is here given to all

the Lord's people, as a motive to their overseers to diligence, and a dissuasive from usurping dominion over them: *neither as being lords over God's heritage.* [10.] That which does much complete the ministers of Jesus Christ, is when with their abilities to teach and rule and other inward qualifications, they have also such an external conversation as may be alluring to the flock to follow, and worthy of their imitation, while they express in their practice the graces of God to be in their heart, such as faith and love, 1 Tim. 4:12, patience under personal injuries, 1 Cor. 4:16, humility, and self-denial for the good of others, 1 Cor. 10:33 and 11:1, for this is the Apostle's last direction without which all the rest (suppose they could be where this is wanting) would do little good: *but being ensamples to the flock.*

4. And when the chief Shepherd shall appear, ye shall receive a crown of glory that fadeth not away.

The Apostle, having cleared the duty of the officers of the church, gives them here in the close of the first part of the chapter, some strong motives to fidelity and diligence therein; as firstly, that there was a higher Shepherd than they, to wit, Jesus Christ the Prince of Pastors, to take account of them; secondly, that if they were found faithful and diligent in their duty they might be sure of an eminent degree of glory from Christ at his second coming; thirdly, that that glorious reward should remain always the same in itself and be eternally possessed by them.

Hence learn, [1.] The most eminent of Christ's servants have no less need of encouragement in their duty than the meanest under their charge; their trials and temptations being often greater than others, Luke 22:31, and they no less subject to discouragement, by reason of those, than others, 1 Cor. 7:5,6. Therefore the Spirit of the Lord finds it necessary here to give them encouragement, as He did to the flock before (4:13,14): *And when the chief Shepherd shall appear, ye shall receive a crown.* [2.] Jesus Christ is the chief Shepherd, the Prince of Pastors, the prime Feeder and Ruler (as the word signifies) of His own flock, from whom all the under-shepherds, the officers of his house, have their commission, Matt. 28:18,19, their furniture[1] or gifts, Eph. 4:8,11, and to whom they must all give an account, Heb.

[1] See page 62.

13:17, who takes the prime charge of His own flock, Isa. 40:11, and will supply to them the defects of the shepherds under Him, Ezek. 34:11. In all which respects He is here called *the chief Shepherd*. [3.] Albeit the Lord uses to give in hand to His faithful servants worth all their pains in His service, either by letting them see some success of their labours, 2 Cor. 2:14, or by giving them inward peace from the faith of His approbation, when desired success is wanting, Isa. 49:4, yet He would have them taking their prime encouragement from what they shall get when He and they meet: for to the consideration of this the Apostle here leads all the servants of Christ: *When the chief Shepherd shall appear, ye shall receive a crown of glory.* [4.] The reward abiding Christ's faithful ministers wherein all the lovers of Christ shall share in their own measure, 2 Tim. 4:8, shall be exceeding complete and glorious, as the metaphor of a crown of glory signifies, and such as shall never fade or wax old, but to all eternity shall remain still in its primitive vigour as if a flower should still keep its fairest lustre and sweetest smell; which metaphor is also in the words: and this may comfort them against the fading of their reputation among men, which is incident to the best, John 5:35, Gal. 4:16, for this is here given to the church guides as their great encouragement, that they *are to receive a crown of glory, which fadeth not away*.

5. **Likewise ye younger, submit yourselves unto the elder. Yea, all of you be subject one to another, and be clothed with humility: for God resisteth the proud, and giveth grace to the humble.**

The Apostle having in the former part of the chapter exhorted the officers of the church to their duty, in the second part he points out the duties of the flock, whom he designs[1] by the name of *younger*, not only because the most part of them are ordinarily younger in years than their officers, but mainly because in their disposition and carriage toward their overseers they should show some resemblance of that reverence and obedience which is suitable in young ones toward the aged. And their duty he holds forth in six directions. The first, which belongs to them considered only as they are under the charge of their officers, is subjection to them in the Lord, which imports obedience to

[1] See page 37.

CHAPTER 5 : VERSE 5

their message and respect to their persons. The second, which concerns them mainly as fellow-members of the church, is mutual subjection of one to another in all the duties of love. The third, which holds forth the special means of attaining to the former two, is that they should adorn themselves with a mean esteem of themselves: and this the Apostle presses by two arguments. The one is that the Lord opposes Himself to them that lift up themselves. And the other is that he gives His favour and grace to them that abase themselves.

Hence learn, [1.] It is the duty of the Lord's people to be subject to their rulers whom He has set over them in His church, by submitting to the duties which they press upon them from the Word, Heb. 13:22, and to the censures they inflict according to the Word, 2 Cor. 2:9, by affording them some means of outward subsistence, Gal. 6:6, and by giving some respect to their persons because of their office, 1 Cor. 4:1, in respect whereof they are lifted up by the Lord above His people, as the word here signifies: for the substance of the duty of the flock to their church officers is here by the Apostle comprehended in this one word, *Be subject*. [2.] Whether the members of the church be younger or elder in years they should, in reference to their overseers, resemble that disposition and carriage which beseems young ones toward the elder, in their earnest desire of the Word, and means of salvation administered by them (2:2), by depending upon them as instruments for counsel in their difficult cases, Mal. 2:7, calling for their help and assistance under their crosses, Jas. 5:14, and by their meek submission to censures from them, Heb. 13:17, for it is mainly in respect of the resemblance that should be between the disposition of the flock in reference to their pastors and overseers and that of children toward their parents or such as have the charge of them, that the Apostle thus designs[1] them: *Ye younger, be subject to the elder*. [3.] The obligation of the Lord's people to their duty toward their overseers is no less strait than that of their overseers to their duty toward them, and therefore their hazard in neglecting their duty can be no less than theirs: for the Apostle bears in their duty upon them toward their overseers, by such a word as imports an equality in the strictness of the tie: *Likewise ye younger, be subject to the elder*. [4.] There is a mutual subjection due by every one of the Lord's people toward another, which consists in their con-

[1] See page 37.

197

descendency to reprove one another in love for their faults, Lev. 19:17, their instructing and admonishing one another concerning their duty, Col. 3:16, in their taking well with reproofs and admonitions one from another, Psa. 141:5, and in their stooping to all the duties of charity one toward another, Gal. 5:13 and the like. All which is comprehended in this second direction given to the members of the church, in reference to their fellow-members: *Yea, all of you be subject one to another.* [5.] However men appointed for destruction do glory in their pride and violence, wherewith they think themselves adorned, Psa. 73:6,18,19, yet the grace of humility whereby a Christian has a mean esteem of himself flowing from the sense of his own sinfulness, 1 Cor 15:9, and of the undeserved goodness of God, 2 Sam. 7:18,20, whereby he is inclined to prefer others to himself, Rom. 12:10, not desiring more esteem from others than God allows him to have, 1 Cor. 3:5 and 4:6, and takes well with all chastisements from God as less than his deserving, Ezra 9:13, is the prime ornament of Christians which they should tie about them and delight to wear, as the word here signifies, and be no less ashamed to appear without than without their clothing: *Be clothed with humility.* [6] There can be no right discharge of any duty that the Lord's people owe to superiors, inferiors or equals, until they get from God that humble frame of spirit formerly described: for this exhortation may be taken for a means of attaining to the former duties: *And be clothed with humility.* [7.] Although the Lord may suffer proud sinners to prosper in their sins for a time, Psa. 73:4,5, yet He does still stand in battle array (as the word here translated *to resist* signifies) against them, and will take His fittest opportunity to bear down all that live in that sin of pride which manifests itself in the slighting of the study of reconciliation with God through Christ, Psa. 10:4, the neglect of clear duties pressed by the Word, Neh. 9:16,17,29, and in unthankfulness to God for His mercies, 2 Chron. 32:25,26; the consideration of which opposition from God should make the study of humility lovely; and pride, hateful to the Lord's people as they would not have God for their party: for this is a reason to press humility: *God resisteth the proud.* [8.] The sweet proofs of God's favour, and the increase of the graces of His Spirit, is that which every humble sinner may expect, which should commend the grace of humility to them, and make them study the exercise of it: for both these are comprehended in this second argument, pressing them to put on this ornament, *God giveth grace to the humble*.

6. Humble yourselves therefore under the mighty hand of God, that he may exalt you in due time:

The Apostle here again urges his former exhortation to the study of humility especially under the cross, by two further arguments; the one taken from the omnipotency of God, which is able to crush the proud and carry the humble through all their straits, the other from the certainty of the humble person's deliverance, which is promised in the season fittest for it.

Hence learn, [1.] Humility is a lesson so hard to be learned that Christ's ministers had need to press the same frequently upon His people and study many arguments to bear it in upon them: for the Apostle, having in the former verse by very strong reasons persuaded them to clothe themselves with that orna-ment, he here again by other arguments, presses the same in substance: *Humble yourselves under the mighty hand of God*, &c. [2.] The consideration of the mighty power of God, which is sufficiently able to protect and bear through all His followers, John 10:28, and to find out and punish all that oppose Him or them, Psa. 21:8,9, should move the Lord's people humbly to submit to their duty and to the hardest dispensation in following thereof: for His almighty power, here signified by His hand, is mentioned as a further reason of His people's humbling of themselves: *Humble yourselves therefore under the mighty hand of God*. [3.] Although the Lord's people who have attained to some approved measure of the exercise of this grace of humility, under their straits, may not expect a present deliverance out of them, Hab. 2:1,3, yet their delivery is made sure for them and they are certified by His faithful Word that they shall be carried through till they meet with it: for though He does not promise here to the humble that they shall be presently[1] exalted, yet He makes them sure of this, that if they humble themselves under His mighty hand, *they shall be exalted*. [4.] The deliverance of the Lord's humble people comes always to them in the fittest time, which is when the Lord has perfected His work intended by their affliction, Isa. 10:12, particularly when they are brought to that

---

[1] See page 15.

measure of humiliation to which by their straits the Lord intends to bring them, Lev. 26:41, when they are prepared by their straits to put a due price upon a delivery, Psa. 102:13,14, and when the cup of their enemies' iniquity is full, Gen. 15:16, for this word signifies both the opportunity fixed and fittest for the exaltation of the humble: *He shall exalt you in due time*.

7. Casting all your care upon him; for he careth for you.

The fourth direction which is brought in as a special means of attaining to the former is that believers should by faith commit to the Lord their through-bearing in their duty, the event thereof, and all their anxiety about these; and that, because the Lord's loving providence does not suffer Him to neglect them or any of their concernments.

Hence learn, [1.] The children of the Lord are subject to much sinful anxiety in following of their duty; which appears when they are hindered from their duty by looking more to their own weakness and the difficulties in the way of duty, than to the sufficiency promised by Him that calls them to it, Exod. 3:11, or when they are discouraged in their duty by the apprehension of probable hazards in the way of it, Isa. 51:12,13, of which evil the Spirit of the Lord would have them sensible, while He finds it necessary thus to exhort them: *Casting all your care on Him*. [2.] Although it be most commendable in Christians to entertain such a care of discharging their duty aright, and of eschewing what may provoke the Lord in their way of going about it, as stirs them up to much diligence and employing of Jesus Christ, 2 Cor. 7:11, yet such a care, whether concerning the manner of their going about their duty or the success and event thereof as does distract their heart in duty and indispose them for it, is sinful, and to be shaken off by all that would discharge their duty acceptably: for so does the Apostle here direct: *Casting all your care upon Him*. [3.] The way to be liberated of anxiety and heart-dividing cares which indispose for duty is by prayer to commend the success and event of our duty and our through-bearing therein to the Lord, Phil. 4:6, and by faith to commit both to him, Prov. 16:3, for this is here the direction of the Spirit of the Lord for attaining to freedom from sinful anxiety, *Casting all your care upon Him*. [4.] The Lord allows His children to cast upon Him all their anxieties, both such as they have about their souls and matters of highest concernment, and those about their

bodies and lesser matters: however small the thing be whereabout their heart becomes anxious, He allows them to commit
the same to Him; for He knows that a very small matter is ready
to occasion much vexation of spirit of His own, Jonah 4:8.
Therefore does He thus direct them, *to cast all their care upon Him*.
[5.] It is not only the privilege of believers that they may dis-
burden themselves of their distrustful heart-dividing cares by
casting them over upon the Lord; but it is also the very great
desire of our God that we should not sink under the insupport-
able burden of our own needless cares and fears. Yea, it is His
peremptory command to put these off ourselves upon Him,
which His people may not disobey, except they would incur His
displeasure and destroy themselves: for this has the force of a
command: *Casting all your care upon Him*. [6.] As no duty can be
rightly discharged by us while the Lord is not trusted with our
through-bearing in it, and with the event and success thereof, or
while the heart is distracted with misbelieving anxiety about
these, so the trusting of God with these is the best way to come
speed in every duty: for the Apostle having exhorted before to
duties toward their overseers, to one another and to God, he
brings in this as a means of attaining to all these, without which
none of them could be attained to: *Casting all your care upon Him*.
[7.] Mis-believing anxiety, whereby Christians break themselves
with the burden of these cares which God requires to be cast
upon Him, is one of the greatest signs of pride in the world; and
to trust God with the weight of these in following our duty is a
prime evidence of true humility: for this is brought in as a
special way how they should prove themselves to be humbled
under God's mighty hand, and as that without which they could
not but declare their pride; as both the construction of the
words and their connection with the former do import: *Humble
yourselves*, &c, *casting all your care upon Him*. [8] Although the
Lord be altogether free of such passions as care, sorrow and the
like, which are in men, Numb. 23:19, yet those of His people
that cast their care upon Him shall find no less proofs of His
love, both in warding off hazards so far as is necessary, and providing every thing needful for them, than if He were as solicitous
for their well-being as they can be for themselves; the consideration whereof should liberate their hearts of their distrustful
cares: for this is here asserted as a reason enforcing the fourth
direction, *He careth for you*. [9.] While the Lord's people take
upon themselves the weight of their matters and have their

hearts distracted with cares about their through-bearing in, and the event of their duties, they do not then believe the fatherly providence of God watching over them for their good, the faith whereof could not but banish their anxieties: as is imported in the connection of this reason with the direction, *Casting all your care upon Him, for he careth for you.*

8. Be sober, be vigilant; because your adversary the Devil, as a roaring lion, walketh about, seeking whom he may devour:

The fifth direction is that Christians should prepare themselves for the spiritual warfare against their great enemy, Satan. And for this end he shows what frame of spirit and carriage becomes a soldier of Christ in two directions preparatory to this warfare. The one is, that they should meddle sparingly with the delights of this present life. The other is, that they should still be upon their watch, lest they be surprised by their spiritual enemies and to move them hereunto, he describes their prime enemy, Satan, from his great enmity, unwearied activity and insatiable cruelty, as so many arguments to sobriety and vigilancy.

Hence learn, [1] They that are most conscionable in their duty and have come nearest to the right manner of going about it have reason to make ready for the hottest battle and sorest assaults from Satan to hinder or discourage them therein: for the Apostle (having directed the flock of Christ in the former words to their several duties and to the right manner of going about them, with humility and confidence) does here exhort them to prepare for a battle in that way, and for this end thus instructs them for it, *Be sober, be vigilant: because your adversary,* &c. [2.] Every one that would be a good soldier in this holy war against Satan must labour for a sober frame of spirit, whereby Christians esteem meanly of their own abilities, Rom. 12:3, they keep down the kything[1] of their passions against those that injure them, Acts 26:25, and meddle sparingly even with lawful delights, the excess whereof becomes fuel to Satan's temptations and overcharges the heart, so as it cannot foresee and guard against hazard from him, Luke 21:34, for this is the first preparatory direction given to soldiers in this spiritual warfare: *Be sober.* [3.] Holy watchfulness, whereby a Christian forecasts hazards and guards against them, is also required in a Christian

---

[1] See page 168.

warrior without which he cannot but be surprised and made a slave to his adversary the Devil: for to prepare believers for this battle the Apostle gives this second direction, *Be vigilant.* [4.] Satan is such an enemy as, in opposing the Lord's people, pleads law and equity upon his side, and by law would carry his point against all that are come of *Adam*, were it not that Christ has freed law-breakers who believe in Him from the curse of the law, Gal. 3:13, for this style of Satan's, *Your adversary*, imports an adversary in some suit of law. [5.] Of all the enemies of the people of God, whereof they have many both within, 1 Pet. 2:11, and without, Psa. 3:1, Satan is the chief, acting in and by all the rest and far exceeding them all in power and policy, and therefore to be especially watched against and opposed: for he is here called *Your adversary the Devil.* [6.] Satan watches all possible advantages of prevailing against the children of the Lord by his temptations, compassing them round about, that he may espy where they are weakest or least afraid of hazard, that there he may assault them: *for he is an adversary that goeth about.* [7.] There is no outwearying of Satan in this warfare, by never so much opposition or frequent disappointments, he is still in action against the Lord's people, which should provoke them to constant watchfulness and employment of Jesus Christ for strength against him: for his constant activity is here set forth by a word in the present time, as a motive to sobriety and vigilancy, *Your adversary goeth about.* [8.] Satan is a very powerful enemy and a terrible, and so cruel that no less than the utter destruction of souls can satisfy him: for he is here described by the similitude of one of the most powerful, terrible and cruel of beasts, *A roaring lion seeking whom he may devour.* [9.] All the activity, power, terror and cruelty of the Devil should be so far from discouraging the Lord's people in the battle against him that the consideration thereof should animate and hearten them to the same, considering that he is an enemy spoiled by Jesus Christ, Col. 2:15, that there is more power to be employed for believers than is against them, 2 Kgs. 6:16, and that victory over Satan is sure and near to all believers, Rom. 16:20, for as an argument to sobriety, vigilancy and the exercise of other graces and duties, formerly pressed upon believers, their adversary is thus described, *he goeth about like a roaring lion seeking whom he may devour.*

9. Whom resist stedfast in the faith, knowing that the same

afflictions are accomplished in your brethren that are in the world.

Here is the sixth and last direction wherein the Aspostle presses the great duty of spiritual warriors, to wit, resistance to their great enemy, Satan; and withal, holds forth the right way of maintaining that holy warfare against him, which is by constant adhering to the truths of the Gospel, and resting by faith upon the promises thereof, notwithstanding of all afflictions in that way; to which the Apostle gives this encouragement, that they had all the rest of the Lord's people in the world for their fellow-soldiers, each of them filling up their own measure of hardship in this battle.

Hence learn, [1.] Although the power and policy of our spiritual adversary be exceeding great, as was shown from the former verse, yet none of Christ's soldiers must think of flying from him or yielding to him in the least, but must make them for a stout and peremptory resistance of him in all his temptations; considering that the more place be yielded to him, he tyrannizes the more, Matt. 12:29, &c, and the more stoutly he be opposed, the more ground he loses, Jas. 4:7, for this is the order which Christ's soldiers have received from their general, Jesus Christ, concerning Satan and his temptations, *Whom resist*, &c. [2.] The principal means whereby believers beat back Satan and his temptations is their constant adhering to the truth of the Gospel, whatever they may suffer for their so doing, and their maintaining of their interest in Christ and the promises: both which are comprehended in this direction, holding forth the right manner of opposing Satan, *Whom resist stedfast in the faith.* [3.] The strongest of Satan's temptations are conveyed to the godly through afflictions, under which his temptations are ordinarily most prevalent with them, to make them quit the truth or their duty, or else to ding[1] them from their confidence in adhering to these. Therefore the Apostle, giving an encouragement to oppose Satan's temptations, suits the same for an afflicted condition, importing that through affliction the greatest temptations are ordinarily conveyed to the godly, *Whom resist*, &c, *knowing that the same afflictions are accomplished in your brethren.* [4.] It is an ordinary and strong temptation which Satan suggests to the hearts of the godly that they are singular and

---

[1] 'ding': beat, knock.

matchless in their sufferings; that so he may make them question their Father's affection and put themselves out of the number of his children because of their afflictions: for this is the temptation which the Apostle mainly guards the hearts of sufferers against, while he says, *Knowing that the same afflictions are accomplished in your brethren that are in the world.* [5] It ought to be a great encouragement to sufferers in that battle against their temptations which accompany their afflictions, to consider that their lot is no harder than the rest of the saints of God through the world, from whom they may expect sympathy and the help of their prayers: for this is here given as an encouragement to the battle against Satan's temptations, notwithstanding of afflictions in the way of their duty, *that the same afflictions were accomplished in their brethren that are in the world.*

10. **But the God of all grace, who hath called us into his eternal glory by Christ Jesus, after that ye have suffered a while, make you perfect, stablish, strengthen, settle you.**

Follows the last part of the chapter which is the conclusion of the whole Epistle, containing several articles. In the first, the Apostle betakes himself to God by prayer for these suffering Christians, that the begun work of grace in them might be carried on to perfection; and for that end, that they might be established in what they had already attained, that their spiritual strength for all their duties and difficulties might be renewed and increased, and their union with Christ the foundation made more and more firm (which is the signification of these several expressions in the Apostle's petition), and for the strengthening of his faith and theirs: concerning the hearing of this prayer he takes hold of the all-sufficiency of grace which is in God, and makes use of the sweet proof thereof, which they had already received in the Lord's calling of them by the Gospel to the possession of His everlasting blessedness through the Mediator, after they had wrestled a little while through a few difficulties in the way to it.

Hence learn, [1]. The ministers of Christ ought not to satisfy themselves with the pressing of pertinent duties upon the Lord's people, and holding forth fitting encouragements to be made use of by them, that thereby people may come to the knowledge and approbation of their doctrine; but they must also by prayer and faith put over upon the Lord to work in the people what

205

they have pressed, and must go before them to the Fountain of furniture,[1] that so the people may apprehend a necessity of divine influence to concur with men's best gifts in order to their profiting, without which neither ministers' pains, nor people's resolutions or endeavours can have success, Rom. 9:16; for so does the Apostle here put over upon the Lord by prayer to work in the people that which was his main scope in preaching and writing to them, *But the God of all grace*, &c, *make you perfect*, &c. [2.] It may be a great comfort to the Lord's people, and encouragement in their duty, when the Lord sends them such messengers as have not only ability to clear their duty and hold forth their encouragements to them, but such as have also skill of wrestling in prayer with God for them, to draw down the blessing upon their doctrine, and by their practice of that duty of prayer before the Lord's people to direct them in the right manner of going about it: for this may be taken for a sweet encouragement to them to study the duties he had pressed upon them, that they had the Apostle, so earnest and skilful a wrestler with God for them, putting up, as it were, in their hearing such pertinent petitions on their behalf, and making use of such strong grounds of confidence as was fitting for the strengthening of their faith and his, that he should be heard, *The God of all grace, who hath called us to his eternal glory by Jesus Christ, after ye have suffered a while, make you perfect*, &c. [3.] Even those of the Lord's people who are furthest advanced in grace are far short of that measure of perfection which is attainable; they are oftentimes like a member out of joint (as the first expression here in the Apostle's prayer signifies) both in regard of their own inward distempers, Psa. 22:14, and of their divisions among themselves; for healing whereof Paul uses the same word in his exhortation to the Corinthians, 2 Cor. 13:11, they are not so hardened against, nor resolute as they ought to be to meet with further difficulties, as the next expression in his prayer imports; they are far from that vigour and ability for their duties and crosses and from that close adherence to Christ the Foundation Stone (as the two last expressions import) that they might be at: of all which defects every one that desires to thrive in grace would labour to be sensible, that so they may be humble and stirred up to greater progress; for which cause, the Apostle makes use of such expressions in his petitions as might represent

[1] See page 62.

to the minds of the people (of whose progress he had spoken much before) their several defects; *The God of all grace make you perfect, stablish, strengthen, settle you.* [4.] It ought to be the great aim and design of ministers in all their labours with God and with the people that those who have attained to some good measure of grace may not rest satisfied with the same, but may be stirred up to aim at progress and perfection therein: and for that end may have their inward distempers and mutual divisions healed, as a broken member is set in joint again, that they may be made able for their duties and hardened against their trials; and that they may be better built upon the foundation Christ, by a more hearty embracing of His offered grace and firm adherence to His truth: for these are the things which the Apostle has aimed at in his writing this Epistle to these persecuted *Hebrews*, and in his prayer to God for them, as is clear by the signification of the words in the original, *The God of all grace make you perfect, stablish, strengthen, settle you.* [5] There is in God an all-sufficiency of every grace, and withal a strong pro-pension[1] to communicate the same freely to unworthy sinners, the consideration whereof should hearten both ministers and people to pray for and expect a more plentiful measure thereof than what they have already received: for this first ground of con-fidence which the Apostle makes use of to strengthen his own and the people's faith for obtaining of what he seeks here, includes both the abundance of grace that is in God and His gracious inclination to communicate the same freely; in both which respects He is here called, *The God of all grace.* [6.] Whether the Lord's people consider that woeful case out of which they are called by the Gospel, Col. 1:13, or that blessed state to which they are called, 1 Cor. 1:9, they may take His calling of them for a sure ground to their faith (if so be they have consented to His call) concerning His willingness to give them every thing necessary for their perseverance, till they come to the possession of what He has called them to: for this is a second ground of confidence which the Apostle makes use of to obtain what he seeks, hereby teaching the people to make use of the same, *that God had called them unto his eternal glory.* [7.] The blessedness which the Gospel calls sinners to possess is such as they that obey the call can never be put from the possession of it; yea, it is of the same kind with that which the Lord Himself lives in, glorious for

---

[1] 'propension': propensity.

ever, so that they share with Him of His own blessedness, so far as they are capable, John 17:22, for that blessedness whereunto sinners are called by the Gospel is here called *His eternal glory.* [8.] It is by Jesus Christ the Mediator that sinners are called to the possession of this eternal glory; He by His blood has purchased it for them, Eph. 1:14; by His Word and Spirit He clears to them the way to it, 2 Tim. 1:10. Yea, He Himself is the way, and He quickens His redeemed ones to walk in it, John 14:6, for we are called to *His eternal glory by Jesus Christ.* [9.] The way to eternal glory lies through sufferings so that none have ground to expect it any other way: for this clause, *after ye have suffered,* may be knit to the words going before, *who hath called us into His eternal glory by Jesus Christ, after ye have suffered.* [10.] Those who get grace to adventure upon sufferings for Christ and His truth with the small measure of strength and grace which they have already attained, may expect a further degree of perfection and a greater measure of strength and stability after they have suffered a while: the Lord makes trials discover to His people the weakness of His grace in them, and that discovery, to chase them to Himself who loves to let out liberally upon sufferers, 4:14, for this clause may be also knit with the following petitions, *After ye have suffered a while, make you perfect,* &c. [11.] Even the hardest of the Lord's people's sufferings are of small weight as compared with the reward, 2 Cor. 4:17, and of short continuance, as compared with eternity, 2 Pet. 3:8, the consideration whereof may hearten the Lord's people under them all: for in both these respects may this encouragement be understood, that they are but for a while, or, *a very little.*

11. To Him be glory and dominion for ever and ever. Amen.

The next article of the conclusion of the Epistle contains a song of praise to God; wherein the Apostle acknowledges Him worthy to be glorified and obeyed by all, as their sovereign Lord to all eternity; and by his so doing expresses his faith of being heard in his former petitions, that so the people for whom he prayed might with the like confidence join with him in the song.

Hence learn, [1.] Christ's ministers should carry a praising disposition in their hearts all along their work and be ready frequently to break forth in some expressions thereof before the Lord's people, especially in a suffering time: for the Apostle raised one song of praise at the beginning of this Epistle in 1:3, another in 4:11 and here in the conclusion he takes it up again, *To Him be glory and dominion for ever and ever.* [2.] While the Lord's people are praying for a further measure of His grace they should join praise therewith, acknowledging Him to be glorious in Himself, and worthy of all glory from others, to have dominion over all, and wishing that His glory may be seen and acknowledged, and His dominion submitted to in testimony of their thankfulness for that measure of His grace which they have already received, and of their confidence grounded upon their knowledge of His gracious nature, and their former experience of His grace already bestowed upon them: for upon these grounds the Apostle, having prayed for the people's perseverance, stability and perfection, does here praise and lead them so to do: *To Him be glory and dominion for ever and ever.* [3.] Whenever the Lord's people see aright how gracious the Lord is and has manifested Himself to be in the offers of His grace to them in the Gospel, they cannot but have their hearts raised to glorify Him and to wish that many might be subject to Him: for the Apostle having set forth the Lord as the God of all grace, who had graciously called sinners to partake of His own eternal glory, does now break forth in praise, as that wherein all that were sensible of what he had said could not but join with him: *To Him be glory and dominion for ever and ever.* [4.] Where there is a real and kindly desire of ascribing glory and dominion to the Lord, it will extend itself beyond all time and ages, even toward the length of eternity; considering that His love and the proofs thereof will follow His own that length; and that His excellency and the worth of His favours bestowed upon His people are such as to all eternity they will not be able sufficiently to acknowledge; and therefore they will desire that *Glory and dominion may be given to Him for ever and ever.* [5.] While we ascribe glory and dominion to the Lord, there should be in our hearts strong desires that His glory may be known and acknowledged, His dominion enlarged and submitted to, and much confidence that it shall be so, He having engaged his faithfulness for that effect, Isa. 45:23, for this word wherewith both prayer and praise uses to be closed, signifies both desire and confidence: *Amen.*

12. **By Silvanus, a faithful brother unto you, as I suppose, I have written briefly, exhorting and testifying that this is the true grace of God wherein ye stand.**

The third article of the conclusion of this Epistle contains two branches. In the first, the Apostle commends the bearer of the Epistle (who was to explain and apply the purpose of it to them, he being a public minister, 2 Cor. 1:19) from his fidelity and near relation to himself and them, as he had good ground in charity to judge of him. In the next, he commends the Epistle itself [1.] from the shortness of it and [2.] from the sweet scope thereof, which was to stir them up to their duty and to bear witness to the doctrine of God's free grace whereunto they did adhere.

Hence learn, [1.] Though saving truth should be heartily embraced, whoever they be that carry it, Phil. 1:15,18, yet it contributes for the better acceptance thereof that those who deliver it deserve and have a good esteem amongst those to whom it is delivered, and be looked upon by them as having a special respect to their good: for to make this Epistle the more acceptable to those to whom it was first directed, the Apostle commends him that carried it and was to open it up to them, as one faithful in his office and loving towards them: *By Silvanus, a faithful brother unto you*. [2.] It becomes those who are of longer standing and more eminent gifts in the ministry, to be so far from undervaluing or slighting those who are of shorter standing and meaner gifts, that they ought to gain to them all the respect and esteem they can among the Lord's people, for the sake of the message which they carry: for this Apostle being among the first of those that Christ called immediately to the service of the Gospel, and eminently honoured by Him to be a pen-man of Scripture, does here commend *Silvanus* (of whom there was no mention in Christ's days, and who was only an ordinary minister, called to expound the written Word) as if he had been in all respects his equal: *By Silvanus a faithful brother*. [3.] It is the great commendation of a minister of Christ that he be faithful in his Master's service by improving his talents whether more or fewer, for His glory, Matt. 25:21,23, and that he have a brotherly affection toward his fellow-labourers, expressing the same by working to their hands in the work of the Gospel, Col. 4:11, and to the people by a humble and affectionate care of their good, as if they were his brethren, Phil. 4:1, for this is the commendation of Silvanus, *A faithful brother to you*. [4.] It is neither safe to withhold our testimony concerning the fidelity of others when we have grounds for charity, that they do deserve it, nor to be positive and superlative in commending of any as if we were infallibly persuaded of their faithfulness: for the Apostle gives this commendation to Silvanus of his faithfulness with such an adjection[1] as signifies a judgment of charity concerning him, which the Apostle had gathered by several probable grounds and reasons; and yet the expression does import an inferior degree of certainty to that which he had concerning his own estate and fidelity in his calling, Rom. 8:38, 1 Tim. 1:12: *By Silvanus, a faithful brother, as I suppose.* [5.] It is a necessary favour to the church and people of God, to have the mind of God given to them in writing to be a standing rule for trial of every thing that is pretended to be His mind, Isa. 8:20, to help their frail memories the better to remember His truth, Isa. 30:8; to prevent mistakes among His people concerning His mind, which would far more readily arise if it had been only delivered in so transient a way as Satan's oracles are; and that His people when they have not occasion to hear His mind preached or spoken by others, may have it with them to read and meditate upon, Acts 8:28. For though this Apostle and others had preached the substance of the doctrine contained in this Epistle to these same persons to whom it is directed Acts 2, 1 Pet. 1:25, and though they had Silvanus, a man able to preach the Gospel coming to them, yet the Spirit of the Lord finds it necessary to write His mind to them: *By Silvanus, &c, I have written unto you.* [6.] It is a commendable thing in Christ's servants, and a special gift of God's to them, to be able to deliver much of the Lord's mind to His people in a few words, providing it be with plainness of speech, for so will people be the more able to comprehend in their judgment, and retain in their memory, what is delivered to them: for the Apostle commends this Epistle which has in it the heads of all saving truths delivered in much plainness of speech, from the shortness of it: *I have written unto you briefly.* [7.] It is necessary for Christ's ministers to make use of several strains of doctrine in dealing with people, sometimes to exhort them and that with much earnestness and vehemency to their duty, sometimes to comfort them against discouragements in the way of their duty; both which are in the signification of the first word, *exhorting*: at other times again, to bear witness to the truths they deliver as a thing themselves know experimentally and believe to be the truth of God, John 3:11, confirming the same from other places of Scripture, Acts 26:22 and 28:23, and

---

[1] 'adjection': addition.

testifying against them that reject or disobey the same, Deut. 8:19, according to the signification of the next word, *testifying*; by both which the Apostle holds forth his several strains of dealing with the people, especially in this Epistle, and these as a pattern to ministers: *exhorting and testifying*. [8.] The sum of the Gospel and of all right preaching thereof is to make offer to sinners of the rich and free grace of God for pardoning, sanctifying and saving of them, to stir them up to embrace that offer, and having embraced it to study the exercise of grace and walking like gracious persons, in the obedience of that doctrine; for here the Apostle gives the sum and scope of this Epistle, which is the same with that of the whole Word: *To exhort and testify that this is the true grace of God.* [9.] The doctrine of the Gospel will deceive none that receive it. They will find the Lord as gracious and His ways as sweet as the gospel affirms: for it is the *true grace of God.* [10.] Even those who have made good progress in grace, and are for the present fixed in their adherence to the truth, are in hazard to be shaken by temptations and made to question the truth of the Gospel and the reality of the gracious offers made therein; as is imported in this, that the Spirit of the Lord finds it necessary to put the Apostle upon writing an Epistle to such, for *exhorting and testifying that it was the true grace of God wherein they did stand.*

13. The church that is at Babylon, elected together with you, saluteth you, and so doth Marcus my son.

Here is the fourth article of the conclusion of this Epistle, wherein the Apostle delivers salutations to the scattered Jews. [1.] From those Christians at Babylon, whom the Lord had chosen out of the world to be a church to himself, and to share with others of His people in spiritual and eternal mercies. This church at Babylon seems to have been made up of the posterity of those Jews who stayed there after the expiring of the seventy years' captivity, whom this Apostle, being a minister of the circumcision, Gal. 2:7, has gone to visit, and planted in a visible church. And next he delivers commendations from Mark who was a public minister of the Gospel, Col. 4:10,11, and being one of this Apostle's old acquaintance, Acts 12:12, has been instructed by him in the Gospel, for which he is here called his son, as Timothy is called Paul's for the same reason, 1 Tim. 1:2.

Hence learn, [1.] It is the duty of the Lord's people (especially in a suffering time) though never so far distant in place, to love and remember one another as if they were present; and embracing one another, as the word of saluting in the original imports, to signify their desires to know one another's condition, their sympathy with one another's suffering, and joy for one another's welfare: all which is imported in the salutation common among the *Hebrews*, 1 Sam. 25:5, 1 Chron. 18:10. And it is likewise the duty of those who are entrusted with the carrying of such salutations to make conscience of the delivery of them: for the church at Babylon remembers their dispersed countrymen and desires the Apostle to signify the same to them, who does it here accordingly: *The church which is at Babylon saluteth you.* [2.] The Lord who reigns in the midst of His enemies, Psa. 110:2, can erect and keep up a church to Himself, even in those places of the world where His enemies are permitted to have all the external power in their hand: for He has here a church at Babylon, where we never read that the civil power was employed for Him. [3.] The Lord has many designs of providence, which will not appear for a long time after He has begun to work in order to the execution of them: for now it appears that when the Jews were carried captive to Babylon, the Lord had a design to have a gospel church erected there before they should all come back again, as is clear by comparing Acts 15:18 with this, that there is a *Church at Babylon*. [4.] The Lord can make the sinful failings of His people subservient to His gracious purposes and yet be holy in all His ways: for the sinful stay of some of the Jews in Babylon, when they had a call and opportunity to return in Cyrus's time, is made to serve the accomplishment of this holy purpose of God, concerning the having of a visible gospel *church at Babylon*. [5.] The constancy of some of the Lord's people who are under the power of wicked men, and the appearance of the grace of Christ in them, especially their love and sympathy with the rest of His people, ought to move others to constancy under their sufferings, and make them confident of the same through-bearing strength: for, that the Apostle may encourage these suffering believers to whom he writes, he sends them here commendations from their brethren in Babylon, in testimony of their love to and sympathy with them: *The church which is at Babylon saluteth you.* [6.] No journey never so long or hazardous ought to be shunned by any servant of Christ to do service to Him who has engaged Himself to be with them, go whither they will, Matt. 28:20. In the faith whereof, Peter has undertaken this

213

long and hazardous journey from Judea to Babylon, from whence he sends this Epistle to the rest of the Christian Jews. [7.] Because all the members of the visible church are chosen out of the world to profess Christ and to have the offers of His grace made to them, and so many of them as do really embrace these offers have doubtless been from eternity chosen to be equal sharers of spiritual and eternal mercies, therefore they may be all spoken of and dealt with by Christ's ministers as the elect of God: for so does the Apostle here speak of the whole visible churches at Babylon and other places: *Elected together.* [8.] It is a special comfort to suffering Christians to know themselves remembered and respected by more eminent Christians than themselves, by whom they are apt to apprehend themselves forgotten and slighted: for which cause we may safely conceive the Apostle here to mention commendations, particularly from *Marcus his son.* [9.] Those who have been instrumental in the conversion or spiritual edification of others ought to entertain a special measure of tender affection toward them, and should have from them a special measure of reverence and love, such as children owe to their parents: for because Mark was instructed by this Apostle in the knowledge of Christ and the Gospel, and did resemble him in faith and conversation, he is here called *his son.* [10.] A penitent's former failings ought not to hinder his esteem with any of the Lord's people: for Mark who, by his separating from the Apostles while they were about the work of the Lord, did occasion a sinful separation of one of them from another, Acts 15:37,38,39, is here particularly mentioned as one dear to this Apostle, and whose love and remembrance should be a comfort to sufferers: *And Marcus my son.* [11.] So careful should the ministers of Christ be to entertain love among the Lord's people and particularly to beget and cherish in their hearts a good esteem of other ministers, though inferior to themselves, that they should willingly condescend to be servants in the meanest offices of love that may conduce for that end. Therefore does this great Apostle registrate[1] in his Epistle the commendations of the *Church at Babylon, and Marcus his son.*

14. Greet ye one another with a kiss of charity: Peace be with you all that are in Christ Jesus. Amen.

---

[1] 'registrate': register (old Scottish usage).

In this article of the conclusion, the Apostle exhorts those to whom he writes to express mutually their hearty affection one to another by such signs as were ordinary in those times and confidently wishes to them all sort of happiness.

Hence learn, [1.] It does much contribute to the success of the Gospel among a people that there be mutual love amongst them, and expressions thereof. Therefore the Apostles do ordinarily close their Epistles with exhortations to mutual love and unity, as that without which the fruit of their pains in these writings would be much hindered; and so does the Apostle here: *Greet ye one another with a kiss of charity.* [2.] Whatever decent expressions of mutual respect and love be the ordinary custom of the times and places where the Lord's people live, they ought not to be scrupled at, but rather made conscience of by them in obedience to Him who commands love and respect, and consequently the expressions thereof, to be among His people: *Greet one another with a kiss of charity.* [3.] All the mutual expressions of love and respect among the Lord's people ought to flow from an inward affection of Christian love in the heart of one of them toward another, and ought not to be performed as fashionable and flattering compliments, which are hateful to God, Psa. 12:2,3, for so the Apostle exhorts: *Greet ye one another with a kiss of charity.* [4.] The occasion of frequent converse and correspondence among the Lord's people ought not to diminish their love, or hinder the expressions thereof, but rather to increase the same; they who live together being more ready to offend or mistake one another, and so to be mutually jealous of the alienation of one another's affection, than those who are at a greater distance, whose love should provoke those that are nearer: for the Apostle, having signified the love of those that were at Babylon to their dispersed brethren, does here exhort them that had more frequent occasion of meeting and correspondence, to *greet one another with a kiss of charity.* [5.] As it is the duty of Christ's ministers heartily to wish all sort of true peace upon all the members of the visible church, who in regard of their external profession and participation of common gifts and benefits from Christ, may be said to be in Him, John 15:2, so true spiritual peace which is the calmness and contentment of the soul, arising from the faith of acceptation with God through Christ, when fears of His wrath and jealousies of His love are in some measure banished, Rom. 5:1, together with as much outward peace and prosperity as shall be for their true good, is the Lord's allowance only to real believers and to all of them whether weaker or stronger, and may be in a good measure attained to in the midst of many troubles by those who are chased out of themselves and by faith planted in the living Vine, Christ Jesus: for as this apostolic benediction may be understood of the Apostle's wish to all the members of the visible church, so it does especially respect true believers therein; *Peace be to all them that are in Christ Jesus*. [6.] As it is the duty of Christ's ministers to press duties upon all professors, so it is their part to guard promises and privileges by qualifying the persons to whom they do belong: for the Apostle, having pressed the duties of love and expressions thereof upon all indefinitely to whom he writes in the first part of this verse, he does in the latter part restrict his wish of *peace*, qualifying the persons to whom it does especially belong: *Peace be to all them that are in Christ Jesus*. [7.] As the ministers of Jesus Christ ought to enter upon every part of their employment with the faith of their calling and commissions from Him, as was observed upon the first words of this Epistle, so they ought to close the same with some confidence in their hearts of the blessing of God upon their labours, and of His granting their desires for that end: for here the Apostle closes his exhortations and prayers in this Epistle with this word of confidence, *Amen*.

2 PETER

THE ARGUMENT

This Epistle may be called the later Will of a dying Apostle and martyr of Jesus Christ: for when Peter wrote it, he knew that he was shortly to seal the truth in it with his blood; as will be clear by comparing the 14th verse of this chapter with Christ's prediction concerning his death, John 21:18. It is not directed to any particular Church, but to all believers, especially believing Jews, scattered at that time through many nations; as appears by comparing 1 Pet. 1:1 with the first verse of this and of the third chapter.

The principal heads of doctrine contained in it make clear the scope and parts of it; and they are three. The first is concerning a Christian's growth in grace and diligence in holy duties, which is cleared and pressed (chapter 1). The second is concerning error, the way of working and hazard whereof is handled (chapter 2). The third is concerning the last coming of Christ, some errors about it being confuted, and the right preparation for it, held forth (chapter 3).

What can be more necessary than to study growth and diligence in so declining and secure a time as this is? To guard against error when it so prevails? And to prepare for the last coming of our Lord when now it is so near, and so much forgotten?

CHAPTER ONE

The parts of this chapter are three. In the first, which is the preface to the whole Epistle, is contained a description of the Apostle and those to whom he writes in the Inscription, (v 1). An Apostolic wish for the best blessings of God to them, to wit, the growing sense of His love, and the fruits thereof, in the Salutation (v 2). Grounds of encouragement that it should be according to his wish, to wit, that there was a saving work of grace already begun in them, which he describes from the cause, nature, parts and way of working of it (vv 3,4).

In the second, which is the first principal part of the Epistle, he exhorts to diligence and the study of growth in grace, reckoning out several steps of their progress (vv 5,6,7), with many moving arguments thereto (vv 8,9,10,11,12,13,14,15). And because there is no growth but by the knowledge and use-making of Christ, and Christ is only revealed in the Word preached and written, therefore:

In the third part of the chapter, there is a commendation of the preaching of the Gospel (v 16), of Christ himself the chief subject thereof, (vv 17,18) and of the whole written Word from the certainty and usefulness thereof (v 19) and from the divine authority thereof (vv. 20,21).

1. **Simon Peter, a servant and an apostle of Jesus Christ, to them that have obtained like precious faith with us, through the righteousness of God and our Saviour Jesus Christ:**

The Apostle describes himself [1.] from two names which design[1] his person. *Simon*, his old name, when he was a fisher; *Peter*, his new surname given him when Christ called him, Mark 1:16 and 3:16. The one minding him of his former ignorant and mean condition; the other, of the honour Christ put upon him, when He made him a lively stone in the church and a believer and preacher of that truth, upon which, as a Rock, He builds His church; which is Christ's own exposition of the name *Peter*,

---

[1] See page 37.

Matt. 16:18. Hence learn, it is very necessary to carry with us to the end of our time the sensible remembrance of what we were before Christ manifested Himself to us, and of what His grace has made us, that we may go to Heaven both humble and thankful. Therefore the Apostle sets down these two names here in the beginning of his letter, *Simon Peter.* Next he describes himself from two styles, which design[1] his office; the one common to all the officers of the Church, the other proper to those who had immediate commission and extraordinary assistance from Christ to publish the Gospel and work miracles.

Hence learn, [1.] It is honour enough for the highest office-bearer in the church to be a servant of Christ; so does this Apostle esteem it who never called himself lord, or head of the church; but discharged[2] it in all ministers, 1 Pet. 5:3, and here takes a lower title to himself, *A servant.* [2.] It is necessary for Christ's ambassadors to know and assert their calling from Him, that truth may have weight with people, and that they may have courage, whatever their faithfulness may cost them: for while the Apostle knows himself to be a servant of Jesus Christ, he dare avow himself by name and surname even when he is publishing truths that cost him his life: *Simon Peter, a servant and an Apostle of Jesus Christ.* [2.] He describes those to whom the Epistle is mainly directed, from the worth of their faith, equal to the faith of the Apostles, for all saving effects; and clears the way how they came by it, to wit, by the virtue of the faithfulness of God and the merits of Christ.

Hence learn, [1.] The Scriptures are not only given for converting sinners and working grace where it is not, Psa. 19:7, but also for their sake who are already converted and gracious; some places being mainly intended for them to further their growth, guard them against temptations, and to fit them for their last meeting with Christ; which are the ends of this Epistle, directed mainly to them that have obtained *precious faith.* [2.] Although some believers are more strong in believing, and so have more joy and peace than others, 1 John 2:13,14, yet is the faith of them all of a like worth, in so far as it unites them all to the same Saviour, from whom the weakest faith shall never shed;[3] interests them all in the same spiritual promises, privileges and glorious reward, and is bought for them all with

[1] See page 37.
[2] 'discharged': that is, pronounced to be altogether unsuitable.
[3] 'shed': be taken away.

the same price: in all which respects the true faith of the meanest believer is *alike precious* with the faith of the Apostles. [3.] The way how saving faith comes to the elect, and is wrought in their hearts, is by virtue of the faithfulness of God who promised to Christ, in the Covenant of Redemption, the bestowing of it upon the Elect, Psa. 110:3, and to the elect in the Covenant of Grace, Psa. 54:13, John 6:45, it being God's righteousness to prove Himself faithful in making all these promises. And it comes also through Christ's righteousness, which is, His doing and suffering to purchase it, and other saving graces for us; and so, although we have it freely, yet Christ bought it dear, and God is righteous in giving what Himself promised, and Christ paid for, 1 John 1:9. So the Apostle makes this precious faith to come to all that have it, *through the righteousness of God, and our Saviour Jesus Christ.*

2. **Grace and peace be multiplied unto you through the knowledge of God, and of Jesus our Lord**.

In this salutation he wishes to them a daily growth in their hearts. [1.] Of the sweet sense of God's free favour, making the graces of His Spirit to thrive. [2.] Of true spiritual peace, flowing from the former and carrying with it every necessary blessing, as the signification of these words, *grace* and *peace*, and their order does import; and all this, through their growing in that knowledge of God and His Son Christ, which has faith, affection and practice with it.

Hence learn, [1.] No less than what is here wished for is the Lord's allowance to all believers; if they get it not they have themselves to blame: for His Majesty does nothing to mar the multiplying of grace and peace upon all that have *precious faith*. [2.] They that would have this rich allowance must not only expect it in this order – *grace*, or God's free favour first, and then *peace*, with every necessary blessing – but they must study to grow daily in the knowledge of the nature and will of God, the purchase, fulness and offices of Christ; so that, by the use-making of all, heart and life may be changed: for such a *knowledge* is this, through which *grace and peace is multiplied*. [3.] It is not formality or vain repetition to use frequently the same expressions to God, or to others, when they flow from a new sense of the worth and need of the things: for this Apostle and others do ordinarily use these same expressions in the beginnings of their Epistles, *Grace and peace,* &c.

3. According as his divine power hath given unto us all things that pertain unto life and godliness, through the knowledge of him that hath called us to glory and virtue.

Follows the ground of his confidence which might also hearten them, that it should be according to his wish, to wit, that God's powerful grace had already begun a saving work in them, by bestowing freely upon them all that is essential to a gracious frame of spirit within, and a holy life without; and this he had done by making them so to know Christ as to consent to His calling them by the Gospel to glory, or eternal life, as the end; by virtue, which is grace and holiness, as the way or means.

Hence learn, [1.] The seen beginnings of a saving work of grace are comfortable pledges and confirmations to faith that that work shall thrive, it being suitable to the Lord's wisdom, power and constancy to carry on and perfect what He has begun: for the Apostle wishes grace and peace to be multiplied: *According as His divine power had begun the work.* [2.] To give grace to a graceless soul is a work of God's infinite power, there being so much unworthiness, guiltiness, and opposition to hinder that work in all the elect. Therefore the cause of this work is here made divine power. [3.] The Lord, in the bestowing of saving grace, works both irresistibly and freely; neither can any for whom it is appointed and purchased, so oppose as to hinder the bestowing of it; for it is *divine power* that works it. Nor can any in nature so use their naturals as to prepare themselves for, or merit the bestowing of it: for divine power works by giving freely all things that pertain to life, and so the very preparations for the new life. [4.] The substance of every saving grace, though not the full measure, and a right to what may enable for honouring God in practice, is given at once in conversion, as a child when it first lives or is new born has all the essential parts of a man. Therefore to these to whom the Apostle wishes increase of grace and upon whom he is to press growth, he affirms to be already given *all things that pertain to life and godliness.* [5.] The very first beginnings of grace are wrought in the heart, by making a sinner drink in the knowledge of Christ: the law indeed prepares for this work by discovering sin and deserved wrath and terrifying the conscience, but the Gospel which holds out Christ the Saviour from sin and wrath, having in Him the fulness of grace, and a heart to let it out freely upon graceless sinners, is the Spirit's instrument of working grace: for as the Apostle wished grace to thrive in the former verse through the knowledge of Christ, so here he says, *it is given at first through the knowledge of Him.* [6.] Then Christ is savingly known and so saving grace wrought, when the heart consents to Him, calling in His Word to eternal life, by grace and holiness the way to it. They may quit their part of glory who come not to Christ to be made virtuous, or gracious and holy: for *He hath called us to glory and virtue.*

4. **Whereby are given unto us exceeding great and precious promises: that by these ye might be partakers of the divine nature, having escaped the corruption that is in the world through lust.**

Both the means of working and the nature of this saving work are here further cleared. The means are the promises of the new Covenant, containing such worthy and dear-bought blessings as the pardon of sin, taking away the stony heart, &c, the fulfilling of which promises to sinners, by the divine power of God, makes them partakers not of the infinite essence of God, which can neither be divided nor communicated to any creature, but of such heavenly qualities as make them in some weak measure like their heavenly Father and so frees them from the disposition, fashions and estate wherein unregenerate men live and perish.

Hence learn, [1.] As the promises of the New Covenant are beyond all expression great and precious, because of the spiritual and eternal riches which they contain, and will be therefore highly esteemed and commended by all that have faith to embrace the gift of them, so the way how the Lord works saving grace at first is by making out these promises, enabling the guilty, graceless and cursed sinner to believe and apply the pardon, grace and blessedness freely offered in them: for so the Apostle expressly affirms, that by the divine power of God these promises are given to us that by them we may be changed. [2.] The receiving of these promises by faith makes a wonderful change upon sinners: for so soon as a sinner gets grace to believe and apply the free promises of the Covenant, as soon does the Lord begin to make out upon his heart the things promised, so stamping it with His own image, that the sinner receiving these promises begins presently to look like God his Father, and in some weak measure to resemble Him in heavenly wisdom, holiness, uprightness, and other of His communicable properties, especially in humility, self-denial, love and pity toward other miserable sinners, zeal for the Lord's honour, and such other perfections as were eminent in the Man Christ; and this is *to partake of the divine nature*. This change kythes[1] also in abhorring and flying from the filthy fashions which flow from the unmortified corruption of those that are yet living in nature, and so eschewing the wrath and ruin which such are liable to; both which may be understood by *escaping the corruption which is in the world through lust*; and is here made the effect of receiving the promises. And where this work is, it proves a right to the Covenant, and gives ground of confidence that that work shall grow. The study of the growth whereof, the Apostle presses in the next place.

5. **And besides this, giving all diligence, add to your faith virtue; and to virtue knowledge;**
6. **And to knowledge temperance; and to temperance patience; and to patience, godliness;**
7. **And to godliness brotherly kindness; and to brotherly kindness charity.**

To the end that this saving work of grace described in the preface may thrive, the Apostle here seriously exhorts gracious persons not to satisfy themselves with the sight of one or some few graces in themselves; but to give more than ordinary diligence that they may see every grace drawn forth to exercise, and kything[1] in fruits: for which cause he reckons forth a number of these graces, in the exercise whereof a Christian's growth consists.

Hence learn, [1.] Even they who discern in themselves a saving work of grace, and know the privileges spoken of before to be theirs, are not now to sit down idle and satisfied, but to be the more active and diligent in the exercise of grace and holy duties: for so says the Apostle: *Besides this* (ye that have precious faith and promises and do partake of the divine nature) *give all diligence*. [2.] As it is not the ordinary diligence, wherewith most professors satisfy themselves, that will be blessed to make a thriving Christian; but such as goes through all means and waits upon all opportunities of profiting that their ability and calling

[1] See page 168.

will permit them to follow, and gets the flower of a Christian's wit, affections and time, which is here called, *all diligence*, so a Christian's end in being thus diligent must not be his own credit before others, of the satisfaction of his conscience only, but that the exercise and fruits of one grace may be still added to another, and so Christ may be honoured in him and by him: *Giving all diligence, add to your faith,* &c. [3.] Saving faith, which grips Christ for pardon and strength, and daily flies to Him for both, must be held fast and renewed in the exercise of it by all that would thrive in any other grace, or be fit for any duty. If either we loose the grips of faith, or do not frequently renew them, we can thrive in nothing: therefore is faith here made the first stone in this spiritual building, to which all the rest are to be added: *Add to your faith,* &c. [4.] With the maintaining and renewing the acts of saving faith, a Christian that would grow must so mind his duty as that he keep himself in the nearest disposition for it: for no less is signified by virtue than the working habit of every grace which keeps a Christian in such a fitness for doing or suffering, that, when he is called to them, both of them are lovely to him, and he is in some measure ready for them; which the Scripture calls elsewhere the having of the heart at the right hand, Eccles. 10:2, and standing with the loins girt, Eph. 6:14, and here is called *adding to faith, virtue.* [5.] There is more than this readiness of disposition for duty requisite to make a growing Christian, even the use of holy reason to time and manage duties wisely, that as the heart lies to duty there may be skill to go about it with prudence and circumspection, as the word, *knowledge,* here signifies, which is to be added to *virtue.* [6.] Because there remain in the best many immoderate and unruly affections and passions, which, as they are ready to exceed bounds even about lawful objects, so the excess of them darkens reason, indisposes the heart for duty, mars the exercise of faith, and so hinders all the former three. Therefore a Christian that would grow must labour to have, by the power of God's grace in him, such a command over his passions of anger, fear, grief, &c and over his affections of love, joy and the like, especially in the use of sensual delights, that he may be able to keep them within the bounds which right reason according to the rules of God's word prescribes to them. Therefore the Apostle exhorts to *add to knowledge, temperance*; which is a grace whereby a Christian's passions and affections are held under the dominion of sanctified reason. [7.] Because all that walk in this way may expect trials and crosses in it, therefore must a Christian that would grow, labour for a rational and willing submission to these, knowing that he deserves worse, that they may come from love, and work together for his spiritual and eternal good, upon which scriptural grounds the Christian patience of believers is built, which is here to be added to the former. [8.] The Christian that would grow, must never conceit himself to be above the necessity of attending the external worship and ordinances of Christ, but must conscionably wait upon these, not resting upon the outside of them but looking especially to the right manner of going about them: for so much does this word *godliness* signify, being distinguished from inward graces and duties to our neighbour, as here it is. [9.] A thriving Christian must with his godliness make conscience of duties to his neighbour, especially of entertaining a kindly and tender affection toward all, whom he is bound in charity to esteem children of the same Father with himself, and kyth[1] this affection to weak and strong, by sympathizing with them in trouble, supplying their necessities, edifying their souls, and every way studying to promote their spiritual and temporal welfare, according to his place and ability. To do this is to *add to godliness, brotherly kindness.* [10.] The duties of love are not to be all confined to the saints only, but if we would prove ourselves growing Christians, we must thirst after and endeavour the true good of the souls and bodies of all to whom our prayers or pains may be profitable, within the compass of our calling, which is *to add to brotherly kindness, charity*, a grace, the exercise whereof, the Scripture presses upon Christians in reference to all men, Gal. 6:10, 1 Thess. 3:12.

8. **For if these things be in you, and abound, they make you that ye shall neither be barren nor unfruitful in the knowledge of our Lord Jesus Christ.**

Because even those who are endued with these graces are ready to become lazy and too contented with their measure, therefore the Apostle, from verse 8 to the 16th verse does by many moving arguments, labour to rouse them up to diligence and the study of growth. The first motive is from the advantage thereof, that the Christian in whom these graces are, and are in lively exercise

---

[1] See page 168.

and growth, shall never be without work, as the word here translated *barren* does properly signify; nor shall his work be without such fruits as shall manifest, for his own comfort and God's honour and the good of others, that he does savingly know and has an interest in Jesus Christ as his own Lord. Therefore the growth and exercise of grace is much to be studied.

Hence learn, [1.] The most unquestionable duties had need to be pressed upon Christians by many arguments: for what we do most easily assent to in judgment we are oftentimes most careless of in practice. Therefore does the Apostle in this following part of the chapter multiply motives to press this one clear duty, that gracious persons ought to study growth in grace. [2.] Even those of whom it may be best supposed that they are gracious, ought notwithstanding to put themselves to the trial, both concerning the truth and growth of their graces. Therefore even those who are before spoken to as having precious faith and other graces are here put to try *if these things be in them and abound*. [3.] Though the grace of sanctification be in and from Christ as the treasure and fountain thereof, yet it is really inherent in the regenerate as the subjects thereof. It is not sufficient to believe that there is abundance of grace in Christ; but we must try and labour to see *if these things be in us* from Christ. [4.] It is a safe and approved way to try the reality and growth of grace by the effects thereof, to wit, a Christian's activity in commanded duties, and his fruitfulness in his conversation, for the honour of Christ and the good of others: for here the Apostle puts them to try if these things be in them and abound, which, he says, they will know by the effects of them: *They make you that ye shall neither be barren nor unfruitful in the knowledge of Christ.* [5.] As grace may be in the habits and seeds of it where it is not lively and growing, so it is not the being of it in us, but the liveliness and growth of it, that makes a Christian busy and in bearing the fruits of cheerful obedience to Christ's commands, edifying and supplying others and the like; which fruits will kyth[1] in some measure where grace is, and is in vigour, and will evidence a saving knowledge of Christ and interest in Him: for, says the Apostle, *If these things be in you and abound, they make you that ye shall neither be barren nor unfruitful in the knowledge of our Lord Jesus Christ.*

[1] See page 168.

9. But he that lacketh these things is blind, and cannot see afar off, and hath forgotten that he was purged from his old sins.

The second motive to diligence and growth in grace is taken from the hazard of the want or decay of these graces. Those that are altogether void of saving knowledge, faith, and the rest of the graces mentioned, are utterly blind in all things spiritual, and cannot be taken up with anything beyond this present world, and so declare that they undervalue that great privilege, the forgiveness of sins, which by their baptism and profession they did seem and were esteemed to have. Yea, and even those in whom graces really are, but are under a decay and without exercise, are so far blind in things spiritual, and intent upon things worldly, that they do for the time walk as if they had forgotten their pardon. Concerning both believers and unbelievers the Apostle's argument may be understood; it has force to move all to diligence and the study of growth in grace.

Hence learn, [1.] How sharp-sighted soever graceless souls may be in things that concern their back and belly, and this present world, yet till Christ make a gracious change upon them they can see nothing of the hazard of their perishing, the worth of salvation, or their need of Christ, that they might fly to Him and give up themselves to His service and so make preparation for death and eternity: *For he that lacketh these things is blind and cannot see afar off.* [2.] While folks are of this temper and way, however they may be esteemed pardoned souls by themselves and others, and dealt with by the church as if they were such, yet by their being wholly taken up with this present life and making no provision for a better, they do declare that they undervalue the forgiveness of sins: for when the esteem of forgiveness does not stir up to thankfulness and holiness, God esteems it forgotten; and he that walks as if he forgot himself to be pardoned cannot comfortably conclude himself to be such a one, however he may be esteemed and spoken of by the best, as one that *hath been purged from his old sins.* [3.] As sins once committed ought still to be esteemed old, as rags that are cast off, or vomits never to be licked up again, so all that either are or do profess or esteem themselves to be pardoned ought to keep the sensible remembrance of the Lord's pardoning mercy so fresh in their hearts, that they may be daily renewing their repentance for their old sins, their thankfulness for the forgiveness of them, and watchfulness against the like; the lack of which lively exercises even in real believers proves them to be much forgetful that they have been *purged from their old sins.*

10. Wherefore the rather, brethren, give diligence to make your calling and election sure: for if ye do these things, ye shall never fall.

Follows the third and fourth motives to diligence and growth in grace. The one is, the more of these a Christian attains to, the more shall be his clearness and certainty that he was from eternity chosen to life and is, in time, effectually called. The other is, that by this means he shall be kept from apostasy and yielding to temptations by the way.

From the third motive, learn, [1.] Although the election and effectual calling of every soul who has fled to Christ can be no surer than they are in themselves, Rom. 11:29, 2 Tim. 2:19, yet may those privileges be very unsure and unclear to the apprehension of those that are both *chosen and called.* Therefore they are here exhorted *to make* them *sure.* [2.] As some comfortable measure of the certainty of both may be attained to, even by ordinary believers, so this jewel of assurance does not fall in the lap of any lazy soul, nor can any expect to attain to it, or yet to entertain it, in whose hearts grace is without exercise, and whose conversation is without fruitfulness; for so the Apostle exhorts to give all diligence to make them sure; importing that, without that diligence, they cannot be made sure to our hearts.

From the fourth motive, Learn, [1.] Although none that are chosen and called can finally or totally fall away from grace, yet are they of themselves subject so to do, and may actually fall into foul and scandalous sins for a time; so much is supposed in this argument to diligence: *If you do these things, ye shall never fall.* [2.] The Lord's way of preserving His own from falling is by helping them to exercise their faith and other graces before named, and to entertain so much of the fear of falling finally or scandalously, as stirs them up to *give all diligence*, that their falling either ways may be prevented: for the hazard of falling is here made a motive to stir up believers to diligence and exercise of grace.

11. For so an entrance shall be ministered unto you abundantly into the everlasting kingdom of our Lord and Saviour Jesus Christ.

231

Here is the fifth motive. The life of a Christian growing in grace and diligent in duties shall be to him a begun heaven upon earth, his clearness concerning his right to it and his feeling of the first fruits of it being a begun entry into heaven, and the blessing of God upon his pains.

Hence learn, [1.] There is a beginning of heaven to be had in this life, even such a clear sight by faith in the Word, of God reconciled with us in Christ, and such foretastes of that sweet life we shall have with Him for ever, as fills the heart sometimes with comfort, makes duties and difficulties easy, as if a Christian were walking in the entry or porch of heaven, and stepping in at the open gate thereof, Psa. 63:5,6, Phil. 3:20, which is to *have an entrance abundantly ministered unto us into that everlasting Kingdom.* [2.] As the reward of well-doing here and hereafter, may be proposed to believers and looked upon by them as a motive to diligence and growth in grace, so the only way to win to the beginning of that sweet life here, and the full possession of it hereafter, is activity in duties, and keeping grace in lively exercise: for the Apostle proposes sweet firstfruits to be had here, and an eternal reign in Christ's company for ever hereafter, as a motive to diligence and the study of growth, without which neither can be expected; for *So,* (says he) *an entrance shall be ministered,* &c.

12. Wherefore I will not be negligent to put you always in remembrance of these things, though ye know, them and be established in the present truth.

As a sixth motive, the Apostle applies his own doctrine, pressing growth and diligence to himself in his calling as a minister, that since the hazard of negligence and the vantage of diligence was so great as he had cleared, therefore he himself would not be negligent in his duty of stirring them up to diligence, although he supposed many of them to be both discerning and solid Christians, by reason whereof they might conceive so much pressing needless.

Hence learn, [1.] While a minister presses duties upon people by arguments or motives, he ought to apply these motives to himself for his own up-stirring in the duties of his calling. So does the Apostle here, while he says, *Wherefore* (to wit, because of the motives whereby I pressed diligence upon you) *I will not be negligent.* [2.] One kindly motive of a minister's diligence and earnestness with people is the sense he has of the hazard or benefit that may come to souls by slighting or obeying the truths and duties pressed. So is it with the Apostle here, as his own hazard and advantage makes him stir them up. [3.] As it is the duty and commendation of Christians not to be still fluctuating and unfixed in matters of opinion or practice in religion, so neither the promise of the Spirit to bring all things to their remembrance, nor people's great knowledge and settledness in the truth, puts them beyond the need of the daily pains of ministers, whose work is not only to point out believers' privileges and to inform them of what they know not, but to inculcate, clear, and press known truths and duties even upon discerning and stablished Christians, whose imperfection in knowledge, forgetfulness, laziness, formality and oftentimes conceit that much pressing of known truths and duties is needless, does require that they should be *put in mind, though they know and be established in these things*.

13. Yea, I think it meet, as long as I am in this tabernacle, to stir you up by putting you in remembrance;

The seventh motive serves both to stir him up to diligence in his place, and those to whom he writes in theirs; and it is taken from the necessity of his so doing, and that, both upon his part who was bound to it by virtue of his calling, as long as he had life with ability, and upon their part who stood in need, not only to be minded of their duty, but to be powerfully roused (as the word signifies) to the practice of it.

Hence learn, [1.] It is neither the credit nor profit of a minister's calling that should move him to painfulness, but rather the consideration of the equity of the work, how just a thing it is as the Apostle's word here signifies, that one so unworthy of so honourable an employment, and many times justly deserving to have been thrust out of it, should yet be employed, furnished and rewarded by Jesus Christ. This made the Apostle, and ought to make every other minister, to stir up himself and others, because he *thinketh it meet*, or just and equitable, *so to do*. [2.] As death is the term-day of a minister's service in his calling, till which time he ought neither to desire to change his calling, nor do it by deputies under him, though he meet with small success and great hardship, so the consideration of his frail, flitting and fighting condition imported by being in a *tabernacle*, should make him stir himself busily while time and strength last. Therefore the Apostle counted it just so to do *as long as he was in the tabernacle* of his body; and was moved to diligence, by taking up his present condition under the similitude of being in a tabernacle. [3.] A minister should not content himself barely to propound truths and mind people of their duty, but by all means should labour with God and his own heart to have such power accompanying his pains, that dead, sleeping and lazy souls may be quickened, wakened and roused up: for no less does this word signify which the Apostle adds to the word he used in the former verse, *to stir you up, by putting you in remembrance*.

14. Knowing that shortly I must put off this my tabernacle, even as our Lord Jesus Christ hath shewed me.

The eighth motive is taken from the nearness of the Apostle's death, Christ having told him, John 21:18, that in his old days he should be martyred; and now knowing the time to be near, he makes use of the warning, both for his own and their up-stirring.

Hence learn, [1.] The nearer our journey's end be, the faster should we run, according to our strength, in serving Christ, and doing good to souls: for when death is near the best will think the great part of their business undone. Thus the Apostle is earnest with them because he knew he was shortly *to put off his tabernacle*. [2.] Learn from this how hard usage, and unpleasant to flesh and blood, those who are most beloved and honoured of Christ may meet with in the world, even such as this Apostle met with, who after much persecution, frequent scourging and imprisonment in his younger days, must, notwithstanding, in old age, when natural vigour is abated, and men use to look for rest, fall into the hands of cruel persecutors: for he *must put off his tabernacle, as Christ shewed him*. The reward makes up all, and the faith thereof can encourage against all. And no doubt this man who had denied his Master did account it his greatest honour to get leave to suffer for Him. [3.] Though every one be not so particularly warned of their personal trials as *Peter* was, yet all, being commanded to make them ready for sufferings, 2 Tim. 3:12, should live mindful thereof, though they be long delayed; and prepare for them, though they be kept off till gray hairs. So the Apostle here minds and prepares for that trial, now in his old age, whereof Christ foretold him in his youth. [4.] Though it be dangerous to slight a message from the youngest minister, fitted for and lawfully called to that work, 1 Tim. 4:12, so a message from an aged and persecuted servant of Christ, who is shortly like to be plucked away from people, should have a special weight with them: for the Apostle makes this an argument to stir them up, *that he was shortly to put off his tabernacle, as Christ shewed him.*

15. Moreover I will endeavour that you may be able after my decease to have these things always in remembrance.

The last motive is taken from the Apostle's zeal for Christ's glory in studying to propagate His truth for the good of souls. And for that end he resolves to take course before he died how the church might reap profit when he was gone; which he did by writing Scripture, putting forth and instructing faithful labourers who did good after him.

Hence learn, [1.] The sense of obligation to Jesus Christ will make His servants and people sincerely studious to do that while they live, that may be some way useful for His honour and the good of others, when they are gone. And though every one cannot leave such profitable monuments as some others have done, yet ought every Christian to endeavour to leave behind them the seeds of saving knowledge, sown in the hearts of those with whom they converse, at least the savoury remembrance of their humble and holy walking, the fruits of their charity and other good works, which may do as much good after their decease as some volumes do. Therefore did the Apostle not only stir them up while he was in his tabernacle, but endeavoured to propagate the truth among them and others, after his decease. [2.] As the best way of serving the generation after us is the study of transmitting pure truth to them, which the Apostle here resolves upon, so the foresight of approaching trials does not abate but increase the zeal of the Lord's faithful servants after His honour, and the good of souls; (the death of the godly, of whatever kind it be, being a perfect outgate[1] [as the word *decease* signifies] from all sin, sorrow and fears). Therefore the Apostle, knowing he was shortly to be martyred, stirs up himself the more to diligence.

[1] See page 144.

16. For we have not followed cunningly devised fables, when we made known unto you the power and coming of our Lord Jesus Christ, but were eye-witnesses of his majesty.

Follows the third part of the chapter containing a commendation of the preaching of the Gospel of Christ, the chief subject thereof, and of the whole written Word. All which may also be taken for so many further motives to press what the Apostle has been upon in the former part. [1.] He commends his own and the other Apostles' preaching from the excellency and certainty of the Gospel which they preached, to wit, that their doctrine which held forth Christ's coming in our flesh to redeem, and His furniture[1] for that work, was not to be looked upon as some witty fiction or pleasant fable, but the most certain and serious purpose under heaven, delivered by those who were eye-witnesses of the Son of God's personal presence in our flesh and of much glory breaking through it, in His miracles and transfiguration.

Hence learn, [1.] There is as much atheism and unbelief natural to all as to look upon the mystery of salvation through Christ incarnate, as upon a fable, invented to kyth[2] the quickness of men's wit, and please the ears of people; so much is imported in this negative part of the commendation of the Apostle's preaching: *We have not followed cunningly devised fables.* [2.] The main subject of the preaching of the Gospel is to point out Christ's coming in our flesh, such an errand as to redeem and save, and his furniture[1] for that work which is encouragement enough for every lost sinner that hears it to fly to Him for salvation, since He is come to seek and save such, and has power to save to the utmost all that come to God through Him: for this is here made the substance of the Apostle's teaching: *To make known the power and coming of Christ.* [3.] As Jesus Christ does not use all His servants alike familiarly in every thing, but oftentimes uses those most whom He minds to try most, so, any special honour any of them gets should never be forgotten, but minded especially when trials are near and brought forth, only to commend Christ and His truth and encourage against suffering, so does the Apostle here, near death, mention that special honour put upon him and other two upon the mount, and

---

[1] See page 62.
[2] See page 168.

makes it an argument to commend the doctrine, and prove the certainty of it: *We were eye-witnesses of His majesty.* [4.] The Lord has used all means that can be expected to make us look upon the business of our redemption and salvation through His Son incarnate as the most certain and real business of any other: therefore though He might have only employed men to write the Gospel who had never seen Christ in the flesh, and commanded us to believe, yet has He condescended for our further satisfaction to make use of such men to write the most part of the New Testament as saw with their bodily eyes Christ glorious in flesh, and so were *eye-witnesses of His Majesty.*

17. For He received from God the Father honour and glory, when there came such a voice to him from the excellent glory, This is my beloved Son, in whom I am well pleased.
18. And this voice which came from heaven we heard, when we were with him in the holy mount.

In the next place the Apostle commends Christ as our Cautioner[1] and Mediator from the high esteem He has with the Father; and from the full satisfaction the Father has with the price of redemption, paid by Him: of both which the Father gave a public declaration from His glorious residence in heaven, before three witnesses who were with Christ upon a hill where He did manifest Himself to be God, glorious in holiness.

Hence learn, [1.] The glory of the Son of God incarnate was so obscured for our sake that He needed a declaration from heaven to show the Father's esteem of Him and to beget a high esteem of Him in the hearts of His own. This is imported in Christ's *receiving from the Father, honour and glory*, which was not an addition of any glory to Christ which as God He had not, but a manifestation of the glory which He had, though obscured under the veil of our infirm flesh. [2.] As glory is so excellent a thing that they that get but a little glimpse of it cannot but remember it and commend it as worthy to be contended and suffered for, as here the Apostle does, so Christ as our Mediator has not only much glory given Him as the fruit of His obedience to the death for sinners, and a pledge to His members that they shall share of the glory of their Head, whereof this upon the mount was a little foresight and taste, given Him for His and His

[1] See page 13.

followers' encouragement under suffering, but also He is in such power and credit with God the Father that He can do in heaven and earth what He pleases for the good of His redeemed ones; and nothing can be done without Him. All which is imported in Christ's *receiving from the Father honour and glory, by a voice from that excellent glory.* [3.] God the Father is so fully satisfied and completely paid by the Mediator Christ for all that fly to Him for refuge, that He seeks no further mends for all their wrongs, nor further price for what they need, only that they do receive Him freely as He is freely offered; and that as the Father speaks down this of Christ to sinners, *He is my beloved Son in Him I am well pleased: Hear Him*, so sinners should answer back again with their hearts, Christ is our beloved Redeemer in whom we are well pleased; Let the Father hear Him for us. [4.] It is not easy for awakened sinners, who are oftentimes much unsatisfied with themselves, to believe and take comfort from this, that God is well satisfied with Christ for them. Therefore, though Isaiah preached and wrote this truth, the Father spoke it down from heaven twice before witnesses. Three evangelists have recorded it, and one of them has set it down thrice, Isa. 42:1, Matt. 3:17, 12:18 and 17:5, Mark 1:11, Luke 3:22 and 9:35, yet the Apostle sets it down here and, to make it take impression, says again, *This voice we heard, when we were with Him.* [5.] It is no sin nor superstition to esteem and speak of things that can have no inherent holiness, and may have no religious worship, so as may most testify our respect to His holiness who manifests Himself in or by these things; for which cause the very ground and house where He manifests Himself, is called *Holy*, Exod. 3:5, Isa. 64:11, though they can have no more than a relative holiness. And several other things such as the Day for His service, the written Word, &c; and here the hill where the Lord who is glorious in holiness did show much of His glory, is called *the Holy Mount.*

19. We have also a more sure word of prophecy; whereunto ye do well that ye take heed, as unto a light that shineth in a dark place, until the day dawn, and the day star arise in your hearts:

In the third place the Apostle commends the whole written Word, [1.] from the certainty of it. He calls it *A Word of Prophecy*, giving to the whole the name of one principal part, most of the

Old Testament being a foretelling of those things concerning the Messiah and His kingdom, which the New Testament clears to have their accomplishment in Him that was born of the virgin *Mary*. He calls it *A more sure Word*, comparing it with *the voice from Heaven*, whereof he spoke immediately before; not as if there could be any uncertainty in the Lord's voice speaking from heaven, but because it is a greater matter to have foreseen and foretold things to come, than to have seen and related the greatest things present. And because a transient voice is more easily mistaken or forgotten than a standing authentic record, therefore the written Word is a more sure ground for sinners' faith to rest upon than a Voice from Heaven could be. Next he commends the written Word from the usefulness thereof, that it should prove to sinners who make it the rule of their faith and manners, a comfortable directory through this dark state of ignorance and misery, until they get such a measure of the promised Spirit, and nearness to the Sun of Righteousness, that they shall not need a prospect of glass, of the Word and or-dinances, which will not be till death and the dawning of the day of eternity.

Hence learn, [1.] The written Word, believed to be the Lord's mind, is the surest ground for faith to rest upon of any that ever has been or can be given to sinners who are subject to forget-fulness, jealousies and mistakes. The general offers of Christ, and free promises of His grace excluding none who will not exclude themselves, give more solid encouragement to self-judging sinners than they could have by a voice from Heaven, calling them by their names; for that would readily be suspected to be another than the Lord's, or spoken to another of that name. Therefore the Apostle, comparing the written Word with the Voice from Heaven, calls it to sinners, *A more sure Word*. As this world is so dark a place that our own reason, the counsel or example of others, will often leave us comfortless, to wander and fall in snares, except we look to the light of the Word which shines in this dark place, so they have the Lord's approbation and commendation who do apply their hearts to and satisfy themselves with this Word, as the only and sufficient ground of their faith, and rule of their manners, to keep them from erring in judgment or practice; for so says the Apostle, *Whereunto ye do well to take heed, as to a light that shineth in a dark place.* [3.] Although the light be now clear in comparison of what was before Christ came, yet being compared with that light we shall have in Heaven, it is but dark; like the light that shines out of a room where a candle is, into a room where the candle is not seen: so much does this similitude of *a light shining in a dark place* import. [4.] Though it be so, yet shall the Word give comfortable direction to all that follow the light of it, under all their crosses, confusions and difficulties. And those who make it a lamp to their feet and a light to their path may be sure to get at last such a clear and satisfactory sight of Christ as shall banish all darkness and doubts; and such a near union and fellowship with him, the bright Morning-star, gloriously present by His Spirit in their hearts and personally also in human nature, conversing with them for ever, that they shall have no more need of Word or ordinances; which is the condition here described by the Apostle, only to be expected in heaven, till which time we will never be above the direction of the Word and use of the ordinances, Eph. 4:13, Canticles 4:12.

20. **Knowing this first, that no prophecy of the Scripture is of any private interpretation.**
21. **For the prophecy came not in old time by the will of man: but holy men of God spake as they were moved by the Holy Ghost.**

Last of all, the Apostle commends the written Word from the divine authority of it. The interpretation or the meaning whereof cannot be found out by the wit or proper invention of any, whereof the Apostle gives a reason, because these truly gracious men who were consecrated and set apart by the Lord for receiving and registering His mind in Scriptures could neither speak nor write, when, nor what things they pleased, but as they were immediately moved and infallibly furnished by the Lord's Spirit, whose mind it is. Therefore the Scriptures are of divine authority; and this the Apostle says must be known first, to wit, as a principle of saving knowledge, without which Christians cannot profit by the Scriptures.

Hence learn, [1.] As the Scriptures do not hold forth to us the device of their heads who wrote it, but the public mind of God, so none can attain to the right meaning, nor be able to hold forth the true interpretation thereof, by their own proper skill or invention, there being in it such *knots* (as the word *interpretation* imports) as cannot be loosed but by humble imploring of the help of the Spirit, whose mind it is, as the pen-men of it themselves did, that they might know what was revealed to themselves, Psa. 119:18, Dan. 2.22, Zech. 4:4–5, and by comparing one place with another, Acts 17:11, and making use of other helps that God has given, Dan. 9:2, 1 Tim. 4:13,14,15, by which means, through the Lord's blessing, we may come to some saving measure of the knowledge of God's mind in His Word, and may have the common or public consent of both prophets and apostles, to every saving truth made known to us therein: for *no prophecy*, or part *of Scripture, is of any private interpretation.* [2.] As it is the duty of all the Lord's people to fix in their minds as an unquestionable truth this principle, *That the Scriptures being the Lord's mind, none can of themselves attain to the true meaning of them,* so till this principle be known at least so far as that it be not questioned, there can be no light or comfort expected from the Word: for the Apostle, having exhorted in the former verse to look to the Word for direction and comfort, adds here, that as they would find these, they must know this first, *that it is not of any private interpretation.* And though only the Spirit of the Lord, the Author of the Scriptures, can fully persuade hearts that they are His mind, yet if men would consider, a great many of these truths that are revealed in Scripture are not only agreeable to nature's light but may be in some measure known by it. The one (to wit, the light of nature) teaches that there is one God, the first Cause of all, omnipotent, wise, righteous and good; that it is reasonable He should be served, and that, according to His own will, which therefore He, being both wise and good, must have some way revealed; that reasonable creatures have immortal souls, and so die not as the beasts; that there is no true happiness in these things wherein men do ordinarily seek it; that since vice and virtue receive not suitable rewards here, there must be punishment and reward after this life: all which, and many other things of this sort, nature's light teaches, though darkly, as the Scriptures themselves, Rom. 1:19,20, and the writings of those that never knew the Scriptures, do witness. The other again (to wit, the Scriptures) clearly reveals these same things, pointing out the nature, will and way of worshipping of the true God; what the reward and punishment after this life is; and the right way of attaining the one and eschewing the other. And though some things revealed in Scripture, such as the incarnation of Christ, the way of salvation by faith in His death, the resurrection of the dead, and other things like these, have not been known by

natural reason, yet none of all these are contrary to such con-
clusions as may be drawn from principles that are naturally
known concerning the power, wisdom and goodness of God.
And withal, if men would consider the wonderful harmony of
the purpose contained in the Scripture; the likeness of the style
thereof, though written by so many several men, living in so far
distant ages and places of the world; the exact answerableness of
so many future events to their predictions in this Word; the
experience of all the lovers of it who (having no less use of their
reason than any atheist ever had) have found so singular a power
in it, to terrify and humble the mind of man and then to give it
true peace and comfort, and so fresh a sweetness that the more it
be studied it delights the more, which no writing in the world
besides can do; the wonderful preservation of it against the malice of Satan and wicked men, who would not have so hated and
persecuted it and the lovers of it if it had been a man's device; if
(I say) men that have the use of reason would ponder these
things they could hardly (except they were plagued with atheism)
force their hearts to contradict this truth, which the Apostle here
delivers, *that the Scriptures are not the mind of man, but the mind of
God.* And the arguments that move to the receiving of this truth
are so much the more to be weighed that the Apostle makes this
a truth to be known first, before Christians can get saving light
or true comfort from the Scripture: *Knowing this first, that no
prophecy of Scripture is of any private interpretation.* [3.] Although the
Lord has employed men void of true sanctification to prophesy
some things, now set down by others in Scripture as His mind,
Numbers 23 and 24, and to preach the Gospel, Matt. 10:4, and
so may yet employ such men in whose hands the Word and ordinances may be made effectual for the salvation of others, as the
laws of a nation, orderly published by an authorised messenger,
are valid, whatever his personal qualifications be, yet those men
whom the Lord employed to put His mind in the public register
of the Scripture, though compassed with many sinful infirmities
registered by themselves, were endued with true holiness, and in
that to be imitated by all, especially those that handle the Scripture, and were infallible in that work, being consecrated and set
apart by the Lord for it. Therefore does the Apostle here call
them *holy men of God.* [4.] Although these extraordinary men did
find themselves bound to wait upon the ordinary duties of
God's service, the means of their salvation such as reading,
prayer, hearing, use of sacraments, &c, even when they wanted

these motions and that assistance of the Lord's Spirit which they desired and sometimes found, as appears by their fixing set times to themselves for those exercises and at them, crying for the motions and influences of the Lord's Spirit, Dan. 6:10, Psa. 119:164, compared with v. 148,149 and Psa. 63:1,2 and 101:2, yet was it otherwise with them while they were employed in that extraordinary work of receiving and publishing the Lord's mind, which now is the Scripture: for they were not bound to see visions or to prophesy except when they were forcibly moved, and had an extraordinary impulse and furniture[1] so to do; in which employment they were so infallibly borne through as that they could not err or miscarry. All which is signified by this word of the Apostle's, *They spoke as they were moved by the Holy Ghost.* Hence it follows also, that although the Lord's Spirit be promised in the covenant of grace to every believer, Ezek. 36:27, and His light and assistance (which He does not vouchsafe when we will, but as He pleases, John 3:8) is to be sought and is necessary, in some measure, for the right performance of every duty, John 15:5, yet is not any ordinary minister or Christian to stay from their duty till they find that measure of the Spirit which they desire, and ought to seek after, but they are to make use of the power which they have as reasonable creatures, Eccles. 9:10, and to stir up the gifts and graces they have as Christians and believers, Isa. 64:7, 1 Tim. 4:6, and in the way of their duty, to wait and cry for the necessary influences of the Lord's Spirit, Canticles 4:16, for the Apostle speaks of this way of the prophets being immediately acted by the Spirit, and their not acting as prophets till then, as singular and proper to them and such as they; and therefore not to be pretended to, or imitated by any other except they would presume to seek out more Scripture from God after He has closed His Book with a curse on them that add to it, Rev. 22:18. They were no ordinary men, nor acted in an ordinary way, who, according to the sense of this place, *spake as they were moved by the Holy Ghost.*

[1] See page 62.

CHAPTER TWO

Because the prevailing of error ordinarily brings with it a great decay of grace and holiness, therefore the Apostle (having in the first part of this Epistle, Chapter 1, pressed the study of growth in grace and diligence in holy duties) does in this chapter, which is the second part, guard against the infection of error. And for this end, [1.] he gives forewarning of the rise and prevalency of false teachers in the church of the New Testament, especially such as under a pretence of liberty through Jesus Christ would loose the reins to all licentiousness, as appears by comparing the first and nineteenth verses. [2.] He at large describes them by such clear characters taken from their abominable doctrine and vile practices as might make them known and hateful to all the Lord's people. [3.] He threatens them with no less terrible judgments than ever had come upon the vilest sinners that ever lived, that so all might be afraid to drink in their errors. And [4.] he holds out to the godly some grounds of confidence to be made use of by them for their preservation both from their errors and plagues. These four are the principal parts of the chapter; which are not handled apart but often intermixed throughout the whole, as will appear by a particular view of the sum thereof. The Apostle forewarns of the rise of these soul seducers, describing them from the strain and tendency of their doctrine, together with the hazard of it to themselves and their followers (v 1), from the success they should have (v 2), from their way of prevailing and certainty of their judgment (v 3). Which last he confirms by a threefold instance of God's judgment upon the angels, the old world and Sodom; intermixing therewith a twofold example of the Lord's preserving of *Noah* and *Lot* as pledges of his respect to His own in all times of the prevailing of sin and judgment (vv 4,5,6,7,8), both which he applies for the comfort of the godly and terror of the wicked (v 9), especially of such soul-deceivers and their followers as had given themselves to the service of their lusts, wherein they were so bold and self-pleasing that they laboured to disgrace all lawful authority that might oppose them (v 10), which sin he aggravates from the carriage of the good angels who honour magistracy (v 11), and

CHAPTER 2 : Introduction

from their likeness to the beasts, by reason of it, in undervaluing that whereof they know not the worth, and violent prosecuting of their lusts of pleasure, gain and glory; for which he threatens that their end shall be worse than the beasts (v 12,13,14); and for their apostasy from the truth for gain, and other idols, which they no less violently pursue than *Balaam* (v 15) when no opposition even extraordinary, could restrain (v 16), and for their many fair pretences whereby they did ensnare poor souls, once brought from paganism to Christianity, (vv 17,18,19). For all which, especially their apostasy after so great a change externally, he threatens them and their followers with more wrath than if they had never known and professed as they did (vv 20,21). Which apostasy, he shows, is not to be stumbled at in regard that they, still retaining their unrenewed nature, are only gone back (like dogs and swine) to their seemingly renounced errors and sins (v 22).

1. **But there were false prophets also among the people, even as there shall be false teachers among you, who privily shall bring in damnable heresies, even denying the Lord that bought them, and bring upon themselves swift destruction.**

The Apostle brings in the forewarning of the rise of heretics both with guarding against offence thereat, upon this ground, that it had been the lot of the church before; and withal, describing them from this, that they should cunningly convey into the church and minds of people such errors as would bring damnation upon themselves, and all that should receive and continue in them; of which errors he gives an instance, *That they should deny the Lord that bought them*; which is not to be understood as if either Christ had died for such men (for then they could not have perished, John 10:11,28), or as if they had expressly denied Christ to be the Redeemer; for then could they not have prevailed as they did with professors of Christ (v 2), nor had their words been feigned, as they are said to be (v 3), but open blasphemy. The meaning therefore is that they, being by profession and in their own and others' esteem, redeemed ones, should vent such errors as would in substance tend to the denial of the sovereignty and Lordship of Christ over His people, by labouring under a pretence of Christian liberty (as it is, v 19) to loose believers from their subjection to Christ's royal Law; for which he threatens speedy judgments to come upon them, as if

245

they had expressly denied Him after they had been redeemed by Him.

Hence learn, [1.] It has ordinarily been and so will continue the lot of the church to be troubled with false teachers, the wise Lord so disposing that He may have a proof of His people's love to Him by their constant adherence to His opposed truth (Deut. 13:3, 2 Cor. 11:13), that He may make His truth the more clear and lovely to His own, Tit. 1:9, that He may justly punish with strong delusion them that receive not the truth in love, 2 Thess. 2:11, and that His own in no time may stumble at what has been the lot of the Church in all times. For to guard against offence at such a lot, and to stir up all to the study and esteem of the written Word, which the Apostle had commended in the close of the former chapter, he thus forewarns, *But* (or *for*) *there were false prophets among the people, even as there shall be false teachers among you.* [2.] The way that seducers bring in error into the church and minds of people is not easily discerned, it being often mixed with many precious truths (v 19), veiled with odd and heavenly-like expressions (Rom. 16:18), with the pretence of singular piety in the venters of it (2 Cor. 11:13) and of much love to the welfare of the souls they seduce (Gal. 4:17), and borne-in mainly upon the simplest sort of professors, 2 Tim. 3:6. By these and the like artifices, do men *privily bring in damnable heresies.* [3.] Error, no less than the vilest practice in the world, may bring damnation upon the souls of people, especially if it be freely and voluntarily chosen, (not for terror or compulsion) as the word *heresy* signifies, if it do either expressly or in substance destroy any of Christ's offices, or the way of salvation through Him, and if it be vented by some professor for the seducing of others, and rending of the Church: all which are here made ingredients of heresy which the Apostle calls *damnable*, and such as will bring upon them that receive, vent and continue therein, *swift destruction.* [4.] Albeit only the elect are redeemed unto life; and none of them who are given to Christ of the Father can perish or finally deny Christ unto destruction, because Christ is engaged to keep them from perdition (John 6:39), yet reprobates who do profess themselves to be redeemed by Christ and are esteemed for such by the church, may be said to *deny the Lord that bought them*, in the terms of *judicial process* (when they say He has redeemed them, and in the mean time, in doctrine and deeds, do deny and betray Him), howsoever in the terms of *historical narration*, they were never redeemed nor written in the Book of Life. Even as apostates in the terms of *judicial process* are said to trample Christ under their feet, Heb. 10:29, which in the terms of *historical narration* is impossible: because our Lord was long before that time that the Apostle did write this, bodily ascended into heaven and was beyond the reach of any such bodily injury. And as the *Amalekite* (2 Sam. 1:16) is charged for killing the Lord's anointed, albeit the history tells us that he was slain before he came to him because his own mouth testified so much against him, so may reprobate hypocrites crept into the Church visible (calling Christ their redeemer and yet proving, in effect, bodily enemies to Him) be charged for *denying the Lord that bought them*, because their own mouths and deeds do testify so much against them.

2. And many shall follow their pernicious ways; by reason of whom the way of truth shall be evil spoken of.

Follows the success of these sectaries, held forth in two branches: [1.] That they should have a numerous party to back them in their soul-destroying courses. [2.] That they and their followers should prevail to bring saving truth into disgrace among many.

Doctrine [1.] It is not strange to see the most dangerous heretics have many followers; every error being a friend to some lust, 2 Tim. 4:3, and having often more of prosperity and applause attending it than truth, 1 Cor. 4:8,10, and because of activity and fair pretences of them that vent it, Matt. 23:15, Rom. 16:18; for these and the like causes *many shall follow their pernicious ways*. [2.] They that are left of God to the leading of the spirit of error do not only enslave their judgments to their seducers, but do also give up themselves to back them in all the courses they take to propagate their errors, and increase their faction, even although these courses, no less than their errors, be destructive to the honour of Christ and welfare of souls: for the Apostle says, *Many shall follow* not only their errors, which he called *damnable* before, but *their ways* which are called *pernicious*. [3.] As error is received, truth goes out of request, the lovers thereof bending all their wit to disgrace those truths that discover the vileness of their errors, Rom. 3:8, and to raise and keep up hot contests among the professors of the Gospel, Gal. 1:7, thereby giving occasion to a third party who resolve to side with none but to slander or (as the word is) blaspheme the whole profession of Christianity, Rom. 2:24, for the Apostle here makes the slandering of truth the consequence of embracing error, and points at a third party who would take occasion from heretics prevailing to slander the truth: *By reason of whom the way of truth shall be evil spoken of.*

3. And through covetousness shall they with feigned words make merchandise of you: whose judgment now of a long time lingereth not, and their damnation slumbereth not.

Follows the way how these false teachers came to have so great success; held forth in two branches. Their immoderate desire of gain and glory made them very industrious. And [2.] their figurative or plaistered[1] language, as the word signifies, made them easily gain a number of poor souls to be completely at their disposal, as wares are under the power of the merchant that has bought them; for which dealing he forewarns that God's watchful providence was framing His decreed judgments for them.

Hence learn, [1.] However they that seduce souls by error may seem to be the most mortified men in the world, Col. 2:23, and most desirous of the good of souls, Gal. 4:17, yet all their pains with people arise from some unmortified lust such as the immoderate desire of gain or applause: for the Spirit of the Lord is in this to be believed, that whatever they pretend, *through covetousness they make merchandise of His people.* [2.] In their way of dealing with souls, false teachers are very like unto cheating merchants, [1.] in their using of much fair and plaistered[1] language to commend their errors; [2.] in their activity and stirring from place to place (as the word in the original, *of making merchandise,* signifies) to vent them. And [3.] in their unsatisfiableness till their followers become their complete slaves, both in judgment and practice. All which is held forth as clear resemblances between them and cheating merchants, in these words, *With feigned words shall they make merchandise of you.* [4.] However the judgment of such men be hardly believed, because of their success and fair pretences, and may be long suspended for the exercise of the godly and punishment of those who, by reason of strong delusion, receive not the love of the truth; yet it is most certain, according to the foreknowledge and

[1] 'plaistered': (plastered), loaded to excess.

decree of God; it is swiftly approaching and shall light upon them by way of surprisal; for *their judgment now of a long time lingereth not and their damnation slumbereth not.*

4. For if God spared not the angels that sinned, but cast them down to hell, and delivered them into chains of darkness, to be reserved unto judgment;

The Apostle proves the certainty of the judgment threatened against these false teachers by a threefold instance, in this and the following verses. The substance of the first, which is in this verse, is that if the holy Lord did not spare the angels, His most glorious creatures, when they sinned against Him, but did presently[1] imprison them in the pit of hell, reserving them for further judgment, these false teachers and their followers have no reason to dream of exemption. Which conclusion, flowing from this and the following instances, the Apostle finds not necessary to express, but leaves to their own conscience to infer.

Doctrine. [1.] Although it be ordinary for sinners to harden themselves against threatenings because of their excellences and privileges conferred upon them by the Lord, Rev. 18:7, yet nothing of that kind can shelter them from the wrath of a provoked God; but the more of these gifts there be, and be abused, the greater measure of wrath may be expected. Therefore is the judgment of God upon these excellent and privileged creatures, the angels, brought to prove the certainty of the like wrath to come upon false teachers who by reason of their excellent enduements and esteem in the church were ready to make light of the Apostle's threatenings: *If God spared not the angels*, &c. [2.] It ought to be esteemed marvellous mercy in God that He does not presently[1] thrust sinners down to hell when they provoke Him, and much more that He has provided a remedy and offers pardon to them. Every moment's sparing after the commission of sin should be thought wonderful indulgence in God, who *spared not the angels, but* (as the words in the original will bear) *imprisoned them while they were sinning*, secluding them from all possibility or hopes of recovery for ever. *He spared not the angels that sinned, but cast them down to hell, and delivered them into chains*, &c. [3.] The fallen angels, who are the devils, are under such a powerful restraint of divine providence that they

---

[1] See page 15.

cannot move or act anything but in so far as the Lord's holy
justice and wisdom permits and orders them, for the punishment of the wicked or exercise of the godly; *for they are reserved in
chains of darkness*, which are nothing else but God's irresistible
power and terrible justice over-ruling, tormenting and
restraining them. [4.] Although the devils, when they are permitted, can appear visibly as if they were at their own liberty, and
can seem jovial as if they were free of torment, 1 Sam. 28:13, that
so they may the more effectually prevail with such poor slaves as
have provoked God to give them up to their delusion, yet, go
where they will, their hell is always with them, they live in the
constant feeling of the wrath of the Almighty, as their being
delivered in chains of darkness imports, and in the dreadful expectation of a more high measure of wrath which they shall get at the
day of judgment when they together with all that serve them and
follow their counsel shall have nothing else to do but endure
torment, and shall torment one another for ever: for they are
delivered in chains of darkness to be reserved unto judgment.

5. **And spared not the old world, but saved Noah the eighth
   person, a preacher of righteousness, bringing in the flood
   upon the world of the ungodly;**

Follows the second instance to prove the certainty of God's
judgment to come upon these soul-deceivers, whereof the sum
is that if the old world, notwithstanding of their multitude and
their long and great prosperity were all, excepting a few, swept
away with the flood because of their wickedness; these false
teachers, notwithstanding their multitude of followers, and long
success in propagating their errors, have no reason to imagine
to themselves an escape from the wrath of God: with which
instance the Apostle intermixes the example of *Noah's* preservation, as a pledge of the Lord's respect to all who keep the way of
truth and holiness in an evil time, as is clear by comparing this
and the ninth verse. Although there were seven preserved from
the flood beside *Noah*, who is therefore called the eighth, yet he
only is named because he was mainly respected in that
deliverance, and the rest for his cause. He is called a *preacher of
righteousness*, because even in that time he did hold forth to the
people the way of free justification by the righteousness of Christ
and the duties of holiness, wherein justified persons ought to

walk; with both which, *Noah* had been well acquainted, as is clear by comparing Heb. 11:7 with Gen. 6:9.

Hence learn, [1.] There are not a few shifts in the hearts of wicked men, prospering in their sinful courses, whereby they harden themselves against the threatenings of the Word of the Lord and put the thoughts of His wrath far away from them: for after the Apostle has, by the former instance of God's judgment upon the fallen angels, cut off the hopes of false teachers evading the wrath of God because of any pretended or real excellency they had, he does by this instance prove, that neither their multitude of followers, nor former success, could avail them, since God *spared not the old world*. [2.] As the Lord uses in times of greatest defection to profanity or error to preserve a few who will bear testimony for His truth, and against the dishonour done to Him by others, so He is never so terrible to the wicked but that He will remember to manifest His respect to His own few amongst them who labour to keep themselves free of, and mourn for, these abominations which provoke Him to let forth His terror: for *Noah* in this instance and *Lot* in the following, are brought in as pledges of a few whom the Lord minded to preserve from that universal infection of error and vileness which was to prevail in the Church of the New Testament, and whom He minded also to deliver from the plagues to follow thereupon, as appears from v 9, *But saved Noah the eighth*, &c. [3.] Even in the very infancy of the Church under the Old Testament, the way of justification by Christ's righteousness had been publicly preached, and the duties of holiness pressed upon justified persons; the study of both which ought always to be much pressed upon people by the ministers of Christ, especially in a time of abounding of iniquity, and approaching of judgment, as the only way to be hid from wrath and enjoy communion with God: for *Noah* in such a time was a *preacher of righteousness*, both imputed and inherent, as was cleared in the exposition of this verse. [4.] The Lord, in the dispensation of His justice, is not bound to keep the ordinary course of nature, but for the illustration thereof He may, and sometimes does make the creatures move contrary to their nature, there being in them all a stronger propension so to do for their Maker's service than to move according to their ordinary course in serving their fellow-creatures to His dishonour: for here in this instance the sea comes out of its channel at His command to drown a profane world; and in the following instance, the fire comes down out of its region to burn up filthy cities: *bringing in the flood upon the world of the ungodly.*

6. And turning the cities of Sodom and Gomorrha into ashes condemned them with an overthrow, making them an ensample unto those that after should live ungodly;

Here is the third instance confirming the certainty of God's dreadful reckoning with false teachers and their followers. The sum whereof is that if *Sodom* and *Gomorrha*, with other flourishing cities beside them, were for their vileness totally and terribly destroyed, and so made lasting copies of divine wrath to come upon all ungodly persons: these soul-deceivers who were guilty of as high provocations and had drawn in their guilt a great number of the Lord's people, could not think in reason to escape.

Hence learn, [1.] The judgments of God upon sinful cities and incorporations, use to be most terrible and exemplary, there being in them a confluence of many mercies and so of many provocations, powerful examples to sin and bold despising of warnings, which provokes God to make them en-samples of much wrath, *Turning the cities of Sodom and Gomorrha into ashes*; condemned with a total and singular overthrow, as the word signifies, *making them ensamples*, &c. [2.] The sins of reasonable creatures provoke the Lord to write His displeasure, not only upon the persons of the sinners, but also upon the sinless and unreasonable creatures which they abuse to His dis-honour: for here the cities, comprehending both the persons of the sinners and all the plantation, store and pleasant things of *Sodom, are burnt to ashes, and condemned with an overthrow.* [3.] However error or heresy be often looked upon with more charity and less abhorrency than profane practices, yet shall not the judgment of heretics and their followers be inferior to the judgment of the vilest of men that ever lived: for God's judgment upon *Sodom* is here brought in as an ensample and pledge of His wrath to come upon all the ungodly, amongst whom false teachers and their followers are mainly eyed, as is clear by considering the connection between the third verse and this. [4.] However sins and judgments in respect of their special nature and circumstances may vary in several times, yet the desert of every sin and the exactness of divine justice remaining still the same, former judgments of what sort soever, executed upon any kind of sinners, are certain pledges of the same wrath or the like for substance, to come upon all that walk contrary to the truth and will of God, though they were never so free of these special sins that formerly did procure that wrath. Therefore is this instance of God's judgment upon the *Sodomites* (as also the two former) brought in here, as certain pledges of God's wrath to come upon false teachers, and their followers; yea upon all ungodly persons, *making them ensamples* (not only to those who should be found guilty of such unnatural uncleanness as the *Sodomites* were, but also) *to all that after should live ungodly*, whatever their particular sins should be. [5.] However they that live in sin under the light of the Word be neither willing to hear threatenings nor to apply them to themselves, Isa. 13:10, yet is the Lord's justice against impenitent sinners so clear in the examples thereof recorded in Scripture, and the witness and deputy conscience which God has in every man's bosom so impartial, that if upon serious consideration of what God's holy justice has done to sinners before, it were put to speak what men, continuing in their sinful courses, have to expect now, they could not be made to apply wrath to themselves, and certainly to expect it, while they compare their own sins with those for which others have been punished; and do consider how impartially and immutably just He is with whom they, as well as others, have to do. Therefore the Apostle does not express the inference which he clearly intends should be drawn from the three forenamed instances, but leaves it to the consciences of those whom he has been threatening, as that which they might easily conclude from thence.

7. **And delivered just Lot, vexed with the filthy conversation of the wicked:**
8. **(For that righteous man dwelling among them, in seeing and hearing, vexed his righteous soul from day to day, with their unlawful deeds;)**

For the comfort of all that mourn for the prevailing of iniquity in those among whom they live, the Apostle subjoins to the former instance the example of *Lot's* preservation, whom the Spirit of the Lord, that indicated this Scripture, commends by several expressions of great respect, for His deep resentment of and sympathy with the Lord's suffering honour and for these vile *Sodomites* amongst whom providence had cast his lot for a time.

Hence learn, [1.] The dearest of the children of the Lord may be put by His providence to have their residence amongst the worst of men, the Lord thereby correcting and humbling them for their too low esteem and little use-making of better society while they had it: of which fault it seems *Lot* was not altogether free, Gen. 13, and thereby also giving them occasion to do good to the souls of their godless neighbours, and bear witness against their wickedness: both which *Lot* endeavoured, Gen. 19:7, who for these and other reasons had his lot among the *Sodomites* for a time. [2.] It is not impossible for the children of the Lord, living among the most profane, to retain their integrity, and have the Lord's approbation for their disposition and carriage; there being much more power in the grace of Christ and his indwelling Spirit in them than there is in the temptations of Satan, or the example of the wicked, notwithstanding all their terrors and allurements: for *Lot* among the *Sodomites* is approved and commended as a *just and righteous man*. [3.] It is the kindly disposition of a true penitent to be so far from taking pleasure in the sins of others as the wicked do, Rom. 1:32, that he will be *vexed* in soul, and will account it his duty to put himself to much grief, as the words here signify, while he ponders and is a witness of His dishonour that has forgiven him: for so was it with penitent and pardoned *Lot*, he was *vexed* (which is a passive word) and *did vex* (which is an active) *his righteous soul with the filthy conversation* and unjust deeds *of the Sodomites*. [4.] This sympathizing frame of spirit with the Lord's suffering honour is much taken notice of by Him, both to reward it graciously and to punish them that occasion that grief to His people. Therefore both the expressions of *Lot's* vexation and of the Lord's respect to him are frequently repeated here, *Just Lot was vexed and did vex his righteous soul*. [5.] It is the privilege of a true penitent to be in no less esteem with a merciful God and to find no less expressions of respect from Him than if he had never sinned against Him: for though *Lot* (not without guiltiness) did separate from *Abraham*, choosing *Sodom* to live in for better worldly accommodation, for which he met with much oppression and soul-vexation (both which, the word in the original signifies), yet the Lord did not only preserve his memory in esteem by these manifold expressions of His respect to him, *He delivered just Lot, that righteous man, who vexed his righteous soul*. [6.] When men are left of God to follow the inclination of their corrupt nature, they will go to such a height of wickedness as ought not to be mentioned without abhorrency; they will not be restrained by any law, they will cast aside all modesty, and avow their vileness in their outward conversation; unnatural sins will become the very element wherein they will not weary to waste themselves daily: all which is signified by these words here in the original whereby the carriage of the *Sodomites* is set forth, and by the Apostle's speaking of it with so great detestation, while he says, *Lot was vexed with the filthy conversation of the wicked, and did vex his righteous soul from day to day, with their unlawful deeds.*

9. **The Lord knoweth how to deliver the godly out of temptations, and to reserve the unjust unto the day of judgment to be punished:**

This verse contains the application of all the former instances in a conclusion drawn from them especially for the comfort of the godly, as also for the terror of the wicked, who ought both to draw the inference which is here from the former examples.

Hence learn, [1.] Although there be now no ordinary warrant to expect such an extraordinary way of preservation from common calamities as some of the saints have found before, yet that same wisdom, power and love in God which wrought deliverance for them, being engaged in the covenant of grace to be forthcoming for all His own, in the way that may be most for His honour and their good; all who imitate these saints in fearing threatened judgments, in mourning for and keeping themselves free of the causes procuring them, and in the use of commanded means for their preservation, may take their extraordinary deliverances recorded in Scripture for pledges to them either of exemption from the outward calamity, if that be for their good, or of the equivalent thereof; or rather that which will be better for them, to wit, such a measure of the Lord's presence under it as changes the nature of it to them; or their full deliverance both from sin and trouble by it: for *Noah* and *Lot's* preservation, which were extraordinary, are here held forth as useful for ordinary believers, whence they might draw this comfortable conclusion, *The Lord knoweth how to deliver the godly out of temptation.* [2.] It is the lot of the truly godly to be brought into many and great straits, not only by outward troubles but by inward temptations; both which come ordinarily together upon

the children of the Lord, that so their manifold corruptions may
be borne down, the several graces of God's Spirit in them tried
and increased by exercise, and the power, faithfulness and love
of Christ manifested and commended in their through-bearing
and deliverance: for they from whose case this inference is
drawn were in both these exercises at once; and the word *temptation* here does ordinarily in Scripture signify both afflictions and
temptations to sin. [3.] While the children of the Lord are exercised with outward afflictions and inward temptations they are
also oftentimes both ignorant of a way of delivery and anxious
concerning it, as if their straits, and the way of their out-gate[1]
were hid from the Lord, as it is, Isa. 40:27; for this consolation,
The Lord knoweth how to deliver the godly, is fitted for such a case and
so does suppose it to be ordinary. [4.] The Lord's taking notice
of the straits of the godly, and His knowledge of the way of their
deliverance, should be to them a sufficient ground of comfort,
both against their straits and their ignorance of a way of out-
gate,[1] His love having engaged His power and faithfulness to
make forthcoming for them everything His infinite wisdom sees
to be most for their good: for, for this very end is this consolation given to the godly, *The Lord knoweth how to deliver them out of
temptation,* that they may be comforted both against their straits
and their ignorance of a way of delivery. [5.] Whether the Lord
spare wicked men or let out the earnest[2] of His wrath upon them
in this life, yet is the full measure thereof keeping to the fore for
them against the day of judgment, when they shall be made able
to endure that wrath; a sparkle whereof would now undo them.
Therefore for their terror is this conclusion also drawn from the
former examples, *The Lord knoweth how to reserve the unjust to the
day of judgment to be punished.*

10. **But chiefly them that walk after the flesh in the lust of uncleanness, and despise government. Presumptuous are
they, self-willed, they are not afraid to speak evil of
dignities.**

The former threatenings and examples of God's judgments
which do concern all ungodly men are here particularly applied

---

[1] See page 144.
[2] 'earnest': forètaste.

to some who did in a special manner incense[1] the wrath of God against themselves, amongst whom false teachers and their followers are mainly eyed; and who are described from this, that they follow their unmortified corruption as their ordinary leader, making a trade of sins against the second Table, particularly the seventh and fifth commandments thereof, wherein they were so bold and self-pleasing that they did not fear openly to disgrace any lawful authority that might oppose them in their wickedness.

Hence learn, [1.] Whatever be the fair pretences of singular holiness that false teachers use to have, 2 Cor. 11:13, yet really and in effect they are nothing else but profane slaves to their lusts: in so far as truth is forsaken and error received, profanity must needs have place and holiness be forsaken; the same Spirit of Christ, being the Spirit of truth and the Spirit of holiness: for these seducers who drew so many after them by their fair pretences, are mainly intended here, while the Apostle says, *They walk after the flesh in the lust of uncleanness.* [2.] Although any one act of sin, yea, the least sinful motion of the heart, deserves God's everlasting wrath, Rom. 6:23, yet there is a singular measure of wrath abiding some sinners beyond others; particularly those who are not only through infirmity overtaken in sin, as the best of the saints have been, but do also make their corrupt inclination their ordinary guide and rule, and their following and satisfying thereof their common trade: for the threatening formerly given out against all the ungodly, is here particularly applied to some, chiefly those that *walk after the flesh.* [3.] The wrath of a holy God is in a special way incensed against the sin of uncleanness, and that not only against the outward acts of that sin such as fornication, adultery, &c, but against the very inward motions of the heart toward it: for there is a special measure of wrath here denounced against them who walk in the lust or (as the word signifies) *the desire of uncleanness.* [4.] Lawful magistracy is a divine ordinance, so precious in God's account that He will let out a special measure of His wrath upon men for want of inward respect to it in their hearts; yea, for any expressions that may weaken the due esteem thereof in the hearts of others, even though they were heathens that were invested with that office: for though magistrates were generally such at this time, yet there is a special degree of wrath threatened

---

[1] 'incense': kindle.

against them who either undervalue in their hearts or disgrace by their expressions that ordinance, especially *those who despise government, and are not afraid to speak evil of dignities.* [5.] Men that are slaves to their own lusts are ordinarily un-friends to lawful magistrates. Pretend what they will, they who live in rebellion against God can never be truly loyal to any Viceregent of His, and therefore ought not to be preferred or countenanced by such, or any that give out themselves to be such: *for they that walk after the flesh, do also despise government.* [6.] The more stout-hearted men are in their sinful courses out-facing all challenges and the more wedded to their own inclination, not fearing to disgrace any that have a calling to oppose them in their wickedness, the more wrath have they to expect from God: for thus is the sin of these men aggreged,[1] who are here threatened with a special measure of wrath: *Presumptuous are they, self-willed.* [7.] Although sedition and disloyalty to lawful magistracy be the ordinary charge which false teachers give in against the faithful servants of Christ, Acts 24:1,5 and 17:6,7, as they did also against the Lord Himself, Luke 23:1,2, yet these false teachers themselves will be found to be the greatest unfriends of lawful magistrates, either denying or weakening their authority, if so be they employ their power any way for opposing their errors or wicked practices: for false teachers are mainly intended here and charged by the Spirit of the Lord with this guilt: *They despise government, and are not afraid to speak evil of dignities.*

11. Whereas angels which are greater in power and might, bring not railing accusation against them before the Lord.

The Apostle aggreges[1] their sin of despising and disgracing lawful authority from the carriage of the good angels, who though they be far above the greatest on earth in power and other perfections, yet do they esteem so highly of magistracy that they are loath to do anything that may disgrace or bring into contempt that ordinance in the person of any, as these base men do, whose guiltiness and wrath must therefore be exceeding great.

Doctrine. [1.] The good angels are some way present at, and employed about, the affairs of the children of men, not only

[1] See page 159.

within the church, as guardians and servants to the saints, Psa. 34:7, as witnesses of their worship, 1 Cor. 11:10, and co-disciples with them in the study of the Gospel, 1 Pet. 1:12; but also without the Church in reference to her good, executing judgment, at the Lord's command, upon her enemies, Isa. 37:36, marring their counsels against her, Dan. 10:20. Although they use not now visibly to appear, since the worshipping of them has so prevailed in the anti-Christian church, yet if they were not some way present and employed, as is said, the carriage of these heretics could not be aggreged[1] from the dissimilitude thereof to the present carriage of the good angels toward magistrates, as here it is: *they despise government and speak evil of dignities, whereas angels which are greater in power and might, bring no railing accusation against them.* [2.] Although the power of angels be finite, as themselves are, it being the Lord's incommunicable property to be Almighty, Gen. 17:1, yet that power which the Lord has given them for the safeguard of the saints whom they attend, Heb. 1:14, and for the terror of the wicked, whom they oppose, Psa. 68:17, does far exceed the power of the greatest on earth: for whether they be compared with false teachers who by reason of the multitude of their followers are very powerful, or with magistrates who are the mightiest on earth, they are, according to this Scripture, *greater in power and might.* [3.] The more nearness any creatures have to God and the more eminent for gracious qualifications they be, the more tenderness and compassion will they bear towards creatures that are void of those perfections wherewith they are endued, and compassed with infirmities whereof they are free; and the less delight will they have in their disgrace, or destruction. Therefore the angels who do, with much alacrity and height of divine zeal, execute the judgments of the Lord when they are commanded, Psa. 103:20, who are witnesses of more of the wickedness and sinful infirmities of magistrates than false teachers can be, and who do far excel both in perfection, do not (as false teachers use to do) *bring any railing accusation against them before the Lord.* [4.] As the eminency of sinners does in some respects aggrege[1] their sins because of the power of their example and their great engagements to God, 2 Sam. 12:7, so also does the meanness of their condition in other respects, Prov. 30:21, they being thereby called to the more humble dependence and duty toward

[1] See page 159.

God: for thus is the sin of these false teachers aggreged,[1] that they being such base and mean creatures, should despise dominion and speak evil of dignities, *whereas Angels that are greater in power and might, bring no railing accusation against them before the Lord.*

12. But these, as natural brute beasts, made to be taken and destroyed, speak evil of the things they understand not; and shall utterly perish in their own corruption;

The Apostle having shown how unlike these false teachers (who despise magistracy and government among Christians) are to the most glorious creatures of God, the good angels, he shows here how like they are in this and the rest of their carriage to the basest of the creatures, the brute beasts: and the resemblances between them which the Apostle's words may lead us to are especially three. [1.] As the beasts are void of human reason, so are they of heavenly wisdom. [2.] As the beasts do readily trample under foot the most precious things, so do they speak evil of the things they understand not: whereby is especially meant their opposing of magistracy and government among Christians, and their slandering of the doctrine of holiness, so much pressed by the apostles, as if it had been contrary to the liberty of Christians. [3.] As the beasts are framed for destruction, so are they for utter perdition: which is not to be understood as if they that have immortal souls could come to nothing as the beasts, but that they are appointed for eternal torment which they do procure to themselves as the beast is appointed for the slaughter.

Hence learn, [1.] However men of erroneous opinions and vile affections may be in so high esteem in the church by reason of their fair pretences and the specious titles they assume to themselves as to draw a very considerable faction therein after them, yet does the Lord esteem such (and will in his own time discover them to be what they are in effect) base and beastly in their disposition and carriage: for here these false teachers who pretended to be the only fountains of consolation to the church (v 17), and patrons of Christian liberty (v 19), by such fair pretences gaining to themselves a numerous party (v 2), are declared by the Spirit of the Lord to be as *natural brute beasts.* [2.] When men are led by their sensual appetite, not by holy reason, and do

[1] See page 159.

become very adventurous in passing most hard sentences against things they understand least, they have then the characters of a beastly disposition and carriage: for both these are here made resemblances between the beasts and false teachers, who *as natural brute beasts speak evil of the things they understand not.* [3.] When men do thus resemble the beasts in their disposition and carriage, it is the clearest evidence that can be that they are appointed for destruction as the beast is for the slaughter; and that however they may, as fed beasts, prosper for a time, yet their end shall be much worse than theirs: for the Apostle makes the resemblance also in this, that as the beast is *to be taken and destroyed*, so shall they *utterly perish.* [4.] The punishment that abides the wicked consists in a thorough and continual torment of soul and body, in the deprivation of all comfort and that to all eternity, without any hope of recovery: which is imported in this, *they shall utterly perish.* [5.] Whatever destruction comes upon wicked men, it is of their own procuring. They do in time by their sins treasure up the wrath and gather the fuel which shall seize upon them and burn them up to all eternity: for, *they shall utterly perish in their own corruption.*

13. **And shall receive the reward of unrighteousness, as they that count it pleasure to riot in the day time. Spots they are and blemishes, sporting themselves with their own deceivings while they feast with you;**
14. **Having eyes full of adultery, and that cannot cease from sin, beguiling unstable souls: an heart they have exercised with covetous practices; cursed children:**

Here is a further amplification of the sin and judgment of these false teachers whom the Apostle has formerly described and threatened. The substance whereof is, that they shall lack nothing of the wrath due to those who count it their heaven to exceed in all carnal delights, notwithstanding of the light of the Gospel, thereby disgracing their holy profession and making but a sport of deceiving their own souls, since they can in the mean time deceive others, insinuating themselves in the esteem and society of the godly, whether in their religious or ordinary feasts (v 13), who are so under the power of their unclean lusts that they cannot but manifest their filthy disposition, being altogether impotent to resist temptations themselves, and ensnaring with their errors and vile practices such others as are not well settled in knowledge and grace: and who are so sold to love of their gain that they make it their heart exercise to attain thereto: for all which, the Apostle pronounces them heirs of God's fearful curse.

Doctrine. [1.] The wrath of God against sin had need to be oft inculcated to the guilty, and knit to the several branches of their sin, that so they may have the more lively apprehensions of that wrath, and may have their hearts accustomed to think upon it whensoever they think upon their sins, that so they may be either stopped in the course of their sin, and hastened to repentance, or left the more inexcusable. Therefore the Apostle, in branching out the sin of false teachers and their followers, does so frequently intermix threatenings, or some new representation of that wrath they have to expect: *They shall utterly perish,* in the former verse, and here, *They shall receive the reward of unrighteousness*: and they are *cursed children.* [2.] When God reckons with the wicked, they shall not lack a grain weight of the wrath due to them; for since they have slighted the use-making of Christ's righteousness which makes sinners righteous; and the study of holiness, which proves them righteous, *they shall receive the reward of unrighteousness*, which, in the original, signifies a due proportion of wrath to their sin. [3.] That which ripens wicked men for wrath is not their sins only, simply considered, but mainly the several aggravations ordinarily attending their sins, whereof there may be seen here nine in number. As, (1). This does exceedingly aggrege[1] men's sins, when they count it their very paradise to satisfy their lusts; for so the word in the original. They *count it their* Eden *to riot.* The more heaven men apprehend in their sins the more hell they will find. (2). When men become so impudently bent upon their lusts that neither the light of the world's knowledge of their sin, nor the light of the Word discovering the evil and hazard thereof, restrains them; both which may be comprehended in this other aggravation of their sin, *They count it pleasure to riot in the day time.* (3). When men by their sins do stain a holy profession that they have made before the world: for, if these men had not had a fair profession and high esteem in the church they could not have been *spots and blemishes while they feasted* with the Lord's people; which is here made another aggravation of their guilt. (4). When men do not only live in sin but do make a sport of it, beguiling their own hearts

---

[1] See page 159.

with groundless apprehensions that there is neither such evil nor hazard therein, as the Word holds forth, and their own conscience sometimes suggests: for this is another aggravation. *They sport themselves in their own deceivings.* (5). When in the meantime of their living in the slavery of their lusts they are careful to keep up their esteem with the godly and attend all occasions of converse with them, that so they may cloak their sins: for it is here made another aggravation of their guilt that all this wickedness is committed *while they feast with the Lord's people.* (6). When men's lusts are so vigorous within that they manifest their predominancy in their very outward carriage: for this is a further aggravation of their sin, *They have eyes full of adultery.* (7). When men become so impotent to resist their lusts that the satisfying thereof becomes their very element, out of which they cannot rest, as the word here signifies, *They cannot cease from sin*: which is also another aggravation of their guilt. (8). When sinners become infectious, ensnaring with the bait of fair pretences (as the word *beguiling* in the original signifies) many others, to swallow down their foul errors and profane practices: this also is a high aggravation of their guilt. (9). When men make it their heart exercise, whereabouts they spend their wit and affections to fulfil their fleshly desires: for this is here the last aggravation of their sin, *An heart they have exercised with covetous practices.*

Doctrine [4.] Although it be possible that the Lord's people may without guiltiness admit into their ordinary and intimate society the worst of men, while they do not discover themselves, as is clear concerning *Ahithophel* and *Judas*; yet does the admission of such into their society oftentimes prove a great snare, especially to those that are admitted, while they take occasion therefrom to harden themselves in those sins, and to count the less of that vileness, the commission whereof does not mar their esteem and society with the godly: for this is one thing that helped these soul-deceivers to deceive themselves and willingly to overlook the evil of their own condition, that notwithstanding of all their wickedness, they were admitted to the society of the godly, and did pass among them for such: *While they feast with you.* [5.] When men labour not to mortify their inward lusts, the Lord oftentimes justly suffers them to manifest the predominancy of these lusts over them in their outward carriage. As grace which is lively within will put some beauty upon the outward man, Eccles. 8:1, so corruptions vigorous within will readily betray the person to be its slave, Isa. 3:9, *Having eyes full of adultery*, or (as it is in the original) *of the adulteress*. [6.] So bewitching is the spirit of error where it enters and so devoted are deluded souls unto their seducing teachers, that though these teachers be judicially plagued of God (as ordinarily such are) with profanity of life, yet this does not make their followers loathe them or abhor their errors: for though *they did riot in the day time* and *had eyes full of adultery*, yet were they still beguiling unstable souls. [7.] Those who are not rooted in knowledge by clear information and frequent meditation of the truth and have not their hearts established with grace by the frequent exercise thereof, will readily be a prey to soul-deceivers: for those whom they beguile are here called *unstable souls*. [8.] No man serves one idol alone, but many at once: he that is wedded to worldly pleasures will be also wedded to his credit; the want whereof mars his pleasure; and if pleasure and credit be two of a man's idols, ready gain will be the third, that so he may the more easily attain to the other two. Therefore the Apostle describes these men here as slaves to all these three idols at once, to their pleasures, which were their Eden; to their credit, which made them hold forth baits to take many followers; and to their gain, wherewith their heart was exercised that so their pleasures and credit might be attained and upheld. Lastly, they who profess themselves to be the children of the Lord, but spend their immortal spirits upon the unworthy things of this present life, not trusting to His care and providence in the moderate use of lawful means whereunto their profession does oblige them, forfeit the right they pretend to have to the privileges of His children and serve themselves heirs to His curse: for because their heart is exercised with *covetous practices*, they are *cursed children*.

15. **Which have forsaken the right way, and are gone astray, following the way of Balaam the son of Bosor, who loved the wages of unrighteousness;**
16. **But was rebuked for his iniquity: the dumb ass speaking with man's voice forbad the madness of the prophet.**

The Apostle, having shown what idols these false teachers set up, shows here two woeful effects that their love to them, especially to their gain, had upon them. The first is their apostasy from the truth and way of Christ. The second is extreme violence in the prosecution of these idols, which he sets forth by comparing them with *Balaam*, who was so mad in the prosecution of these same idols that even extraordinary opposition could not restrain him.

Hence learn, [1.] However men that *really* enter the way of Christ can never totally or finally fall from it, by reason of the Lord's undertaking, John 10:28, and unchangeableness, Rom. 11:29, yet they who have been once in opinion sound and in external practice blameless, remaining in the mean time without any inward saving change, may make apostasy from both: for such had these men been, of whom the Apostle says, *They have forsaken the right way.* [2.] Love to some unmortified lust, especially covetousness, is the prime cause both of much apostasy and of extreme violence in sinful courses; for so was it with these false teachers and their followers. Their heart was exercised with covetous practices in the former verse, and therefore *they forsook the right way*, imitating *Balaam* in the violent prosecution of that idol. [3.] When the right way, which is the way of truth and holiness, is forsaken, men can keep no certain course, but must needs be like wandering stars or planets (as the word here signifies), ever seeking and never finding that true satisfaction they might have had, and have forsaken, by forsaking the right way; *And are gone astray.* [4.] When the Lord's ordinary means to reclaim sinners from their lusts does not prevail with them, the Lord is justly provoked to give them up to go on in their own way, over the belly of more than ordinary opposition, if they have it, till they perish: for *Balaam* was not restrained by means more ordinary in his time and therefore he is not reclaimed by means more extraordinary; *He loved the wages of unrighteousness though he was rebuked for his iniquity by the dumb ass.* [5.] Covetousness being once rooted in the heart, and proposed as a man's main end, it is so powerful and imperious an idol that it will make the covetous man adventure upon any course, though never so unrighteous, and go over never so much opposition in the way of his gain: for though the wages that *Balaam* desired were wages of unrighteousness, because they could not be had but by cursing the people whom God had blessed, yet *he loved* them and pursued them *though the dumb ass forbad his madness in so doing.* [6.] The more opposition from the word or dispensations of God men do go over in the prosecution of their lusts, the greater is their guilt, and the more wrath have they to expect from God, especially when they trace the steps of sinners, whom

God has by His word and providence opposed before them: for it is here made an aggravation of sin, and cause of a special measure of wrath, that these men followed the way of *Balaam* who would go on after his lusts, *though the dumb ass, speaking with man's voice, forbad his madness.* [7.] It is in some respects more easy to work the greatest miracle in nature than to stop the course of a sinner violently pursuing his lusts; the reasonless creatures who have no active opposition in them to their Maker's will being more prone to obey Him, contrary to their ordinary course, than reasonable creatures without special grace and assistance can be, either to follow the direction of His Word or their own reason, contrary to their corrupt and vile affections: for while *Balaam* goes on in his sinful course, *The dumb ass, speaking as if it had a man's voice, forbad his madness.* [8.] A cross providence meeting sinners in a course contrary to the revealed will of the Lord has a language to them, proclaiming their madness, and prohibiting them to go on in their sins, which they ought to hear and obey, although it be not so express as when one man reproves another (see Micah 6:9), for though we read not (Numbers 22) that *Balaam's* ass did either expressly call him mad or prohibit his course, yet here the Spirit of God puts that commentary upon what it spake, which also *Balaam* should have done, *That the dumb ass speaking with man's voice, forbad the madness of the prophet.* [9.] It is the height of madness to walk contrary to the revealed will of God, how much use of reason soever men may have to cover their wickedness, and attain to their idols: for though much carnal reason and policy did appear in *Balaam's* way, yet the *dumb ass forbad the madness of the prophet.* [10.] A man who is mad in the pursuit of his lusts and so incorrigible that even extraordinary means do not reclaim him, may, notwithstanding, be employed by the Lord for revealing of His will to His people, and for the edifying of His church; and in the discharge of that employment may be furnished with much heavenly matter and suitable expressions, and ought to be heard and obeyed by the church in the discharge of his employment, while he is not discovered to be what he is, and is not according to the order established in the house of God put from that employment: for such a man was *Balaam*, whom the Lord did employ, and by whom He did deliver most comfortable and edifying truths to His church: all which is clear by comparing this place of Scripture with Numbers 21 and 22.

17. These are wells without water, clouds that are carried with a tempest; to whom the mist of darkness is reserved for ever.

In this and the two following verses the Apostle holds forth several of those means which false teachers make use of for attaining their forenamed idols, especially their gain and applause. The first, which is in this verse, is their fair promises of doing much good to the church: they give out themselves to be well-springs of comfort to the Lord's people and clouds to drop down their doctrine as rain, to make the church fruitful while in effect they did but disappoint poor souls and darken the truth; for which the Apostle threatens them with everlasting darkness, as their portion.

Hence learn, [1.] They that do most hurt to the souls of the Lord's people by venting most dangerous errors among them make oftentimes the fairest promises of doing most good to them, that so they may feed people with vain expectations of more than ever they can find from them. Faithful ministers, being sensible of their own insufficiency, 2 Cor. 3:5, and of the necessity of a divine concurrence with their pains, 1 Cor. 3:7, are more ready to express their fears of people's disappointment, 2 Cor. 11:2,3, than to make such large promises of much comfort and profit to people by their means, as false teachers use to do: for here these seducers give out themselves to be what faithful ministers ought to be, *wells* of consolation, receiving from Christ the Fountain and giving out to His people what may comfort them; and *clouds*, to drop down their doctrine as rain in season, to make them fruitful. [2.] Whatever be the fair pretences and promises of false teachers, the Lord's people can meet with nothing but disappointment from them; and whatever esteem they may have among the best for a time, God will take His own time to manifest what they are in effect, and to undeceive His own people: for here they that gave out themselves and were esteemed to be the chief instruments of the comfort and fruitfulness of the church, as the similitude of wells and clouds, whereby they set out themselves, do import, are here discovered to be such as did disappoint and in disappointing increase the anxiety of those that expected comfort from them, as *wells without water* to the weary traveller; and to be such as are acted by the restless spirit of Satan into every airth[1] where their fore-

---

[1] 'airth': direction, point of the compass.

named idols of gain and applause can be had, as *clouds that are carried with a tempest.* [3.] The judgment of false teachers whereof their followers shall get a share shall be very proportionable to their sin; for they promise to be wells of consolation to the Lord's people and do disappoint them; they themselves delight to walk and to lead others in the works of darkness: they darken the truth of God; and in this course they are restless as *clouds carried with a tempest*: and therefore the threatening is exactly suited to these sins: *For them the mist of darkness is reserved for ever.*

18. **For when they speak great swelling words of vanity, they allure through the lusts of the flesh, through much wantonness, those that were clean escaped from them who live in error.**

Here is the next course which soul-deceivers take to ensnare poor souls by their errors, to wit, a high and lofty style of language which their love to their lusts made them to affect, and whereby they were very taking with unmortified wanton professors, especially such as have been turned from paganism to the profession of Christianity.

Hence learn, [1.] They that vent error do ordinarily hold it forth under some lofty strain of language and high-bended expressions beyond what is ordinary, such as may be most taking with and admired by the hearers; whilst faithful ministers can trust Christ to make plain truth spoken in the simplicity of words, effectual for the salvation, comfort and edification of His own, which is their main scope, 1 Cor. 2:4, for it is here a character of false teachers, *they speak great swelling words.* [2.] When the veil of odd and soaring expressions, wherein false teachers delight, is laid aside and the naked purpose held forth under them is considered, it will be found of no worth, but either some untruth, or that which makes nothing to the true advantage of souls; both which are vanity: for here their *great swelling words* are *words of vanity.* [3.] An affected lofty style of language in uttering things divine ordinarily flows from some unmortified lust in the speaker, especially the love of applause; and is also mainly taking with wanton unhumbled souls when it provokes to more vanity and lightness, by diverting them from the study of their natural vileness, their need of Jesus, and the necessity of the mortification of their heart evils: for they who speak great swelling words of vanity, *allure through the lusts of the flesh, through much wantonness*: both which last clauses may be understood of the principle which bends the preacher to that strain, and also of the qualification of those hearers with whom it is most taking. [4.] There may be a very remarkable external change from vile and blasphemous opinions, idolatrous and profane practices, to a profession of truth and suitableness of the outward conversation to it, where there is no saving or inward change made of the heart, from the love of secret lusts to the love of Christ and His grace; the one without the other may be occasioned by the power of example, the majesty and clearness of truth, which is in nothing contrary to nature's light, the beauty of holiness shining in the conversation of professors, and outward advantages which sometimes may attend the profession of truth and holiness: for these here who were yet given *to the lusts of their flesh* and *much wantonness* had once *clean escaped from* the blasphemous opinion and profane and idolatrous practices of those without the church, who are here called *them that live in error*. [5.] Whatever change of this sort be wrought upon men, unless they labour to find the power of Christ's Spirit changing their nature, and mortifying their inward lusts, they will easily be a prey to seducing spirits, and carried to those sins which are no less dishonourable to God and destructive to their own souls than those wherein they lived before: for here those who had once clean escaped from the vile opinions and wicked practices wherein pagans live are now, by the seduction of false teachers, turned profane and licentious Christians.

19. While they promise them liberty, they themselves are the servants of corruption: for of whom a man is overcome, of the same is he brought in bondage.

The last of those means whereby false teachers do ensnare so many of their hearers is their pretending to make clear to them, and possess them of, that Christian liberty whereof the gospel speaks, which they could not at all perform, for they themselves were complete slaves to their lusts, as captives in war are servants to their conqueror.

Hence learn, [1.] The doctrine of Christian liberty, which is in itself most sweet and saving, holding forth our freedom from the law as a covenant of works, Rom. 7:4, and from the curse thereof, Gal. 3:13, from the dominion of Satan, Heb. 2:14,15, the terror and allurements of the world, Gal. 1:4, and the dominion of our own lusts, Rom. 6:14, has been and yet is much abused, while it is stretched to give liberty to sin, and to loose Christians from the holy commandments of the moral law, as they are now pressed in the Gospel: for so does the Apostle forewarn it should be abused during the time of the Gospel, as is clear by comparing this with the first and twenty-first verses. [2.] They that are much in crying up Christian liberty, and little or nothing in pressing the holy commandments of Christ upon His redeemed ones, the obedience whereof is a great part of our Christian liberty, and one main end of our liberation from our spiritual enemies, Luke 1:74,75, cannot but be slaves to their lusts; and so must those be that embrace that doctrine: for *while they promise them liberty, they themselves are the servants of corruption.* [3.] Although every man be bound in law to be the servant of Christ, who can make the worst thing that men can do subservient to His ends, Psa. 119:91, yet he who does voluntarily and ordinarily give up himself to serve the devil and his own corruption, without resistance or crying to Christ for help, is then in a manner a lawful captive to Satan, to be detained by him till the supreme Judge execute deserved wrath upon him, as one that renders himself to a conqueror is his bond-slave, according to the law of nations, to which the Apostle alludes while he says, *Of whom a man is overcome, of the same is he brought in bondage.*

20. **For if after they have escaped the pollutions of the world through the knowledge of the Lord and Saviour Jesus Christ, they are again entangled therein, and overcome, the latter end is worse with them than the beginning.**
21. **For it had been better for them not to have known the way of righteousness, than, after they have known it, to turn from the holy commandment delivered unto them.**

The Apostle proves the condition of these apostates whom he supposes to have attained so much of the knowledge of Christ, as had power upon them to cleanse their outside, to be much worse than it was before that change, because their sin and judgment had been less if they had never known anything of the way of justification revealed in the Gospel, than it will be now, after that has been cleared to their understanding, and yet in doctrine and practice do cast off another part of the gospel, to wit, that which presses the duties of holiness upon justified persons.

Hence learn, [1.] Even those who are destitute of the saving knowledge of Christ, and strangers to the mortification of heart pollutions, may find so much power in the knowledge of Him as to make them cleanse their external conversation. The knowledge of Christ is so ravishing a subject, able to divert even an unrenewed mind from many sinful speculations, that even a hypocrite, living in love with his secret lusts, may *escape the pollutions* that are breaking forth in *the world, through the knowledge of the Lord and Saviour Jesus Christ.* [2.] They who have not attained to a heart-outcast with sin and some inward mortification thereof, will, upon fit occasions and temptations, be readily ensnared again and made slaves to these same sins which were externally reformed, and from the outward acts whereof only they had made an escape: for these here spoken of, having only escaped the pollutions that are in the world through the knowledge of Christ, *are again entangled and overcome.* [3.] Before men be overcome by temptation, they are first enticed with the apprehension of some pleasure, profit or the like, to be had by their sins; with which apprehension the hazard and danger of committing the sin is covered and hid, as the fisher's hook is by the bait, which is the metaphor in the Apostle's expression, *they are again entangled and overcome.* [4.] The guilt and deserved wrath against those who after illumination by the truth, and external renunciation of their sins, do return back again to them, is much greater than if they had never been so far enlightened and reformed, their sins being now against light and some tastes of sweetness, which is sometimes let out even to those who do but externally renounce their sins and betake themselves to the way of Christ, Heb. 6:4, &c, for of such the Spirit of God says here, *The latter end is worse with them than the beginning.* [5.] Those to whom the Lord makes known the way of free justification by the righteousness of Christ, to them also He delivers His holy commandments, the obedience whereof they ought to set about in His strength: for so much is imported in the Apostle's words, that having *known the way of righteousness,* there was *a holy commandment delivered to them.* [6.] It is less difficult, and more ordinary for men to adhere in their opinion and profession to the way of free justification by Christ's imputed righteousness, when that way is once cleared to their minds, than it is for them to insist in the constant practice of holy duties which Christ presses upon them, and offers them strength for, there being even in corrupt nature, which is most averse

271

from holy duties, some inclination to be made blessed, and that freely; which is imported in the Apostle's changing of the expression: for he does not say that after they had known the way of righteousness, they had turned from it; importing that these false teachers did still profess and preach justification by His righteousness; but *after they had known that way, they turned from the holy commandment delivered to them*; their adhering to the one without the other, made their guilt greater than if they had never known that one, and no less than if they had turned from both.

22. But it is happened unto them according to the true proverb, The dog is turned to his own vomit again and the sow that was washed to her wallowing in the mire.

In the last place, the Apostle guards against any offence which might be occasioned by the apostasy of these false teachers and their followers, in regard they had now proved themselves never to have been inwardly renewed, as the true sheep of Christ are; but only by their baptism and profession to have externally renounced that vileness, whereunto they are now returned again, after the custom of dogs and swine, according to that common proverb which is made use of in Scripture, Prov. 26:11.

Doctrine [1.] Sin ought to be represented by the Lord's ministers in its abominable vileness, especially when men labour to palliate their filthy practices with fair pretences. Therefore these vile practices, which these false teachers called their Christian liberty, the Apostle here calls a *licking up of their vomit*, and a *wallowing in the mire*. [2.] They who after external reformation and great profession of holiness do return to and continue in their renounced sins, do thereby give evidence that they were never inwardly or really changed in their nature: for these of whom the Apostle speaks here, being still dogs and swine, were only washed externally, and did vomit up by confession and seeming renunciation, their filthy practices, to which they did return again, *as the dog returneth to his vomit, and the sow that was washed to her wallowing in the mire*; and so this place can make nothing for[1] the apostasy of the saints. [3.] It is lawful for the ministers of Christ to make use of common similitudes or

---

[1] 'make nothing for': supply no proof of.

proverbs to clear the truth and fix it in the minds of those that are led by sense, providing they make use especially of such as are scriptural, and propose all their similitudes in a decent and cleanly way, suitable to the majesty and purity of truth and apposite to their present purpose, and bring them forth only for illustration of truths otherwise proved: for so does the Apostle here make use of such a similitude as he found in Scripture, which, though it be taken from things in themselves vile, is expressed in the most honest terms that can fitly set out the vileness of apostasy, the evil whereof he had clearly proved before: *It is happened unto them according to the true proverb*, &c.

CHAPTER THREE

Because the believing consideration of Christ's second coming is a special means to make Christians thrive in grace and holiness and to guard their hearts against temptations, therefore the Apostle, having pressed growth in grace and holiness in the first part of this Epistle, chapter 1, and guarded against the infection of error in the second part, chapter 2, does in this last chapter wherein is the third part of the Epistle, [1.] defend and clear the doctrine of the last judgment, and [2.] show what use believers should make thereof.

In the first part of this chapter the Apostle, having put them in mind of his main scope in both the Epistles, which was to keep the substance of the gospel fresh in their minds (vv 1,2), gives forewarning of the rise of profane mockers of Christ's second coming, who, that they might serve their lusts with the more quietness, would plead for an eternity of this present world, because they had never observed any appearance of such a change as was foretold to be at that day (vv 3,4). Which blasphemous opinion, together with their seeming reason for it, the Apostle confutes by several reasons drawn from the works of creation and providence, which prove there will be such a day as will be very terrible to profane mockers of it (vv 5,6,7), and holds forth to the godly, satisfying reasons of the delay of that day, to wit, that it is very small, being compared with eternity (v 8), that the delay is mainly for the gathering of the elect (v 9), which being done, that day will come suddenly and with much terror (v. 10).

In the second part of the chapter the Apostle makes use of his former doctrine concerning Christ's second coming, for the up-stirring of the Lord's people to the study of holiness (v 11), to wait and pray for that day (v 12), when they had ground to look for so excellent an estate (v 13) as might provoke them to much diligence in making ready for it (v 14), and to esteem the delay thereof to be granted for the furtherance of their salvation, in which strain *Paul* had insisted much in his Epistles (vv 15,16). And upon the consideration of all, to labour for steadfastness and progress in grace and in the knowledge of Christ, who is worthy of eternal praise (vv 17,18).

1. **This second Epistle, beloved, I now write unto you; in both which I stir up your pure minds by way of remembrance:**
2. **That ye may be mindful of the words which were spoken before by the holy prophets, and of the commandment of us the apostles of the Lord and Saviour:**

The Apostle here presents to them his chief scope intended by him in both the Epistles, which was the wakening and rousing of these sincere-hearted Christians to whom he writes, to an actual consideration and constant practice of known truths, that had been delivered to them by the prophets, himself, and other apostles of Jesus Christ.

Hence learn, [1.] The ministers of Christ ought not only to intend as their scope some particular advantage to the souls of the Lord's people by all the messages they carry to them; but also in their delivery of them frequently to make clear to the people what their main intent is, that so themselves may be engaged to direct all they deliver toward that scope, the people may have it the better fixed in their minds, and all that they hear relating to that scope may be the better understood, and have the greater weight; otherwise the greatest variety of truth and most taking expressions can have but a slender and soon vanishing impression upon that hearer who cannot be able to condescend upon[1] the principal scope of the speaker: for here the Apostle has proposed their up-stirring as his scope and by his frequent mentioning of it in the first chapter and this also, did tie himself to speak to it and make his hearers able to judge how all he delivered did make for it: *This second Epistle, beloved, I now write unto you, in both which I stir up your pure minds.* [2.] A minister's main scope ought not to be the acquitting of himself before men in his duty so as he may be free of censure, neither only the clear information of the minds of the Lord's people in the truth, neither yet the bringing forth of some new things which they that live under the Gospel have not formerly heard, but more principally he must study the quickening and wakening of the affections of the Lord's people to a delight in and resolution to walk

[1] 'condescend upon': to arrive at.

in the practice of truths they have formerly known and remembered: for it is here the Apostle's scope *to stir them up*, a word frequently used in the New Testament of raising the dead, and wakening those that are asleep by *putting them in remembrance*, which signifies to represent anew to the mind and memory truths formerly known and remembered. [3.] A minister that would prevail with the Lord's people ought both to keep love to them, that his pains may flow therefrom, and in his dealing with them to express his love and high esteem of any measure of sincerity he has discerned in them. Therefore does the Apostle style these whom he intends to stir up, *beloved*, and acknowledges that they had *sincere and pure minds*. [4.] Even those who for sincerity of heart and honesty of their aims and intentions may abide the trial of gospel light, have great need of many messages to the same purpose, and of much up-stirring to the right use-making of them, there being in them that have the clearest understanding, much darkness, and many mistakes concerning the truths of God; and in the sincerest believer whose heart is most lively and forward in duties, a great remnant of hypocrisy, deadness and unwillingness to the practice of many known duties: for the Apostle finds it necessary to write two epistles *for the up-stirring of pure minds*, or as the word in the original signifies, minds so sincere that they may be judged by sunlight. [5.] The Word of the Lord has most weight with people when not only they that carry it to them are holy and so esteemed by the people, but the minds of the hearers are carried above the messengers to Jesus Christ, and their hearts in hearing or reading are filled with some sense of His sovereignty who employs those messengers and of His usefulness to them in all His offices. Therefore, that the Word which the Apostle here exhorts them to study may have the more weight, he leads them not only to look upon the messengers that carried it as holy men, but to consider the sovereignty, excellency and usefulness of Christ in His offices to which He is anointed: *Be mindful of the words which were spoken by the holy prophets, and of the commandments of us the apostles of the Lord and Saviour Jesus Christ*. [6.] The way to keep life in the affections of the Lord's people is to have their wit and memory actually exercised about the truths of God, both the prophecies and promises of good to the church and people of God and to press the precepts enjoining their duty: for that the Apostle may gain his principal scope, to wit, the rousing up of their affections, he makes this his speech subordinate thereto,

That they might be mindful of the words that were spoken before by the holy prophets, and of the commandments of the Apostles of the Lord and Saviour Jesus Christ. [7.] Although the Lord has let forth His mind to His church little by little, in several ages of the world and by several messengers, Heb. 1:1, yet is there such a complete harmony among all the parts of His mind that all serve for one and the same principal scope, the up-stirring of the Lord's people to a hearty receiving and use-making of Christ and His truth: for unto this scope the Apostle here affirms that the whole doctrine both of the prophets and apostles did harmoniously tend.

3. **Knowing this first, that there shall come in the last days scoffers, walking after their own lusts,**
4. **And saying, Where is the promise of His coming? for since the fathers fell asleep, all things continue as they were from the beginning of the creation.**

That the Apostle may attain his fore-mentioned scope, he forewarns of the rise of profane mockers toward the end of time, who, that they might sin the more securely, should question the second coming of Christ and plead for an eternity of this present world, pretending this reason for it, that since the whole frame of nature had kept one constant tenor and course since the death of *Adam, Seth, Enos* and the rest of the first fathers, it was not to them credible that ever there should be such a change as was foretold to be at the day of judgment.

Doctrine, [1.] A variety of very fierce and discouraging opposition in the way of Christ, and that from several sorts of enemies, is the lot wherewith the church and people of Christ may resolve to be exercised: for the Apostle, having forewarned of and guarded against open persecutors in the former Epistle, and subtle and fair pretending heretics in the former chapter, he here forewarns of and guards against a third sort, to wit, profane *scoffers* of Christ's second coming. [2.] The consideration of the hazard that the best are in of being drawn aside some one way or other from the truth and way of Christ, by such variety of opposition as they ordinarily meet with, ought both to stir up ministers carefully to warn and guard people against the same; and people to the use-making of their pains: for after the Apostle had guarded against open persecutors and cunning deceivers, he here brings in the forewarning of the third sort of enemies, *scoffers*: which may be taken both for a reason of his pains in writing two Epistles, as also for a reason why they should be stirred up by what he had written: *Knowing this*, that besides furious persecutors and subtle deceivers, they should also be exercised with profane *scoffers*. They who have not been terrified by the first sort, nor deceived by the second, are in hazard to be discouraged by the third. [3.] The certainty and necessity of being exercised with variety of opposition in the Way of Christ is one of the principles of Christianity which ought to be held in the first place by all that resolve to adhere to any other saving truth; they who do not first know this, and notwithstanding thereof resolve upon adherence to the truth in Christ's strength, will readily, when they meet with such a lot, be surprised therewith, and either forsake the truth or faint in their adherence to it. Therefore the Apostle would have them *knowing this first*, that after several other sorts of enemies, there were also to *come in the last days, scoffers*. [4.] There are no such pure or peaceable times to be expected by the church and people of God within time wherein the fore-mentioned lot is not to be expected; they who dream of the best times to the church on earth look for them toward the end of time; yet the Spirit of God here forewarns that beside the rage of persecutors and prevailing of heretics, *there shall come in the last days scoffers*. [5.] It is clear evidence that men are slaves to their lusts when they do strongly desire an eternal enjoyment of this present world and labour to banish out of their own hearts the thoughts of a day of judgment. Yea, their so doing is also the cause why they give up themselves to the service of their lusts, the believing consideration of the terror of that day to the wicked being a special help to mortification and of the sweetness thereof to the godly, a special encouragement in the battle against corruption: for their *scoffing at the promise of Christ's second coming* may be looked upon here both as the evidence and cause of their *walking after their ungodly lusts* [6.] When men are left of God to vile opinions for not receiving the truth in love, they are then oftentimes plagued further, not only with devilish wit, to find out seeming reasons for the defence of them, very plausible to themselves and others like themselves; but also to take manifest falsehoods for undeniable grounds of their errors: for these mockers here lay all the weight of their blasphemous opinion upon this seeming reason, that *since the fathers fell asleep, all things continue as they were*, &c, which appears from the Apostle's contrary instance, (v 6) to be a manifest falsehood. [7.] Although it be a sweet mercy much to be acknowledged by the Lord's people, that things in nature do ordinarily keep one constant course, and that they are not terrified with the frequent change thereof, but may be thereby confirmed in the faith of the Lord's constancy and faithfulness, as David was, Psa. 119:90,91, yet men that are in love with their lusts do make a woeful use of the consideration thereof, hardening themselves in their conceit that there shall never be a change, that so they may sin the more securely: for thus did these scoffers abuse this mercy, taking occasion therefrom to question the promise of Christ's second coming and to walk the more boldly after their ungodly lusts; *since all things continue as they were from the beginning of the creation.*

5. **For this they willingly are ignorant of, that by the Word of God the heavens were of old, and the earth standing out of the water and in the water:**
6. **Whereby the world that then was, being overflowed with water, perished:**
7. **But the heavens and the earth, which are now, by the same Word are kept in store, reserved unto fire against the day of judgment and perdition of ungodly men.**

Because these mockers did pretend reason for their blasphemous opinion, the Apostle takes pains to confute it by several reasons, such as they did not love to understand. The first, taken from the work of creation, is that the whole fabric of the heavens was set up by a word of God's. The second, taken from an ordinary and daily work of providence is that the earth, being the lowest and heaviest of the elements, is by His Word kept from being overflowed by the waters that go about it and cover it in many places (v 5). The third, taken from an extra-ordinary work of providence, is that by a word of His, letting out the waters to their natural course, the whole earth was once overflowed in the time of the flood (v 6). The conclusion drawn from these three is that His Word is a sufficient ground for us to believe that He shall come again to judgment, and that this whole frame of nature is keeping to the fore, as fuel to burn up all the ungodly, especially profane mockers of that day, (v 7).

Hence learn, [1.] When vile blasphemies are not only boldly vented but maintained with some show of reason to make them taking with people, they ought then to be solidly confuted, and borne down with strength of reason, grounded upon the Scripture; though otherwise, when they are only simply or rashly asserted and are not taking with hearers, it is sufficient to reject them with detestation, and expressions of our abhorrency of them; for because this blasphemy had a seeming reason to back it with, the Apostle takes pains to confute it by many solid reasons, drawn from the Scriptures. [2.] They that are in love with their lusts and errors, love also to be ignorant of these truths, the knowledge whereof might disquiet them in following their lusts, and maintaining their errors. Yea, they would willingly be ignorant of what they do know, that so they might sin the more securely: for these men here, whom the faith of a day of judgment could not but terrify, are discovered to be *willingly ignorant* of these things that might have helped them to believe it. [3.] As the whole frame of nature had its being and has its subsistence by the word of God, so the believing consideration of this is sufficient to make the most unlikely thing that God has promised to be credible to us. They who look rightly upon what God has already done by a word, will never think anything He has promised or foretold impossible; for the Apostle gives this as a sufficient confutation of their blasphemous mockery at the promised appearance of Christ; that since *by the word of the Lord the heavens were of old, and the earth standing out of the water and in the water*, it is not incredible that all shall be taken down with as little difficulty as it was at first set up, and has hitherto been upheld: which is the force of the Apostle's reasoning here. [4.] It is a standing miracle of nature that the earth is not overflowed by the water, while one part of it is covered therewith and another not, whereof, though some probable natural reasons may be given, yet all will not satisfy, till we look to God's decree of providence and His executing thereof by His word, by which *the earth is standing out of the water, and in the water*. [5.] However error, when it is looked upon alone as the cunning craftiness of men usually represents it, may seem to have a kind of likelihood and probability, yet when it is compared with the clear light of the truth shining upon it, it manifestly appears to be a lying deceit: for that plausible assertion, *All things continue as they were from the beginning* (v 4), wherewith these scoffers laboured to weaken the faith of a day of judgment, is clearly discovered to be a manifest lie, by this contrary instance (v 6), *The world that then* (to wit, before the flood) *was, being overflowed with water, perished.* [6.] Particular judgments upon some wicked men while others are spared prove that there shall be a general judgment; for seeing some are justly punished here, and others, deserving no less, are spared, He who is immutably and impartially just, must have a day for judging these afterward, who are spared in time. Therefore the Apostle brings in the instance of the flood upon the ungodly world, not only as a contradiction to their assertion (v 4), but as a proof against them of a day of judgment; *the world being overflowed with water, perished*. [7.] The day of Christ's second coming will be a most dreadful and terrible day to all ungodly men, who banish the thoughts of it, and desire eternally to possess this present world, and the pleasures thereof, when they shall see all those creatures which they have abused to serve them in their serving of their lusts, burning fuel to kindle (as it were) that flame which shall burn them up for ever and ever, and shall not be so happy as to be destroyed with the rest of the creatures, but shall then enter into their never-ending torment: for *the heavens and the earth which are now, are kept in store, reserved unto fire against the day of judgment and perdition of ungodly men.*

8. But, beloved, be not ignorant of this one thing, that one day is with the Lord as a thousand years, and a thousand years as one day.

The Apostle having, by strength of reason drawn from Scripture, overthrown the opinion of these mockers of Christ's second coming, in this and the two following verses he holds forth three reasons which may satisfy the godly concerning the delay thereof. The first, which is in this verse, is that the delay ought not to be judged of according to our sense or apprehension, but according to the duration of God, with whom that space of time which seems very long to us is but as one day, and to whom all those differences of duration which to the creatures are longer or shorter, are all alike, and always constantly present.

Doctrine, [1.] There is so great affinity between the hearts of the godly, who are but in part renewed, and the vilest temptations to the greatest blasphemies or errors, especially such as patronize the lusts of corrupt nature, that when they are boldly vented with pretence of reason, there is great hazard that there be some impression left upon their hearts, inclining them to the same. Therefore for the preventing or removing of this, the Apostle takes pains to satisfy the godly concerning the causes of the delay of Christ's coming, which had not been needful except they had either received, or had been in hazard to receive, some bad impression from the bold assertion and seeming reason of these mockers. [2.] Although it has pleased the Lord to condescend so far to our shallow capacity as to set forth to us in Scripture, and to give us leave to take up His duration in our own terms, while He calls Himself, *Yesterday, and today and for ever*, Heb. 13:8, *Which was and is and is to come*, Rev. 1:4, *the Ancient of Days*, Dan. 7:9, *Whose years have no end*, Psa. 102:27, yet all these differences of time, which to us are longer or shorter, are all alike to Him, whose duration admits of no beginning, succession or ending, but consists in a constant presentness of all that which seems to us past, or to come: *for one day is with the Lord as a thousand years, and a thousand years as one day.* [3.] The servants of Christ ought to have a far different esteem of those who mock at the truth of God and scoffingly vent their errors contrary to it, and of those who through infirmity may have some inclination toward error and therefore stand in need to be guarded against it; and accordingly their carriage ought to be different toward the one and the other: for of the one the Apostle spoke in the former words with indignation and contempt, as they deserved, calling them *scoffers, walking after their ungodly lusts*; but to the other he speaks here with love and tenderness, *But, beloved, be not ignorant of this one thing.* [4.] There are some things revealed in Scripture concerning the Lord which must be understood by faith, as the Apostle's expression is, Heb. 11:1, although they cannot be comprehended by us to the satisfaction of our shallow reason: for here the Apostle would not have them ignorant of this one thing, *That one day is with the Lord as a thousand years, and a thousand years as one day*; which is a truth that none within time can well comprehend; only faith can assent to and make use of it, in judging as He judges, that many years' delay to us of the performance of a promise is but a very little time compared with eternity, only it may foster a holy longing to be with Him, when we shall partake of His duration as well as of His glory, when there shall not be such a thing as any sad reflections upon past sweetness, or any painful langour for sweetness to come, but a constant present possession thereof: our duration resembling His with whom *one day is a thousand years, and a thousand years as one day.*

9. The Lord is not slack concerning his promise, as some men

count slackness, but is long-suffering to us-ward, not willing that any should perish, but that all should come to repentance.

The second ground for satisfaction of the godly concerning the delay of Christ's second coming is that that delay does not proceed from any such thing in God (whatever men may judge) as usually makes men slow in performing their promises, but only from His patience toward His elect, whose temper requires time and pains for working grace in them, that they may be fitted for glory.

Hence learn, [1.] We ought not to frame our thoughts of God as one man uses to do of another, especially when we think of the delay of performance of promises, as if that delay did flow from want of foresight of possible difficulties, weakness, forgetfulness or fickleness, whence delay among men ordinarily flows. All such thoughts of Him as our hearts are very apt to entertain, Psa. 50:21, we ought to remove far from us, and to persuade ourselves of the contrary, that He is most mindful of His promises, Psa. 111:5, and so swift in performing of them that He will not stay a moment after He has wrought what is necessary before the performance, Mal. 4:2, for such negatives as this here concerning God, do in Scripture both import an aptness in us to imagine the contrary affirmative of Him, and likewise that the contrary of what is denied is, in a superlative degree, His property; *The Lord is not slack concerning His promise, as some men count slackness.* [2.] The true and satisfying reason of the delay of the second coming of Christ is the Lord's long suffering toward His own elect, who must be dealt with in order to their conversion in a way suitable to their temper which requires time and pains to work upon each elect soul come into the world, and to the years of discretion, by commands, threatenings, promises, and alluring motives, every one of these being multiplied after another, and by these same means every elect person brought to that measure of grace which God has determined to work in the converted, that they may be fitted for glory: for this is here given as the satisfying reason of the delay of Christ's second coming, that the Lord is *long-suffering to us-ward*. [3.] The Lord does not soon nor easily gain His point even with His own elect, but after many refusals of His renewed offers and slighting of His pains, His patient and powerful love does at last overcome all opposition in them, and so brings them to repentance: for before they are brought to it He is *long-suffering to us-ward*. [4.] The Lord cannot fall short of His intention toward any upon whom He takes pains, nor does His good-will to save reach to any sinners but those whom He does really make partakers of salvation: for the Apostle says here, *He is long suffering to us-ward*, that is, to us believers and others, elected as we are, not as yet born or not as yet converted, not willing that any such should perish, but that all of that kind should come to repentance; so that the Scripture *all* is not always to be understood of all and every individual person in the world, but oftentimes it is put (here comprehended in *us*) for all the elect only, as is clear by comparing Jer. 31:34 with John 6:45 and this present Scripture. [5.] Although the Lord only intends the salvation of His elect by His long-suffering and pains, yet He is pleased to express His desire of their salvation in the largest terms that can be, that so He may the more effectually prevail with His own and render the rest the more inexcusable, who, except they will exclude themselves, are not excluded by such large expressions of the grace of God as are here, *He is not willing that any should perish, but that all should come to repentance.* [6.] All those whom the Lord minds to save in an ordinary way are first brought by Him to a sensible sight of sin and deserved wrath, and to such apprehensions of mercy in God for them through Jesus Christ as makes them turn in to Him, grieving for and forsaking their sins and giving up themselves to His service: *for those whom He willeth not to perish, He willeth and maketh to come to repentance.*

10. But the day of the Lord will come as a thief in the night; in the which the heavens shall pass away with a great noise, and the elements shall melt with fervent heat, and the earth also and the works that are therein shall be burnt up.

The third thing whereby the Apostle labours to satisfy the godly about the delay of the day of judgment is that that day will be very unexpected and terrible to secure sinners, as the coming of a thief in the night uses to be to a sleeping family; and that there will be then a great change and dissolution of the whole frame of nature, and of all things wherein most men place their happiness; the inference from which not being expressed, but to be collected from the Apostle's scope, is that it is the wisdom of the Lord's people rather to prepare for that day than to complain of the delay or to be anxious concerning it.

Doctrine, [1.] Similitudes made use of in Scripture do not justify the actions of men whence these similitudes are taken, only they do much commend to us the Lord's condescendency and desire to have us taking up His mind, while he demits[1] Himself for our capacity to compare His most just and holy actions to these actions among men which are most abominable and hateful to Him. Therefore is the suddenness and terror of Christ's second coming set forth here by the coming of a thief in the night; which practice, though it be in itself sinful and condemned by the Lord, yet it is made use of by Him because the terror and suddenness of it is so well known to men that they by it the better conceive the manner of Christ's second coming: *but the day of the Lord will come as a thief in the night.* [2.] Christ's coming at the last day will be a great surprisal to the most part of the children of men, who will not be wakened out of their security by the Word, to make preparation for it. As for those foregoing signs of that day which the Scripture speaks of, such as the destruction of Antichrist, the conversion of the Jews, and that great alteration of the whole course of nature, some of them may be done in so little time, and so immediately before that day, and others of them so little taken notice of, or believed, as signs for that day, that notwithstanding of them all, the most part shall be surprised with it as with the coming of *a thief in the night.* [3.] That day of judgment will be a most terrible day to all who do not expect and prepare for it. There will be a strange sight and a dreadful noise when this great workmanship, being on fire, shall all rush down, and all the delights of wicked men shall be burnt up before their eyes, the Lord thereby testifying His displeasure against men's placing their happiness in these things, and their defiling of them by making them subservient to their lusts, mean time signifying His purpose to give a more cleanly and glorious mansion to His own to dwell in: *In that day the heavens shall pass away with a great noise, and the elements shall melt with fervent heat, the earth also and the works that are therein shall be burnt up.* As for questions which may be stated here, it is much more safe for us to give time and pains that we may be found of Him in peace at that day, than to be taken up in enquiring and determining whether the visible heavens and the earth, and the rest of the creatures of that kind, shall then be totally and for ever annihilated; or whether there shall be a new edition of them

---

[1] 'demits': humbles.

all, or of some of them only, to be lasting monuments of the power and glory of the Maker, and so ravishing objects of the saints' delight, who may through that new world follow the Lamb wheresoever He goes.

11. Seeing then that all these things shall be dissolved, what manner of persons ought ye to be in all holy conversation and godliness,

In this second part of the chapter are contained the several uses which the Apostle draws from his former doctrine concerning the last judgment, and they are especially six. The first, which is in this verse, is that the consideration of that day should make all the Lord's people very inquisitive how they may be more and more forthcoming for His honour, in the discharge of all the duties of holiness, especially those whereby He may be glorified in their conversation.

Hence learn, [1.] The ministers of Christ ought not to satisfy themselves to draw the Lord's people to a naked contemplation of the truth which hypocrites, yea devils, may attain to, Jas. 2:19, but they ought to draw every truth they propound to them to some practical use for the promoting of holiness in the hearts and lives of their hearers, without which people's condemnation will be greater than if they had not heard or known these truths, 2 Pet. 2:21. Therefore the Apostle does not think it enough to have defended by reason the second coming of Christ, and to tell them of strange events to fall forth at that day, but does here and to the end of the chapter apply all to them for their use: *Seeing then that all these things shall be dissolved, what manner of persons ought ye to be*, &c? [2.] The whole creation is now in a manner imprisoned, and in bondage, while they are abused, contrary to their inclination, to the service of men's lusts, and dishonour of their Maker; from which slavery they shall be loosed at Christ's coming, Rom. 8:21, for the word in the original here is used to signify the loosing of a captive, or prisoner, out of his bonds, Acts 22:30. *These things shall be dissolved.* [3.] The consideration of this dissolution of the creatures should make those of the Lord's people that are furthest promoted in holiness very inquisitive after, and still aspiring toward, a further degree of holiness than what they have formerly attained; knowing that the greater degree of holiness they attain to, the more comfort shall they have now and the more glory when Christ comes: for the Apostle puts this question to his own heart and the hearts of all the Lord's people, *What manner of persons ought ye to be*, &c.? [4.] That holiness which should be aimed at by the Lord's people and which will be comfortable to them and approved of God now and hereafter, must be manifested in all the parts of their conversation, both in their outward carriage and secret practice, in their common affairs and religious performances, in duties of God's immediate worship and in duties relating to their neighbour, as is imported in this, *What manner of persons ought ye to be in all holy conversation and godliness?* [5.] In the discharge of all the duties of holiness, Christians ought to look much to the qualification of their persons, that they be reconciled with God through Christ, and daily renewing the friendship by the exercise of godly sorrow for sin and a living faith in the Mediator, and by keeping their hearts in frame for the particular duties of holiness they are called to: for the Apostle does not put the question, How holy ought our conversation to be? but, *What manner of persons ought ye to be in all holy conversation and godliness?* [6.] If the holiest on earth would put their conscience to speak to them, after serious consideration of the terror and glory of the second coming of Christ, they would be much unsatisfied with their present measure of holiness, and would have their desires quickened and their endeavours strengthened after a further measure thereof, as is imported in this question of the Apostle's, put to his own and others' conscience, *What manner of persons ought ye to be in all holy conversation and godliness?* including himself (v 13).

12. **Looking for and hasting unto the coming of the day of God, wherein the heavens being on fire shall be dissolved, and the elements shall melt with fervent heat?**

The second use of the former doctrine is that the consideration of so dreadful and glorious a day should make all the Lord's people live in the constant expectation thereof, by their prayers and pains furthering those works which must be done before it come: which use, together with the former, the Apostle bears in by a new representation of the glory and terror of that day.

Hence learn, [1.] To live in the constant expectation of Christ's glorious appearance is both the duty of all the lovers of Him, and a special means to make them grow in holiness. Therefore is this expectation pressed here by a word of the present time, importing that it is both a perpetual duty in itself, and a special means of attaining to what is pressed before: *What manner of persons ought ye to be*, &c, *looking for the coming of the day of God?* [2.] Although the time of Christ's second coming be so fixed in the decree of God as that it cannot be altered, Acts 17:31, yet ought the Lord's people to be no less earnest in hastening their own preparation for it, and by their prayers and other means competent to them in their stations, furthering these great works to be done before, than if that day could be hastened by them: for the word in the original signifies not only our hastening toward that day but also our hastening of it; see Isa. 16:5, *Looking for and hasting the coming of the day of God.* [3.] It is safe for the Lord's ministers frequently to represent to His people those truths that are much contradicted by enemies of truth, that are but little considered by His people, and which have greatest influence upon their practice to restrain them from sin and provoke them to duty: for such is this truth concerning the terror and majesty of the last day which the Apostle, having spoken of before, repeats here again: *Wherein the heavens being on fire shall be dissolved, and the elements shall melt with fervent heat.*

13. Nevertheless we, according to His promise, look for new heavens and a new earth, wherein dwelleth righteousness.

Here is the third use of the former doctrine and it is for the consolation of believers against all their pains and sufferings in Christ's service and especially against the loss that they may apprehend to be in the forementioned dissolution of all things; they have a more excellent state to look for, a new world when the old is destroyed, where only righteousness shall have its constant abode. This promise of the new heavens and the new earth was first given out to the church by Isa. 65:17 and 66:22 and had some accomplishments, as these places make clear at the return from Babylon, which was a new world to the ruined and exiled state and church of the *Jews*. It is also made use of by the Apostle *Paul* as having spiritual mercies in it; such as conversion, regeneration and the like, which is as a new world to sinners: for he marks it to have accomplishment this way, 2 Cor. 5:17. And yet this Apostle here leads believers to expect more out of that same promise, not any worldly or temporal felicity, as millenaries dream, because it is a state promised after the day of judgment, as fully satisfactory to believers, where no sin but only righteousness shall have its constant mansion; which cannot agree to any earthly happiness, but must be understood of everlasting blessedness, set forth under these borrowed expressions.

Doctrine, [1.] One and the same promise may contain several sorts of mercies, both temporal and spiritual, to be let out at several times to the Lord's people, and yet may have its full accomplishment only in heaven: for such is this promise of new heavens and a new earth, out of which *Isaiah* has drawn temporal deliverance, *Paul* spiritual mercies, and *Peter* here everlasting blessedness. Many promises in Scripture are of the same nature, as, for example, that promise, *The Lord God will wipe away tears from off all faces,* Isa. 25:8, was in part accomplished when the mourning church came rejoicing home from their exile in Babylon, as is clear, Psa. 126. That same promise has also been often made good in the Lord's comforting of particular persons, humbly mourning for their sins, as appears by Psa. 116:8. And yet that promise is to have its full accomplishment in heaven as is clear by Rev. 21:4. The consideration whereof may serve to direct us to a right use-making of many promises. [2.] The state of believers in the other life will be wholly new, their bodies will be new like Christ's glorious body, Phil. 3:21, their spirits also new, 1 John 3:2, their duration new, a constant presentness of enjoying the Lord, 1 Thess. 4:17. Their exercises shall be new, to sing new songs to the Lamb, Rev. 5:9, and to follow Him wherever He goes; Rev. 14:4. Their clothing shall be new, glory and immortality, 1 Cor. 15:53. New food and refreshment, to eat of the Tree of life and drink of the Water of life, Rev. 22:1,2; and a new light and sun to shine upon them, the glory of God and of the Lamb being the light of that new world, Rev. 21:23. All which are but borrowed expressions to set forth the glory of that estate which cannot be fully set forth: for even the Apostle, not having time nor ability to reckon out all the particulars of that new and blessed estate, sets it out by a new world which comprehends many new things in it: *We look for new heavens and a new earth.* [3.] In that new world there shall neither be sin nor temptation to sin; there shall be no wrong, nor oppression, nor affliction, which are the consequences of sin; there shall neither be any change, nor any possibility or fear of change: for righteousness, which often falls in the straits now and cannot get entrance, but is banished out of the most parts of this world, Isa. 59:14, shall have a constant mansion there, as the word here signifies, *Where righteousness dwelleth.* [4.] They that would have a well-grounded confidence of attaining to this better world, must take hold of it in the promises thereof in Scripture, which ordinarily contain both the qualification and duty of the person that may expect it, as is clear by comparing 2 Cor. 5:17, John 3:16, 1 John 3:3 with this present text: *We,* according to His promise, *look for new heavens and a new earth.* [5.] They who have laid sure hold upon eternal life by faith in the promises thereof, will not be shaken out of their confident expectation of it, either by profane men's scoffing at the ground of their confidence, or by the sight of never so strange events falling forth before they possess what they believe: for, the Apostle, having foretold believers that they should hear much bold mockery of the last judgment and a better life than this, and that they should see all this world on fire before they did possess that better world, expresses here what should be their hope and language notwithstanding of both; *Nevertheless we, according to His promise, look for new heavens and a new earth.*

14. **Wherefore, beloved, seeing that ye look for such things, be diligent that ye may be found of him in peace, without spot, and blameless.**

From the consideration of that comfortable state that believers have to look for beyond time, the Apostle exhorts them to serious and constant diligence in making use of the blood and Spirit of Christ for the doing away of their sinful spots, as the only way wherein they may expect true peace when Christ comes, which is in substance the same with the first use of his former doctrine (v 11).

Hence learn, [1.] The lively hope and expectation of everlasting blessedness should be so far from making them that have it negligent and remiss in holy duties, that it should be a special motive and engagement to the same, that so they may honour Him who has made sure for them that heavenly inheritance after time, and allows them the comfortable expectation of it in time: for this exhortation to believers is inferred upon their confidence, *Wherefore, beloved, seeing ye look for such things, be diligent,* &c. [2.] They who have an approved and well-grounded confidence of heaven are so subject to laziness in their duty, and thereby in hazard to lose or weaken their assurance, which is only maintained in the way of diligence, 2 Pet. 1:10,11 that they have much need to be frequently roused up by the word of exhortation to diligence in their duty: for it is those whose confidence of heaven the Apostle questions not, but supposes to be well-grounded, whom he does here (as often before) exhort to *give diligence*. [3.] It is not unlawful for the Lord's people to look upon the excellency of the reward which free grace has prepared for them, and thereby to provoke their own hearts to diligence in their duty. Though the reward be neither the main nor the only motive of a Christian to his duty, yet it is one that may warrantably be made use of, as here the Apostle does, *Wherefore, beloved, seeing ye look for such things* (to wit, the new heavens and the new earth, spoken of in the former verse) *be diligent*. [4.] The main thing whereabout Christians' diligence ought to be exercised, is the washing away of the spots of their past guiltiness, by the frequent application of the blood of Christ and the changing of their polluted natures, whereby they are inclined to defile themselves further, by the virtue of the Spirit of Christ; both which may be comprehended in this, *without spot, and blameless*, which is here held forth as the object of Christians' constant and serious diligence. [5.] Although there be now many spots, and much to blame in the best, who may, so long as they are in time, cry, *unclean, unclean*; yet those who get grace to be seriously diligent (as the word here signifies) in employing of Christ for pardon of past guiltiness, and for strength in the battle against sin for time to come, shall be found by Him when He comes, *without spot, and blameless*. [6.] Much sweet peace and quietness when Christ comes, whether at death or judgment, will be found in the spirits of those who make it their serious work in time to have their daily guiltiness washed away by the application of the blood of Jesus, and their filthy natures changed by the power of His Spirit; and, on the contrary, much fearful unquietness and bitter anxiety will be at that time in their hearts who carry their unpardoned guilt and unrenewed nature to their end with them, without any serious diligence for removal of either: for the words in the original are, *That ye being without spot and blameless may be found by Him in peace*; importing that these, and none but these, will have peace when He comes. [7.] The thoughts of that peace which diligent believers will have at Christ's coming, and of that unquietness which will be then in the hearts of others, ought to provoke all that love their own peace, to much diligence in making use of Christ for pardon of sin and victory over it: for the Apostle makes this an alluring motive to diligence, that such, and none else, shall be *found in peace, without spot, and blameless.*

15. And account that the long-suffering of our Lord is salvation, even as our beloved brother Paul also; according to the wisdom given unto him hath written unto you;

The fourth use of the former doctrine both concerning the delay of Christ's second coming and the manner thereof, is for up-stirring of the Lord's people seriously to ponder what work the Lord is about while His second coming seems to be delayed, to wit, the working and promoting of saving grace in His own, and fitting of them for that eternal salvation which He is to bring with Him, for which work, time and pains are necessary; and this use the Apostle bears in upon them as a thing that had been much pressed from the same ground upon these same *Hebrews*, by the Apostle *Paul*, of whom he speaks with much love and respect as a man dear to him and faithful according to his talent.

Hence learn, [1.] The way to quiet our hearts under the delay of the performance of promises is to have them much exercised with the consideration of that work which the Lord is about during the delay, how much it serves for the advancement of our spiritual and eternal welfare: for this way would the Apostle have the Lord's people to lay their reckoning, that every day's sparing of the world is given to them for making fast-work of their peace with God, and fitting of them for glory, that so their hearts might be quieted under the delay: *And account that the long-suffering of the Lord is salvation.* [2.] These truths which have been often and by several of the Lord's ministers harmoniously pressed upon the Lord's people ought to have a special weight with them, as being attested by many witnesses to be the mind of God, more fully cleared and offered with a new relish, from several hands: for by this the Apostle bears-in the study of holiness and preparation for the day of judgment, that both he and the Apostle Paul had agreed in substance upon the use that was to be made of the doctrine of Christ's second coming: *Even as our beloved brother Paul also hath written.* [3.] All the faithful ministers of Christ ought to be so far from lifting up themselves above their fellow-labourers, or lessening the reputation of their persons and labours among the Lord's people, even although their fellow-labourers be in some things inferior to them, or differing from them, yea, and have sharply rebuked them for their failings, that by the contrary, they ought to entertain and to express love and esteem of them and to conciliate respect to them, and to their gifts and labours among the Lord's people: for this Apostle, who had the advantage of Paul in the priority of his calling to the ministry and acquaintance with Christ in the flesh, whom Paul had withstood to the face and whose failings he had registered in one of his Epistles, Gal. 2:11,14, does not lift up himself above Paul, nor labour to weaken his esteem, but writes of him as his equal, beloved by him and faithful according to his gifts, and commends his writings as useful for this people, *Even as our beloved brother Paul also, according to the wisdom given unto him, hath written.* [4.] The Lord has not given a like measure of gifts and qualifications for His service to all his faithful servants, but to some more, to some, fewer talents, that every one may make use of another and none may expect fulness but in Christ Himself: for that there were diverse measures even among the apostles is imported in this, that *Paul, according to the wisdom given unto him, hath written.* [5.] Whatever measure of gifts or graces any have more than another, it is a free gift of God's, and therefore ought to be humbly and thankfully possessed, and carefully employed for His honour, who ought to be acknowledged as author of these gifts, not only by those that have them, but by every one who discerns them in others; for while this Apostle speaks of Paul's wisdom, He calls it the *wisdom given him.* [6.] It is the prime commendation of a faithful minister that he has faithfully employed his measure, whether it be less or more, in serving Christ and doing good to the souls of His people: for here it is Paul's commendation that *according to the wisdom given him, he hath written.* [7.] Although it be the duty of one faithful minister to keep up the credit of another among the people, yet ought their commendations one of another to be in sobriety, such as may not detract from the due esteem of those whom they do not commend, and such as may lead people's thoughts above them that are commended, to God as the author and free giver of anything commendable in them: for this Apostle sufficiently commends Paul and his writings while he says of him, *According to the measure given him, he hath written.* [8.] Although it be both the sin and the character of false teachers to steal the words and lessen the estimation of other ministers that are more in esteem than themselves, that thereby they may cloak their own laziness, and want of God's calling, Jer. 23:30, yet it is very lawful, and the duty of the most eminent ministers of Christ to make use of the gifts and writings of their fellow-labourers, for clearing of the truth to themselves and others, and sometimes to cite their testimony for gaining the greater credit to truth with people: for so does this Apostle here, who not only presses the same truth that Paul had pressed, but is not ashamed to avow that he had perused Paul's writings to those *Hebrews*, as also all the rest of his Epistles, wherein he had found that which did agree with his doctrine, *Even as our beloved brother Paul hath also written.* [9.] Although the Apostle Paul has not put his name to that Epistle to the Hebrews, which is extant in the New Testament, either because he was hateful to the unconverted Jews, or suspected by weak converts, who were too much addicted to the Levitical law, or because he was sufficiently known and of unquestioned authority with the stronger sort, yet this place of Scripture puts it out of doubt that he is the Author thereof: for it is clear that this Apostle writes both his Epistles to the twelve tribes, by comparing 1 Epist. 1:1 and 2 Epist. 1:1 with 1 Epist. 2:12 and here he asserts that Paul also had written to them; which writing of Paul's can be no other than that Epistle to the Hebrews which is extant: [1.] because the purpose in Paul's writing to which this Apostle here relates, is clearly held forth there in Heb. 10:35,36. [2.] because that which this Apostle speaks in the following verse concerning the difficulty of understanding some passages in Paul's writing especially agrees to that Epistle; and [3.] because that writing of Paul's to the Hebrews whereof this Apostle here speaks, cannot be supposed to be lost except we would reflect both upon the providence of God and upon the fidelity of those to whom the oracles of God were committed, Rom. 3:2, whose faithfulness in that matter the Lord has never challenged; *Even as our beloved brother Paul hath written unto you.*

16. As also in all his Epistles, speaking in them of these things; in which are some things hard to be understood, which they that are unlearned and unstable wrest, as they do also the other scriptures, unto their own destruction.

The Apostle, having confirmed his doctrine from Paul's Epistle to the Hebrews, takes occasion to commend all the rest of his Epistles as confirming the same truth; and withal removes a prejudice which had been at that time rife against Paul's writings, as dark and obscure, showing that there were only some few things in his writings hard to be understood, which none but un-humbled and wanton spirits would pervert and mistake, as they would do much more of the Scripture, to their own damnation.

Hence learn, [1.] Although the frequent pressing of necessary truths upon people be oftentimes a burden to their corrupt nature, Jer. 23:33, yet must not the Lord's ministers weary to repeat and inculcate one and the same truth to them not knowing when life and power from God may accompany that truth to their heart, which has been often told them before, and as often slighted by them; see Phil. 3:1, for this Apostle presses the same truth upon the Hebrews which he knew Paul had pressed before upon them and upon all others in all his Epistles, which were all intended for the common good of the whole church in all ages: *As also in all his Epistles speaking in them of these things.* [2.] It has pleased the Lord so to express some parts of His mind in His Word that the sharpest-sighted will not at the first, nor easily, take up the meaning thereof, that all that study the Scriptures may be made humble in the sense of their own blindness, earnest in imploring Christ for His Spirit, and may be quickened to pains in meditation, comparing one Scripture with another, and the use of other commanded means, that after the use of all, any insight they get in places formerly dark to them may be the more esteemed of; for there are in Paul's Epistles *some things hard to be understood.* [3.] Although no man without special illumination from God, can savingly take up any truth revealed in Scripture, 1 Cor. 2:14, yet is there much of the Lord's mind revealed therein, in itself plain and easy to be understood by them who humbly depend upon Christ's teaching in the use of His own means: so that the simplest, who desire to know as much as may save and comfort their souls, ought not to be hindered or discouraged in the study of the Scriptures, in which, the Apostle says, there are *some things hard to be understood*, impor-ting that there are therein many things plain, and such as may be easily understood. [4.] Those truths which are most darkly pro-pounded in Scripture are not impossible to be understood if men would seriously exercise their wit about them, and humbly ask Christ for understanding, as the saints have done, Psa. 119:33,34,97, for the Apostle says only, there *are some things hard* (importing not only that there are many things plain, but also that there is nothing impossible) *to be understood.* [5.] Although human learning, being sanctified in the use thereof, may prove a blessed means of fitting men for the service of God, Dan. 1:17, Acts 7:22, and 22:3, yet it is not so much the want thereof, nor yet any obscurity that is in the Scriptures, which causes men dangerously to mistake and wrest the Word of God, as that men will not become humble disciples of Christ, renouncing their own wit and giving themselves up to Christ's teaching: for the word here in the original, *unlearned*, is not that which is made use of in Scripture, Acts 4:13, to signify the want of human literature, but it is a word that signifies to be undiscipled, or not taught by Jesus Christ; in which sense, *they that are unlearned do wrest the Scriptures.* [6.] Another special cause of wresting and mistaking those things in Scripture which are hard to be understood, is that men labour not to fix themselves in the knowledge, love and practice of truths that are plain, but have their hearts distracted with the cares and pleasures of this present world: for it is *they that are unstable* in this sense that *wrest the Scriptures.* [7.] To wrest the Scriptures is to endeavour to force them to speak contrary to the intent of the Spirit that indited them, in defence of vile errors or profane practices: for there is a metaphor in the word which is translated *wrest*, taken from those who by tortures labour to compel the innocent to speak against their mind. [8.] They that wrest one place of Scripture will readily wrest many more, there being a connection between one error and another, as there is between one truth and another: for they that wrest *Paul's* Epistles, *wrest also other Scriptures.* [9.] The hazard of men's forcing a sense of their own upon the Scriptures contrary to the mind of the Spirit that indited them, is no less than the everlasting destruction of them that do it: for they that wrest the Scriptures do it *to their own destruction.*

17. Ye therefore, beloved, seeing ye know these things before, beware lest ye also, being led away with the error of the wicked, fall from your own steadfastness.

The fifth use of the Apostle's former doctrine is an exhortation to constancy. The sum whereof is, that since they had been clearly forewarned of their spiritual dangers and informed concerning the remedies thereof, they should be the more wary, lest they be drawn away from that way of truth and holiness wherein they had been, through the Lord's grace, in some good measure established.

Hence learn, [1.] Clear forewarnings of spiritual dangers and informations concerning the remedies thereof, do lay upon the Lord's people strong obligations to watchfulness; it being a great aggravation of their guiltiness, if after these they be ensnared: for the Apostle makes the fore-knowledge they had of these things by his former doctrine a special motive to watchfulness, *Wherefore, beloved, seeing ye know these things before, beware.* [2.] There is no error nor temptation so gross that has overtaken others, whereof those that are dearly beloved of God and His saints ought not to entertain so much fear as to make them very strict in watching, lest they be ensnared with the same, considering that there is a friend to these in their unmortified part: *Beloved, beware lest ye also be led away with the error of the wicked.* [3.] Although the Lord's people can neither totally nor finally fall away from truth or holiness, John 17:11,12, yet those who have been in some good measure established in the knowledge of the truth and practice of holy duties, may for a time and in a great measure, fall from both; as is imported in this warning, *Beware lest ye also, being led away with the error of the wicked, fall.* [4.] The possibility of believers falling for a time should provoke them to much circumspection, and as the word here signifies, to keep very strict watch over themselves, which exercise the Lord has appointed to be a special means of His people's preservation, *Beware lest ye also, being led away with the error of the wicked, fall.* [5.] The Lord's people have a steadfastness proper to themselves, which no hypocrite can attain to, whereby they do adhere to the truth and way of Christ, not for the applause or example of others, or any worldly advantage whatsoever, but because their minds are enlightened to know and their hearts renewed to believe and love the truth for its own worth, and for his authority that reveals it: for the words in the original are, *Beware lest ye fall from your own proper steadfastness.*

18. **But grow in grace, and in the knowledge of our Lord and Saviour Jesus Christ. To him be glory both now and for ever. Amen.**

The sixth and last use of the former doctrine is an exhortation to the study of a continual growth and progress in grace and knowledge: and this the Apostle presses as a special means to attain to that which he pressed in the former use, to wit, steadfastness; and closes with a song of praise to Jesus Christ.

Hence learn, [1.] It is not enough for the Lord's people to

maintain that measure of grace which they have already attained; but they must labour to find the lively exercise and daily growth of every grace: for the Apostle, having exhorted to steadfastness in what they had already attained, adds this, *But grow in grace.* [2.] Growth in grace is a special preservative from apostasy, there being no possibility to keep what we have attained, except it be improved and be upon the growing hand, Matt. 25:29, for this exhortation is added to the former as a special means of attaining to steadfastness, *Grow in grace,* &c. [3.] They that would have grace to thrive in their hearts, must labour for a daily increase of knowledge in their minds concerning Christ's sovereignty, His offices, and the benefits we have by Him: for as growth in grace is here pressed as a special means to steadfastness, so growth in knowledge is pressed as a special means of attaining to growth in grace: *But grow in grace, and in the knowledge of our Lord and Saviour Jesus Christ.* [4.] It is the duty of all who have any right thoughts of Christ to break forth some way in His praise, and to ascribe glory to Him who, being the Sovereign Lord of heaven and earth, is become the Saviour of sinners and has clothed Himself with offices answerable to all their necessities, as is imported in the names of Christ that are here: for the Apostle that knew Him well to be such a One, takes up the song which all that know Him should follow and keep up in their hearts, *To Him be glory.* [5.] Praise is a duty wherewith all our other duties should be closed, both for the help we find in them and for the pardon we believe to obtain for our failings; upon both which grounds the Apostle closes his Epistle with praise: *To Him be glory.* [6.] Praise is an exercise for the discharge whereof, not only all our time, but the long age or day of eternity, as the word here signifies, is little enough: *To Him be glory, both now and for ever, Amen.*

GLOSSARY OF OBSOLETE WORDS
(or words of changed meaning).

Adjection: addition
Admiration: wonder, perplexity
aggreage (aggrege): to make to appear greater, or more grave
airth: direction, point of the compass
bensell: determination
characters (to make characters of): to characterize
cautioner: (in old Scottish law) a guarantor
compellation: appellation (style of address)
(to) condescend (upon): to arrive at
conversation: manner of life
decerned: (in old Scottish law) a judicial decree
dehort: to dissuade
demit: to humble
design: to designate, indicate
ding: to beat, knock
discharge: to pronounce to be altogether unsuitable
entertaining: sustaining
furniture: provision, equipment
harbour: a shelter
hold throng: to be associated
imported: implied
incense (verb): to kindle
kythe (kithe): to make known, or make manifest
(to) make nothing for: to supply no proof of (a thing)
midst: middle way
outgate: a passing from one state to another (usually to a better
    state)
plaistered (plastered): loaded to excess
presently: immediately
propension: propensity
registrate: to register
respective: respectful
set (against): to contend against
shed (verb): to be taken away
shift: to decline, escape from

299

sit up: to sit in judgment upon (another)
stand to: to refrain from
uncouth (take uncouth): to view ignorantly
untimeously: unseasonably, inopportunely
wail (wale) out: to pick out, to choose